# Eating for Britain

*Also by Simon Majumdar*

Eat My Globe

# Eating for Britain

### A Journey into the Heart
### (and Belly) of the Nation

## SIMON MAJUMDAR

JOHN MURRAY

First published in Great Britain in 2010 by John Murray (Publishers)
An Hachette UK Company

I

© Simon Majumdar 2010

A CIP catalogue record for this title is available from the British Library

ISBN 978-1-84854-226-6

Typeset in 12.5/15 Monotype Bembo by Servis Filmsetting Ltd, Stockport, Cheshire

Printed and bound by Clays Ltd, St Ives plc

John Murray policy is to use papers that are natural, renewable and recyclable
products and made from wood grown in sustainable forests. The logging and
manufacturing processes are expected to conform to the environmental regulations
of the country of origin.

John Murray (Publishers)
338 Euston Road
London NW1 3BH

www.johnmurray.co.uk

*To Gwen and Eva for teaching me how to cook
and to Pratip and Arthur for teaching me how to eat.*

# Contents

\* \* \* \* \*

## Afternoon Tea

\* \* \* \* \*

## Snacks

\* \* \* \* \*

## Supper

### Starter

### Main Course

*Pudding*

\* \* \* \* \*

## Drinks

## Introduction
# Whetting the Appetite

As I write this introduction, I have just completed an interview with a German radio station. The interviewer's first question was the almost inevitable, 'Tell me, Simon, why is British food so dreadful?'

I resisted my first urge to circle my eyes with my fingers and respond with a childish refrain of *The Dambusters* theme and began to argue our case. She was having none of it and as she signed off, finished by saying, 'So, now you want to be the saviour of British food? The best of British luck to you.'

I don't want to be anyone's saviour, thank you very much. I doubt anyone would have me anyway. But constantly having to defend British food from the barbs of foreigners is one of the more tiresome elements of travelling around the world and writing about food. *Eating for Britain* is my own small attempt to restore the balance, a chance to prove to myself as much as anyone else that, while we have much to be apologetic about when it comes to food in Britain, we also have some truly exceptional dishes that are prepared from fabulous ingredients by people who really give a damn about what they are doing.

Although this is not a history book, I hope along the way you will glean at least one or two useful little facts and stories about the origins of some of our national dishes that you can bore your friends rigid with on a rainy day. It is not a sociology book although I hope it will give you some insight into the state of our nation through the prism of the food I sampled. It is not a recipe book although you will certainly find a handful in here where I have decided that your life would not be the same without them. Bloody good they are too: trust me, I have prepared them all any number of times.

*Eating for Britain* is quite simply my attempt to discover Britain's most wonderful foods and from that to construct the perfect day's eating if, by chance, I could bring any and all of them to my table without concern for price, seasonality or, God help me, carbon footprint. It is the result of a journey that has taken me the best part of a year and has involved over 13,000 miles of driving in a battered Ford Focus, from the coast of Cornwall in the south-west of England to the coast of Moray in the north-east of Scotland; from the rural idylls of the Gower Peninsula to the grim urban sprawls of London and Birmingham.

It was a trip that brought moments of incredible luxury as I tasted whisky costing £10,000 a bottle and it was a trip that also brought unmitigated horror as I practised projectile vomiting for seven long hours off the coast of Norfolk. It was a trip that challenged many of my preconceptions as I met those who hunt for sport, and confirmed my worst prejudices as I encountered dishes for which their manufacturers should be dragged before the local beak.

It was a trip that brought back wonderful memories of my childhood growing up in Yorkshire: memories of Sunday lunches centred around a huge joint of pork or beef; memories of fish and chips on weekend trips to the coast; and visits to my grandparents in London where my own passion for food was nurtured by my Welsh grandmother's love of baking. And it was a trip that brought me up to date with the state of our nation's food in this modern era, our love of celebrity, the power of our supermarkets and the decline of so many of our renowned food industries.

Despite the dubious reputation our food has earned itself around the world I discovered that we are beginning to fight back and rediscover dishes of which we can be really proud: classic dishes like hot pot in Lancashire; dishes of ancient tradition like the famous clotted cream of Cornwall, brought to our shores by Phoenician traders; and dishes of recent immigration like chicken tikka masala in Glasgow and balti in Birmingham. Some dishes are instantly familiar and recognized worldwide as being British: fish and chips and roast beef and Yorkshire pudding. Dishes for so long debased by the use of poor ingredients, but when done well, as good as anything I have eaten anywhere in the world. Then there are the foods you may not have sampled or may never even have heard of such as Staffordshire oatcakes in Stoke or Arbroath smokies in Scotland, which still sell by the bucketload but only to locals in their home region.

It certainly wasn't all positive news. Tales of our declining fishing industry and the struggles of farms and small food retailers all over the country were a constant and depressing refrain. Depressing too was some of the food I was asked to eat and you should all get together and write me a big thank you note for eating a macaroni and cheese pie at the Great British Pie Awards, so that you never have to.

The sighting of the words 'Chicken Tikka Lasagna' on a hotel blackboard in Buckie, in Scotland, was not only enough to send me scampering out into the rain in terror, but also enough to convince me that despite our culture of celebrity TV chefs, farmers' markets, dedicated TV channels and cookery magazines, we still have a huge fracture between what we produce and the food that many people are happy to put in their mouths. During the day I might meet people dedicated to producing food of the highest quality they could, but I found precious little sign of it in the procession of takeaways, pizza restaurants and kebab shops as I walked the high streets of our towns in the evenings. With its roots buried in the ethos of quantity versus quality that sprang from the necessity of years of post-war rationing it is a fracture that will take a long time, if not generations more, to repair.

Despite these horrors and disappointments, it was still a journey from which I returned filled with enthusiasm and hope for the future, certain that although I may not ever be able to defeat the prejudices of so many towards food in Britain, I can at least counter them with knowledge. Knowledge of just how delicious some of our produce and our dishes are and knowledge that there are thousands of people out there who are determined to continue to improve in the face of the very tough opposition from economics and ambivalence.

In the end, as it has proved on all my food travels, *Eating for Britain* was a journey to meet people. As I drove those 13,000 miles I met farmers, fishermen, bakers, cheese makers, hunters, shop owners, chefs, distillers, brewers and fish smokers to name but a few off the top of my head. I met Pakistani businessmen running restaurants as part of their empire and plump Scottish ladies who had been making oatcakes all their lives. I met the chairman of one of the most famous Scotch whisky distilleries in the world and a fourth-generation farmer who produces bacon so good you want to make a suit out of it and wear it to church. I met two young Brummy boys who served me fish and chips as good as I have tried anywhere and a genial chef who turned out the best Yorkshire puddings ever while turning the air blue with his views on ramblers. I met the men who strove towards European PDO (Protected Designation of Origin) status for Craster kippers and the Melton Mowbray pork pie and the people trying to do the same for Bakewell pudding.

All had one thing in common: they gave a damn and so too, I hope, will you. We have so many things to be proud of in this country and it is about time we realized that food is one of them. So, even if it means cooking a blow-out Sunday lunch for friends, searching for the finest fish and chips in town or simply making the best bacon sandwich ever, I hope the tale of *Eating for Britain* splashes it with a dash of inspiration. If this book can contribute to your own desire to get out there and find the best of British, eating that macaroni and cheese pie will have been worth it.

Just about.

Simon Majumdar
London, 2010

# 1
# Eating for Britain

What does it mean to be British?

It's an odd question to ask yourself as you hit your fifth decade, and it took my American fiancée to bring it into sharp focus. Although her take was that I was 'such a Brit' because, and I quote, 'you have a huge stick up your ass' it did make me wonder what being British might actually mean in the twenty-first century, particularly at a time when our formerly great nation is struggling to find its place in the ever changing world.

For once it wasn't just about me, however. Even the Brits I asked about their own identity were not much help, with one particular friend boiling down our entire culture to nothing more than 'just saying sorry a lot'. There had to be, I decided, more to a whole nation's identity than a permanent state of atonement and I knew that if I was to come to any conclusion about my own sense of identity, I had to try to find out what it meant to be British in the first place.

What better way than through my lifelong obsession, food? By looking at the nation through its stomach and constructing the perfect day's eating in Britain, I was sure I could discover a useful picture of what it means to be an inhabitant of these sceptred isles, not just for me but also for their growing and increasingly cosmopolitan society.

To construct the perfect day's British eating meant that I would have to consider all the options from the moment I opened my eyes and thought about breakfast to the last snatched snack I grabbed before hitting the hay. Along the way there would have to be pit stops for that all too British institution, elevenses, and for lunch, whether it be a long lingering meal when time permitted or a hurried bite on a busy workday. There would be, of course, a break in the afternoon for a little something to refuel for the long drag until the evening meal. This would be a more filling repast of many courses finishing with a gloriously decadent dessert of the sort that only Britain can provide. And there would, naturally, be no other choice than to finish my day with a final dram of Scotch whisky. I am not a savage.

Whether we are a branch on the most aristocratic of family trees or a recent immigrant, whether we kneel before God in an English village church, a mosque, a synagogue or not at all, we all have to eat and my assumption was that what we eat would reveal much about who we British are and where we come from. Dishes are not created in a vacuum, however. Well, in fact, some are, but you would have to buy a book by Heston Blumenthal to read about that. They develop over time and with changes in people's economic and political situations, with the influence of immigrants historical and modern and, of course, with the insatiable British desire to travel and explore, which led to the expansion of the British Empire and, on my part, even a journey around the world for my previous book, *Eat my Globe*. It would not just be about the outbound journey, however. More than almost any other nation, the British have a desire to relive travel experiences on their return. The production line of tapas bars reflects our ongoing love affair with Spain, and, more recently, the explosion of Thai and Mexican restaurants speaks to our more recent travel trends. Most obvious of all, the thousands of curry houses, which dot our high streets, were initially evidence of the desire of returning expats to recreate the Anglo-Indian dishes of their time in the Raj, and more recently the influx of immigrants from the sub-continent.

As I ate, it would be important too to delve into the roots of the dishes I sampled. I did not want to write a history book, but it would be impossible to taste a dish without putting it in the context of its origins. Was it the result of trade? Was it the result of invasion? Was it the result of immigration, both historical and modern? All have had an impact on the way we eat today.

It is no great revelation that Britain's relationship with food is a complicated one. It has been formed by its geography and religion, its wars and rationing, and has been subjected to years of verbal abuse from just about every other nation on earth for its lack of passion and skill. Had we as a nation lost touch with our food so that it could decline to this extent? Or is the unspoken truth that even before post-Second World War rationing changed everything our food was pretty lousy anyway and the dishes we look to as classics deserve the insults hurled at them by other nations?

What about religion? A few years ago, a food writer once told me, when I was complaining about the dearth of good places to eat in Scotland, that 'John Knox has a lot to answer for'. Did the victory of Protestantism over Catholicism condemn us always to think of food as fuel, or is it the simpler truth that if you live in a damp, cold, northern European country you are always going to think about food in more functional than celebratory ways?

Some might argue that the recent emergence of a new generation of chefs who had travelled the world heralded a new golden age for British cuisine; others that they were merely feeding the nation's love of celebrity rather than teaching the nation to feed itself. And what about the growing power of the supermarkets? Did it sound the death knell for independent high street shops and serfdom for the nation's suppliers? Or did they bring with them all the benefits of vast ranges of product, great prices and convenience?

I turned my attention to what it might mean to eat for Britain. Which regions of the country should I visit and what dishes should I look for? I did what I always do when faced with such a challenge: I began to make a list. I knew that there would be meat involved. I had eaten enough of it in my forty-five years to know that Britain produces some of the finest anywhere. Superb lamb and pork and, most famous of all, the roast beef of Old England, so renowned a dish that the French sobriquet for the British, 'les rosbifs', was, I was told, originally offered up in admiration for our animal husbandry rather than in damnation of our lack of culinary talent. Not just the fine cuts, however; what about the offal, the blood and the dishes made from what is left after the prime pieces have been taken away? What about pies? My God, pies. How could you write about Britain and its food and not write about pies: pork pies, steak and kidney pies and steamed savoury puddings? Then there would be seafood, caught off the coasts of Norfolk, Scotland or

Ireland, where the quality is incomparable and considered so highly abroad that much of what is landed never finds its way to our tables but is rushed to the markets of Spain and France. I wondered what happened to the fish that remained on our shores and whether anyone actually wanted to eat it.

There would be traditional dishes in the day's menu, of course, both sweet and savoury: Lancashire hot pot and Bakewell tart – or as I found out more correctly, Bakewell pudding – Cornish pasties and spotted dick. There would be dishes that had their origins in the Middle Ages and whose recipes had changed little in the intervening centuries. There would be dishes that were a direct result of Britain's pre-eminent military and trading status through the eighteenth and nineteenth centuries and there would be dishes whose recipes had been handed down from generation to generation.

However, as in other areas of life, Britain's cuisine is not ossified like a museum relic. New arrivals from other countries have always brought their ingredients and culinary skills with them, so my journey would also take me in search of dishes brought to our shores by immigrants. Nordic invaders, for instance, brought their knowledge of smoking fish, which gave rise to the production of kippers and Arbroath smokies. Also from the same region came methods of slow-cooking simple ingredients, which gave us lobscouse, Irish stew and cawl, the lamb stew that brings a happy tear to every Welshman's eye. Jews fleeing Portugal in the eighteenth century brought with them the ability to fry fish and by happy accident combined with Huguenot refugees from Belgium and France bringing their own passion for fried potatoes. End result, Britain's and my favourite dish. Without the Dutch, we would not have jellied eels. Some may consider that a good thing, but if they dare to say the same about gin, for which we owe the same nation a debt of gratitude, they will incur my violent and vengeful wrath.

More recently, immigrants from the Asian subcontinent brought with them versions of dishes that had proved popular during the days of the empire and altered them to work with local ingredients and appeal to local tastes. In Glasgow, cubes of marinated chicken, normally served as a dish on their own, were combined with a spicy tomato sauce to become chicken tikka masala, now considered as a contender for our national dish.

In modern Britain, an invitation to a meal could just as easily see you sit down to a bowl of cholent stew, challah bread and some chopped liver as it could a roast dinner. It is just as likely to see you being offered a bowl of fiery curry with a wicked slick of ghee or a glistening piece of jerk chicken as it is to include a dainty cucumber sandwich and a stiffening gin and tonic. And you are just as likely to be presented with a Chinese New Year moon cake as a Christmas card. Our food, like our country itself, never stands still.

One thing that I fully expected to remain intact, however, was the much admired British eccentricity. Britain is, quite frankly, a nation of oddballs, freaks and nut jobs. Nowhere is this more in evidence than when it comes to our food. Other countries might be true nose-to-tail eaters, making sure that no bit of the animal gets wasted, but none would turn a mixture of lung, heart and livers in a lamb's stomach into a living 'beastie' to be serenaded by the skirl of bagpipes and the lamentations of a poet. No other cuisine would take a century-old condiment containing over fifty ingredients and simply dub it 'brown sauce' and I defy anyone to find the French equivalent of the Bedfordshire clanger, a hefty suet pudding with meat at one end and jam at the other so no time is wasted between courses. I hoped that the people I met on this journey would have a story to tell: the farmers and fishermen, the brewers and the distillers, the Michelin-starred chefs and the café owners, in fact anyone who could give me a glimpse into our relationship with food, whether they were directly involved with its production or simply as passionate about it as I was.

I was also certain, however, that it was not all going to be good. To many people, meals are still predicated on cost rather than quality and, added to a deeply embedded puritan ethic that had people sailing to worlds unknown to escape it, it is easy to see why Britain and the British have never been known for treating food with passion and joy in the same way that some of our European neighbours, France, Italy or Spain, have done for centuries. I knew that among the great there would be the God-awful, the badly made and the downright shameful, the sort of dish that once had me staring open-mouthed at a pub blackboard near Victoria Station in London that offered a daily special of a 'Thai Vegetarian Schnitzel'. None the less, I dared to hope that such horrors would be few and far between, but I was far from certain.

At the very least, I hoped that on the *Eating for Britain* trip I would get to fill my face with some delicious foods and, if that was the case, it would all have been worthwhile.

# — Breakfast —

Many would argue that breakfast seems to have lost its place in the hierarchy of British meals. They would claim that it was once a lavish affair, which has now lost ground to lunch and even more so to dinner as the major dining event of the day. But this would not be taking into account that for many, particularly the working classes both before and after the Industrial Revolution, breakfast was as hurried an event as it is for today's office workers, a bite snatched at dawn to provide fuel for the morning's labours.

In fact, it was in the nineteenth century that the Great British Breakfast began to come into its own and only then for those whose wealth allowed the time to take it at leisure. Almost inevitably all Victorian breakfast roads lead to Isabella Beeton, who believed that 'The English breakfast, even when taken at an early hour, is usually a fairly substantial one, and rightly so, for a good meal, if enjoyed and digested, gives the support necessary for the morning's work.'

Her comments, taken from *The Book of Household Management*, were aimed at affluent upper-middle-class households, who could afford not only the time to linger over their morning meal, but also the cost of the dishes she suggests. Her instructions for breakfast show that it was a family ritual to be observed and enjoyed on a daily basis by the wealthy, rather than being the act of necessity it was for those heading to the factories.

The list of dishes she offers up is astonishing to modern eyes, even mine. For a fitting breakfast, there would be a sideboard covered with cold dishes including joints of meat, pies, potted fish and pressed meats of tongue and ham. Yet these were merely the bit-part players to the main events, which consisted of 'Broiled fish, such as mackerel, whiting, herrings, dried haddocks; mutton chops and rump-steaks, broiled sheep's kidneys, kidneys à la mâitre d'hôtel, sausages, plain rashers of bacon, bacon and poached eggs, ham and poached eggs, omelets, plain boiled eggs, oeufs-au-plat, poached eggs on toast, muffins, toast, marmalade, butter etc.' While Mrs B is not suggesting that all of these should be available at the same meal, there is little doubt that the Victorian breakfast would have contributed a major part of the day's calorific intake.

Such substantial breakfasts are now a thing of the past even for the rich and idle. For most, the morning meal may be a rushed bite of a piece of toast on the way to the bus, a bowl of instant oatmeal taken at the desk while checking e-mails or may even be skipped altogether in favour of a strong cup of coffee or a cigarette. Understandable given the hectic life we all seem to lead and it is only at the weekend, when schedules are more relaxed, that breakfast is given any attention at all.

Breakfast has always been my favourite meal of the day. From the moment I wake up, my first thoughts are about what food I can shovel into my mouth. This probably stems from a rare condition of early morning ebullience. I am told by just about everyone that I am unbearably chirpy in the morning. I usually wake by 5 a.m. no matter what time I go to sleep. I find it almost impossible to stay in bed and usually leap from beneath my *Battlestar Galactica* (Original Version) duvet ready to face the world the moment my eyes are open. My cheeriness, so I'm told, can be a little on the annoying side and one university flatmate even informed me that if I continued with my early morning brightness, he would, 'hit you in the face until my hand breaks'.

However, being such an early riser does present me with the opportunity to indulge myself in a proper breakfast. On the rare occasions I am being healthy, it could be a bowl of cereal spiked out with fresh fruit or, even more likely, a beautifully creamy bowl of slow-cooked porridge with a large spoonful of crunchy peanut butter stirred through it and then topped off with berries. If I have more time, I will give breakfast the attention it so richly deserves, and retrieve the frying pan from the kitchen cupboard to prepare a lavish meal, which will often be big enough to see me through to evening. What dishes, I wondered, would make their way on to my shortlist for the perfect breakfast?

There could be golden kippers, herring that has been cold-smoked on the Isle of Man or on the blustery north-east coast of England. Simply grilled with a poached egg on top, they would be hard to beat. There could be an Arbroath smokie haddock that has been hot-smoked over the embers of oak chips in a whisky barrel half buried in the ground. Perfect on its own, leaking oily fish juices on to the plate, or flaked in a kedgeree for something more substantial. There could be a bulbous ring of black pudding, from Bury of course, with its traditional seven blobs of pork fat to add to the richness of the blood, barley and spices. What about Staffordshire oatcakes? There's a truly local delicacy eaten in the thousands but seldom seen more than a few miles from Stoke-on-Trent.

Best of all, I anticipated, would be the fry-up. Call it what you will, the Full English, Scottish or Welsh Breakfast or even the Ulster Fry, there can be few more enjoyable, if artery-challenging, ways of beginning your day than with the classic combination of eggs, sausages and bacon alongside an assortment of mushrooms, tomatoes, beans and a few slices of toast and a mug of thick brown tea. The fry-up is always good for what ails you, not just because of the undoubted guilty pleasure of consuming fat-laden calories, but because the sounds and smells of its preparation and the tastes of eating it also come laden with wonderful and comforting memories of times past. Times when the smell of bacon frying downstairs persuaded you to climb from your pit before midday on a Sunday morning, or times when a fried egg and a sausage slapped between two slices of white bread were the perfect antidote to the student revelry of the night before. Like all the most comforting dishes, it is as much the memories of meals past as the plate in front of you that make your mouth salivate for the meal to come.

## 2
# The Full British Breakfast

The Walworth Road forms a grimy arterial passage between the two London neighbourhoods of Camberwell and the Elephant and Castle. For the first year of my university life in the early 1980s I would walk this unlovely street on my way from my hall of residence on Camberwell Hill to King's College on the Strand. At least twice during every week I would set off early, eschewing the grim breakfast offer in the hall canteen, and make a pit stop at a typical greasy spoon on the way. They are all but gone now, replaced by more modern versions and chain coffee shops, but only twenty-five years ago London was littered with such places, often run by Greek or Italian immigrants. The one on the Walworth Road was a perfect exemplar of the genre. Its exterior windows were framed with wood, the inside filled with booths whose faux leather covers were ripped and had seen better days. The Formica-clad tabletops were chipped with an amalgam of dirt and grease filling the cracks. The whole atmosphere was of an era rapidly coming to its natural conclusion.

After buying a morning paper, I would squeeze myself into a booth at the back and consider my breakfast choices. Behind the counter was the man who I always assumed was the owner, but never bothered to find out in over one hundred visits. He would be practising the fine art of short-order cooking while dangling a cigarette from one corner of his mouth, ash teetering precariously over the food sizzling on the hotplate. He almost always wore a string vest, which, because of the amount of hair that covered every inch of his back and chest and stuck out in thick tufts through the holes in his chemise, did not appear to come into contact with his body at any point. He never smiled at me, not once, but he certainly knew how to flip an egg. On the wall above the counter was the menu. It comprised a board on to which clip-on letters and numbers could be attached and moved around as the menu changed. It never did, so neither did the letters. Over the years, some had fallen off, never to be replaced, leaving customers faced with the tempting offer of 'Live & Onins' or 'piechips&ps'

The breakfast options were legion and required a degree in calculus or a lifetime spent in the bookies to figure them out as you decided what combination of eggs, beans, black pudding, bacon, sausages, fried slice, mushrooms, tomatoes and chips best fitted your mood that day. Then you had to decide if you wanted to enjoy tea, coffee and brown or white toast with your meal. None of this concerned me greatly as I was eighteen and seemingly able to burn off however many calories I consumed just through the simple act of being. So I went for the 'The Full Breakfast No1' which contained all of the above, two slices of toast and a huge mug of tea, all for the impressively low, even then, price of £1.10.

A few minutes after my order had been shouted across the room, a loaded plate would be delivered by a rotund woman who I assumed was the wife of the owner if only because she too found it impossible to crack a smile. My abiding recollection of the meal was that every item on the plate was the same colour, covered in a thin grey sheen lifted from the flat grill, which I assumed had been given no more than a quick scrape clean in the previous decade. The assorted breakfast items sat in a slick of the grease in which they had been prepared and would slide around the plate like Torvill and Dean if you wobbled it a bit.

The other strong memory is of the tea: thick, dark, builder's tea. It would have been tea of the 'so strong you could stand your spoon up in it' variety if the café had believed its customers could be trusted with such luxurious items as spoons without spiriting them away with them down the Walworth Road. Instead, a single spoon was attached to each table by a long, thick chain. Ever with a thought for hygiene, the grumpy, fat, possible spouse of the owner would come along and give it a flick with a ragged cloth every once in a while. It was a horrible, greasy, dirty, grim hole of a café that has probably long since rightly disappeared. I loved it and the breakfasts they served with all my fatty heart.

That's the thing about the Great British Fry-Up. Whether it is made with great ingredients or lousy ones, we know it is wrong but we can't live without it. We know it will be reducing our life expectancy by minutes with every bite of crunchy bacon rind. We can feel our valves seizing up with every yellow slick escaping from a punctured egg yolk that we mop up with a piece of golden fried bread and we know, with every scoop of baked beans that we mix with HP sauce and lift to our mouths, that no good can ever come of it.

Why do we do this to ourselves when we know the

consequences? Simply because a well-prepared fry-up is arguably the best meal in the world and, although it might make nutritionists in the UK come out in hives, it also has the magical ability to cure a whole world of hurt. What hangover is not sent scurrying into retreat when faced with a plump sausage? What broken heart can't be glued back together with the grease from a circle of fatty black pudding? What weekend, when all you have to look forward to is a dose of spousal earache and an afternoon in the houseplant section of B&Q, can't be given a rosy hue from wiping clean your plate with a folded piece of toast? There is, quite plainly, absolutely nothing that a full fry-up cannot do.

It is also one of the few dishes that can be found in every corner of the country. Different parts may append the name of their region in an attempt to make it their own, but with the exception of a few local items, the Full English, Full Welsh, Full Scottish breakfasts and the Ulster Fry are essentially the same beast. Its existence has much more to do with the rise in tourism around Britain since the 1960s than it does with any great historical significance, but its place in the heart of our nation is secure, even if now, in the face of the wailings from nutritional harbingers of doom, it is an occasional treat rather than a regular repast.

Over the journey of *Eating for Britain*, I experienced well over one hundred fry-ups on your behalf. You can send a 'Get Well Soon' card when I have my first heart attack. Some were exceptional, served in bed and breakfast accommodation across the country and made with fantastic ingredients. They were delivered in gargantuan portions by my hosts and the scrawled notes in their visitor books, many from guests from abroad, showed that it is not only the locals who enjoy the challenge and benefits of a full British breakfast.

Some breakfasts were just downright odd. One morning at 5 a.m. I found myself in the basement of the Cock Tavern in the heart of London's Smithfield Meat Market. I stared down at a large plate, which, unsurprisingly given the location, contained plentiful slabs of dead animal and little else. I washed it all down with a pint of Guinness. It was the breakfast of champions, or at least of the champion meat porters who surrounded me in the busy dining room and rapidly expanded my vocabulary of curse words as they discussed their day's work and politics. I shall never be able to watch Peter Mandelson on television again without laughing out loud at the thought of what one wag suggested should be inserted into his rectal region, causing me to spray a mixture of toast and ketchup across my table.

Some breakfasts were horribly, horribly nasty and I offer in evidence an early morning meal I experienced at the Little Chef in Popham as I headed down from London for a few days in Dorset. It had recently undergone a television makeover at the hands of molecular gastronomist Heston Blumenthal. An odd marriage and one designed as much, no doubt, for its high-concept appeal to TV executives as for the culinary benefit of mug punters like me. As a marketing exercise it had worked beautifully. The café had become a destination and, when I arrived, I had to squeeze my ratty car in between a Jaguar and a brand-new Range Rover. The inside redesign too seemed to push all the marketing buttons with lots of bright Day-Glo colours replacing the faded old design and counters with stools for single diners. Irony and food are seldom joyous bedfellows and the Little Chef at Popham just screamed out with the knowing wit of its overpaid design team. Bright red tables were archly adorned with little round ketchup bottles, dangly bright lights hung from the ceiling and my heart went out to the waiters who were forced to wear bright red shirts with the word 'WAITER' stencilled in enormous letters on the back.

Blumenthal's schtick during the television programme had been to source the very best ingredients he could find and then to try to teach the staff the basics of short-order cooking. He had succeeded in his primary aim as the ingredients in the 'All New Olympian' were obviously well sourced. The menu trumpeted free-range eggs, Wiltshire cured bacon, and even a bit of Scottish black pudding. Unfortunately he obviously failed in his secondary aim, and a major disconnect had occurred between the joyful denouement of his TV show and my early morning arrival. Although the breakfast plate that was placed before me looked adequate when viewed from above, a quick peek at its dark underbelly told a different and more unpleasant story.

A failure to clean the hotplate properly meant that every element of the meal had a nice brown sheen underneath not unlike the one I had encountered at my 'go to' café in the early 1980s. Except that here, a whopping £13 would change hands for this desultory affair when I added a thimbleful of decent orange juice and a cup of tea, a huge price differential, even taking inflation into account. Two sausages rolled over to reveal a burned underside. A few misplaced strands of thyme, that greatest of all breakfast staples, had been fried to a cinder on the underside of an equally blackened mushroom. Two semi-cooked halves of tomato tasted as if they had been drenched in oil allowed to go rancid from being kept too close to the stove. Worst of all, the flipside of the eggs revealed a thick, almost impenetrable crust, which took a vigorous sawing motion of my knife to break through. Only some excellent bacon shone despite the mishandling by the staff and I made a note to find out who the producer was for later in my journey.

After a quick visit to the sparkly toilets, decorated with tiles covered in cookery tips (here's a tip, show them to the chef, see if he can learn something), I slunk out of the über-Little Chef to the sounds of Lionel Bart's 'Food, Glorious Food' ringing in my ears from the piped music. God, it would seem, has a sense of humour.

What was my favourite fry-up of the many I enjoyed and sometimes endured? Well, if I were forced to pick just one, my mind would head back to a weekend spent enjoying the lush, green beauty that is the six counties of Northern Ireland. I arrived with a friend at the end of the marching season. As we drove from the airport to the small town of Comber to the east of Belfast, Union flags and those bearing the Loyalist Red Hand of Ulster were still proudly displayed outside the majority of houses and from the tops of lampposts. I knew that across the city, flags would also be waving, but they would be the tricolours of the Republican movement. The Troubles may be slowly fading into the recent history of Northern Ireland, but the divisions that caused them were still very much in evidence.

Comber seemingly consisted of a few houses and shops

around a small town square. To one side was a freshly painted building, which I determined to have been constructed during the Georgian period. The giveaway was a large sign dangling from the front of the building which read 'The Georgian House'; very little escapes me that way. The Georgian House was a relatively new enterprise run by chef/owner Peter McConkey who had worked at many of Belfast's major hotels and restaurants over his near thirty years in the business. Although his venture had been open for only a few weeks it was already receiving rave reviews for its food and in particular for its memorable Ulster Fry.

The Ulster Fry is arguably the *ne plus ultra* of the fried breakfast world, comprising all the usual suspects but often accompanied by the added glories of soda bread and potato cakes. All too often it can be a greasy mess of a meal involving watery bacon, sausages made from reclaimed meat and eggs that have popped out of the backsides of some very unhappy chickens. However when prepared well, as it was at the Georgian House, it beat its English, Scottish and Welsh challengers hands down.

The chef ambled out of the kitchen for a chat, just as we were finding a seat in the corner of an airy, bright dining room with high ceilings and large windows. Peter McConkey was exactly the sort of chef whose company I enjoy. After his long service in the business, none of his efforts was directed towards his own ego, but all towards the enjoyment of his customers and the ingredients he used. It told in the food he served. When our square breakfast plates were delivered, the layout of their components was a testament to Peter's old-school chef's training. We were admittedly slightly bemused by a carved tomato and a small pile of mushrooms in the corner, which had been 'turned' to give them swirling little indents like the pinched top of a Sichuan dumpling.

'Why did you do that?' my friend asked Peter.

'Because I can,' he replied, which was as good an answer as any.

The rest of the breakfast may not have included any more chef's surprises, but every element was as good as it possibly could be. A single egg had been cooked so the edge was crisped up, the white was firm and the golden yellow centre was still soft and ready to be freed by the prong of a fork. The sausages were dense and meaty. The bacon was just like you remember bacon used to be before they started injecting it with the water that leads to the white sludge in the pan we have become all too used to. There were even three little rounds of local black pudding, spicy and studded with creamy fat. Best of all, however, were the corner pieces of fresh soda bread and potato farls, cooked in butter until they reached a deep, turmeric-golden hue. 'This is the best breakfast I have had in God knows how long,' my friend said as he wiped his plate clean with a remaining piece of soda bread. I found it hard to disagree. If all fry-ups were as good as this, breakfast would definitely be the most important meal of the day.

After we had finished and had slumped back in our chairs Peter came out to join us again. He was excited about our visit. Not because he wanted to show off his own skills but because of the quality of the ingredients. 'A lot of folk around here think my fry is a little dear,' he told us as I glanced down at the menu and saw that it cost all of £5.95. 'That's about £2 more than local people are used to paying, but then the places that serve those fry-ups don't use the ingredients I do,' and he went on to spend the next half-hour listing his suppliers. It is a useful rule of thumb that if a chef spends more time talking about his ingredients than he does about himself, his food is usually going to be good.

I had come a long way for my breakfast that morning, but I had also come a long way since the greasy spoons I used to enjoy as a student. Down the years I had sampled hundreds, possibly thousands of examples, many decent, some appalling, but my early morning meal in Comber reminded me why I love a cooked breakfast so very much and why it is held in such affection in Britain. The fry-up takes time to prepare properly. It is not something that can be rushed, which is why it is now reserved for a leisurely weekend treat. A meal best shared with friends and family, the perfect way to start the day.

# 3
## Black Pudding

Andrew Holt's face looked a very peculiar shade of grey as I sat opposite him in the works canteen of the Real Lancashire Black Pudding Company.

'I am not goin' to lie to you, Simon. I'm feeling a little under the weather this morning.'

I hoped against hope that 'under the weather' was not a Lancastrian euphemism for 'I drank a skinful last night and if you come too close I am going to throw up all over you'.

I had driven a long way and had singled Andrew out because of his amazing reputation in the black pudding world (yes, folks, there is a black pudding world) where he was known not only for producing fine examples of Lancastrian Classic, but also for his extraordinary knowledge of blood sausages and their history all over the world. So renowned is Andrew Holt among the cognoscenti that in 1998 he was granted the title Chevalier du Goûte-Boudin, a Knight of the Blood Sausage. Who could possibly be better to talk to me of matters black pudding-related? However, on a cold Friday morning as Andrew stared down at his mug of tea and gave out a slight moan, I was beginning to doubt that he would be capable of telling me anything at all, let alone ponder on the mysteries of blood, fat and barley in a sausage casing, without providing a sample of his own interesting stomach mixture all over the floor or, even worse, me.

He perked up a little at the 'ping' of a microwave and nodded silently as one of his junior staff members placed a plate in front of us both. 'Have you ever had a rag pudding?' he asked, nodding again at the plate. I hadn't; in fact I had never heard of rag puddings. 'It's a Lancashire speciality,' he added, cheering up immeasurably now that he had a chance to show off some of his local knowledge. Rag puddings apparently consist of minced beef and onions wrapped in a suet pastry that is then boiled or steamed. 'Traditionally they were wrapped in bits of cloth left over from the textile production,' Andrew told me, lifting the pudding to his lips and taking a large bite. If I am honest, I could go a whole lifetime without trying another one, but I was pleased that it seemed to restore his good humour somewhat. Now that a few words had escaped his lips, the floodgates had opened and there was no stopping him.

Although formerly a butcher, Andrew is a relative newcomer to the world of black puddings and only entered the business in the early 1990s when he bought a thriving business from well-respected butcher Richard Ireland. He kept the name R.S. Ireland to assure customers that the quality of the black puddings would not be diminished and he persuaded Richard to stay on to make sure that what he had promised would actually be the case. Only when Richard was convinced that his protégé knew all there was to know was he happy to retire, leaving Andrew to run the company. Andrew continued to run R.S. Ireland so well and built it into such a success that he had to move from the original site to a purpose-built unit in Haslingden, some ten miles up the M66 from Bury, where I now sat watching him recover from his hangover. He decided at that point to change the name to the Real Lancashire Black Pudding Company to help promote his product outside the county.

Andrew was not the first black pudding maker I had ever met, but he was arguably the most knowledgeable and passionate. In just under twenty years his puddings have won countless awards, the certificates for which cover the walls of the canteen, and he has dedicated much of his time to promoting our own home-grown version at international competitions around the world to considerable success. We spent the next hour talking about the history of blood sausages and his search to find the perfect recipe for every one he had encountered to date.

Apart from those cultures whose religions prohibit the eating of blood, just about every country can offer up an example of a blood sausage, developed by necessity as a way to use up every part of the animal. Because blood contains so many nutrients, they were also lauded for their health benefits and I recall my Welsh grandmother once telling me that in her youth pregnant women were advised to eat black pudding on a regular basis to increase the iron in their own blood. My mother was given similar advice, when carrying me, but this time was told a daily pint of Guinness would do the job. That, if you know me, explains a lot.

He talked to me excitedly about our joint passion for spicy Spanish morcilla, melting German Blutwurst and the slightly sweet blood sausages of the Nordic countries, only pausing when I inevitably mentioned the French boudin.

33

'Ah, the French.' Andrew shook his head at the very mention of the boudin. 'I've stopped going to the competitions in France, because it doesn't matter how good your product is, they will only ever award the prizes to a French sausage. There's no point even bothering.'

Other countries celebrate their blood sausages, they dress up in silly costumes and hold festivals in their honour and prime examples can often be found in pride of place in the supermarkets and butcher's shops. Unfortunately, after years of abuse from home and abroad, Lancashire black pudding has never received the praise it is due and has a real image problem. Its very mention can conjure up images of cloth caps, whippets and the theme to *Coronation Street* playing in the background. This reflects the all too common ability of people in Britain to dismiss our own food out of hand in favour of something more fashionable or exotic, even if, as I am sure is the case with most when it comes to black pudding, they have never even tried it. Such prejudice puts the Lancashire pudding at a massively unfair disadvantage.

Fortunately, in the last few years, some chefs have been rediscovering the joys of our indigenous pudding, as they have with so many other great British products, and they have now been making regular appearances on menus throughout the country since the turn of the millennium. This is generally a good thing although, in the name of all that is holy, someone please tell chef and professional Yorkshireman Brian Turner that black pudding should never, ever be used in a spring roll.

There are many theories for the origins of the black pudding in Britain. Some link it to the arrival of Nordic traders and invaders, others to the visits of proselytizing monks from Europe to the shores of Yorkshire, and others still link it to the Roman *botulus*, a sausage which they claim is also the origin for the haggis. The only plausible explanation I could find as to why the black pudding industry found a home in the Lancashire area focused on the quality of the grazing land for cattle, which proved perfect for raising dairy herds. Good dairy herds give great milk, great milk makes excellent cheese, cheese-making produces whey as a by-product and that whey is perfect for feeding pigs. And pigs, as we know, are good for all manner of things to keep a man happy.

Originally, black puddings were made as a way to use up the blood released during slaughter, and at the tail end of the nineteenth century there were dozens of pork butchers in Bury and the surrounding villages, each of whom would have a small abattoir to the rear of the shop and as well as butchering the meat would make their own black puddings. Some housewives would even buy containers of blood from their local butcher to make their own versions at home. Over time, some butchers proved more adept at producing puddings and, demand outstripping supply, would buy blood from others and provide them with finished puddings to sell in return. You can still see remnants of the trade today in Bury, where makers like Chadwicks and the Bury Black Pudding Company sell puddings hot out of the boiler for you to eat with a spread of mustard as you walk around the famous town market. Andrew may not have been in the business as long as some of his neighbours, but the recipe he uses is one that Richard Ireland could trace back as far as the 1800s.

After the tea and rag pudding had served up its restorative magic, Andrew led me down to the shop floor where the ingredients for a new batch of black puddings were laid out and ready for the day's production. Having seen puddings made before, I was not surprised at how spotlessly clean and efficient the process was. Despite Andrew's best efforts and because of European Union regulations, very few of the contents of modern black puddings can be sourced locally. 'There is just not the consistency of supply,' Andrew explained, showing me containers of dried blood from Belgium, tubs of pork fat from Holland, casings of cow stomach from Uruguay and spices from all over the globe. 'It's a shame that we can't get locally sourced blood, but the end result is just as good and we need consistency for our customers to trust us.' It was a story I was to hear more than once during my travels.

If the origins of the products had changed over the years then the method of production had not. The process remained much as it would have been when puddings were made in the back of a butcher's shop, only now in greater volume. The barley is soaked overnight and then mixed with the blood, which has been rehydrated with water. The resulting mixture is then laced with cubes of pork fat and a measured amount of spice mix. The recipe, of course, is a secret, but from a deep sniff I could certainly detect a hefty amount of white pepper.

This results in an unfortunate-looking slurry, which is piped into casings, traditionally made using the stomach of a sow but now more likely to be made using ox stomach. The puddings are then tied into their traditional and instantly recognizable shape, resembling miniature clown's trousers, and boiled once in plain water to make sure they are cooked through and once more in water with soda crystals to give their outer skins that unmistakable black sheen. They are hung in nets to dry and to become firmer before they are chilled for storage. The process of making them may be similar to that of other pudding producers, but it is the care and attention to detail that make Andrew's puddings such award-winning beauties. If there is too much blood pumped into the casings they will burst. If the water in which they are boiled is too hot, the same result will occur. Too little seasoning will lead to a bland result, too much and all you will taste is that strong hit of pepper.

Back in the canteen, Andrew had selected a prime specimen from the batch we had just watched being made. 'It's still warm,' he said, handing it to me to fondle, which I did rather too lovingly. 'It doesn't need anything else doing to it.' He split it open along its length into two horseshoes, revealing the seven blobs of fat which I was told are a prerequisite of a classic Lancastrian black pudding.

I hacked off a chunk with the side of a fork and began to eat. It was not a new taste to me; I had eaten hundreds of black puddings in my time and I am sure I shall eat hundreds more, but to eat one fresh from the boiler and sitting in the works canteen with the people who made it added to the experience. For the uninitiated, the first surprise is the texture, which is firm like a good meaty sausage rather than the slime people anticipate. The spices soften during the boiling to give a definite kick, but more subtle than you might anticipate, and the overall flavour is savoury and remarkably complex. There is little wonder that the walls of Andrew's factory are covered with certificates and the website page listing their awards seems to go on for ever. These are fantastic. I have had other great puddings, but I can honestly say that this one was right up there with the best I have ever tried. Although a Lancastrian may shudder at such heresy, they are even better when reheated, fried in the residual fat of some breakfast bacon so the edges begin to crisp and the pudding releases its aroma.

'Sorry I wasn't on top form,' Andrew said as he led me back to my car carrying a goody bag filled with his range of puddings for me to sample at home. I don't think he did too badly. I had spent nearly three and a half hours with him, in which time he had gone from silence to a man who was so passionate talking about his subject he convinced me that if there were any donkeys in Haslingden, then certainly none of them had hind legs.

Andrew Holt was just the sort of producer I was hoping to meet on my trip. Passionate, funny and up to the task of fighting black pudding's quarter both at home and abroad. What's more, he didn't even throw up all over me, which, if you knew anything about my life, you would realize I usually consider somewhat of a bonus.

# 4
# Craster Kippers

I once spent a long afternoon chatting with a chef friend of mine at his restaurant in London. Service had finished and he was taking the opportunity to grab a break before he had to fire up the stoves again for the evening. He spent the best part of two hours talking passionately about how his style of cookery was dedicated to the two current buzzwords of 'seasonal' and 'local' and how much he hated supermarkets. At the end of the impassioned diatribe I asked him how he was enjoying his tea (from Darjeeling) and which part of Hackney was able to grow the lemongrass and bird's eye chillies used in some excellent crab (from Cornwall) cakes. He stammered for a moment and then angrily muttered something about having to 'prep for the evening' and disappeared back into the kitchen.

Although I am obviously a jerk and he did lay himself wide open, it does raise the question of what makes a product local? At first it seems like a very easy point to answer. And, given the way it is bandied about by celebrity chefs and on television cookery programmes with such abandon, you would hope that by now we would have a good concept of what being 'local' entails.

Literally, of course, having local food means that the product and all its ingredients are sourced and made within a radius of a few miles of where it is served. There you go, easy-peasy, lemon-squeasy. Except, unfortunately, these days it really isn't so cut and dried and it's perfectly possible to argue that it never has been. So many of the raw ingredients used in food manufacture in Britain have always come to our shores from all around the world, that you would be hard pressed to name many products that meet this notional criterion of being truly local.

Britain as a small island has always relied on trade for profit and to supplement what it can produce itself. The arrival of goods and the people who traded them has had a profound impact on British culture and its food over the centuries. Without trade we would not have our daily cuppa, most of the fruit we love to eat or even be able to exercise our right to a glass of wine and a nice large snifter at the end of a hard day.

Our current idea of what is local appears to be based on a romanticized notion promulgated by the media and television that, at some point in the past, which nobody can ever quite pinpoint, we lived an idyllic lifestyle where everything we ate came from within a few minutes' walking distance. In rural areas there may well have been a certain level of self-sufficiency. However, goods have always entered Britain and, certainly since the Industrial Revolution and the growth of the railways, produce from one part of the country has often found itself on sale in another. Even before then, there are records of foods from all over the country finding their way to the capital.

This golden age of local produce, as far as I can tell, simply never existed. It also promulgates the myth that local food is better than something that isn't, merely because it has not had to buy a bus pass. This is, of course, total and utter nonsense. The first rule of food production is 'Be Any Good'; after that so much of it is just media-generated nonsense, and while I am in favour of supporting local industry, local industry in return has to come up with sufficient quality, a fact all too many of them have yet to come to terms with. What have always existed, however, are dishes synonymous with certain areas. Dishes that, because of the economic or geographical circumstances of the location, developed to meet specific requirements. Looking at my list I could see that I had plenty such dishes to explore, including two of my own favourites, Melton Mowbray pork pies and Bakewell puddings.

Both, I noted, had recently been awarded PGI status (Protected Geographical Indication), a designation awarded by the European Union to foods that can demonstrate they are closely associated with a certain area. They must be produced in that district and also show characteristics that can only be found in that area. It is a fairly recent notion, beginning in 1993 and taking its lead from the wine industry, particularly in France where the *appellation contrôlée* system of naming according to local region is central to wine production and the maintaining of standards.

Gaining this award and its sibling PDO (Protected Designation of Origin) is a lengthy and mind-numbing process which not only involves filling out myriad forms but also usually the efforts of a determined individual to bring together all the disparate producers to agree on a standardized recipe. That's easier said than done, because if you have met as many producers as I have, you will know that they are not always an easy lot to get on with, often secretive and loath to offer up the goods on their production methods and ingredients. However, if they can find their way through a forest of forms and the inevitable infighting, gaining this protected status can prove to be an incredibly worthwhile exercise.

Not only do PGI and PDO status prevent others from using the precious regional name to sell their own debased versions of the product, they also ensure that the recipe is codified, maintaining standards and protecting it for future generations. The desire to gain PGI or PDO was a refrain I heard all over the country, not just from producers of classic dishes with centuries of history, like the pork pie, but also for dishes whose existence is linked with Britain's recent history of immigration, like the balti in Birmingham and the chicken tikka masala in Glasgow. That such enthusiasm exists for gaining this protected status is a positive sign that we are now taking our food and its production more seriously than we have at any time since before the First World War. The fact that, at the last count, we have only thirty-eight PGI status products and dishes in the UK compared to over three hundred combined in France and Italy tells you we still have a long way to go.

Which brings us, in case you thought I had forgotten, back to kippers, or more specifically to kippers produced in the small fishing village of Craster on the blustery Northumberland coast. I had arranged to meet Neil Robson, a fourth-generation producer of kippers and current custodian of L. Robson & Sons who have been making the cold-smoked beauties in the same location for well over one hundred years. When I visited, Neil had just begun the long process of applying for PGI status. Although he was garnering lots of support from the local council, which recognizes the importance of the last remaining smokehouse in this famous village, he was encountering a major stumbling block because the key ingredient of his product, the herring, was no longer sourced in regional waters.

'We can't get herring locally,' Neil explained, going into a brief lecture about the history of kippers and the decline of the British fishing industry. Evidence of smoking fish for preservation can be traced back as far as records are kept. The precursor to the kipper was the 'red herring' which was brined and then cold-smoked for up to ten days, preserving it to be kept over the winter months when boats could not put to sea and for long sea voyages where they would provide sustenance to the crew.

The long smoking partly cooked the fish and gave it the red colour from which it drew its name. It also gave it a powerful aroma, which, according to the fourth edition of Nicolas Cox's book *The Gentleman's Recreation* published in 1697, could be used to form a trail to train hunting hounds. Later anecdotal stories can be found of criminals using the fish to throw dogs off their tracks and the phrase 'red herring' entered the language.

The more gentle process of kippering is often credited to local fisherman and smoker John Woodger, who lived in the village of Seahouses in 1843. It is inevitably linked with the story that the process was discovered by accident when brined fish were left too close to an open stove, which had not been doused properly. However, both the process and the term 'kippering' pre-date him, with claims for the name coming from the old English word *kipe*, a type of woven basket in which herring were caught, or *Kuppen*, the Dutch word for spawning. It was certainly at about this time that their popularity caught on and by the end of the nineteenth century there were dozens of smokehouses in the fishing village of Craster supplying Victorian breakfast tables around the country.

As herring stocks declined due to intensive over-fishing in the twentieth century, so too did the fortunes of both the herring fishermen and the smokehouses. In 1977, with stocks dwindling to alarming levels, a full ban was placed on the fishing of herring, which certainly preserved them from almost certain extinction, but also destroyed both the herring fishing industry and the nation's taste for this exquisite oily fish. By the time the ban was lifted in 1983, the fishing boats lay idle as their owners had found other ways to make their livelihood and so too did many of the smokehouses.

L. Robson & Sons persevered during the ban, turning their attention to other more plentiful fish like salmon and haddock. When the ban was lifted, they could no longer source their herring locally and had to look further afield. 'For a while we could get them from the west coast of Scotland,' Neil told me. 'But then the fishermen there realized they could make a lot more money catching seafood to sell to Spain, so that supply dried up. Now we have to bring most of them in from Norway.' It was this last fact that had thrown a spanner in the works of Neil's application for PGI and, as far as I am aware, the debate is still going on.

If the fish he uses now have to come from a new

source, the way he treats them is little changed since the inception of the company. Neil took me from his small office into the smokery where trays of frozen herring were being unpacked and washed to remove loose scales. 'We may have to get them from Norway' – Neil held one up for me to see – 'but the quality is as good if not better than we used to get. It's the same as anything else, the end result is only as good as the raw materials.' The decapitated fish were beautifully plump and would produce lots of oils as they smoked slowly. Traditionally, the fish would be cut open by a line of chattering 'herring girls' who would gut and split the fish into the familiar flat shape. Now the girls have been replaced by a machine that can achieve the same effect at the pace of dozens of fish every minute. After splitting, the herring are brined in a solution of salt and water overnight and then hung on sharp metal tenterhooks to be placed in the kiln.

The development of modern smoking techniques means that kippers can now be prepared in four hours or less by huge commercial machines. Neil, however, still insists on hanging his fish in the same smoking chimney that has been in place for over 130 years. The modern machines may give a consistent product, but with the traditional chimney the end result is down to the skill and knowledge of the smoker. Neil walked me into the smoking room, which towered above us with thick beams running its length all the way from the floor to the ceiling and a small window at the top from which wisps of smoke were already escaping. The beams were black as night, caked in the combined residue of smoke and fish oil that had built up for over a century. 'Kippers are cold-smoked,' Neil went on. 'We leave them over smouldering oak chips for about eighteen hours, more or less depending on the weather outside.' The slow smoking process has two main benefits, he explained. The first is that the smoke obviously imparts flavour to the fish while giving it the familiar colour. The second is that, as it smokes, the fish begins to dry slightly, which acts as a preservative.

Unlike Arbroath smokies, which are hot-smoked and can be eaten fresh from the fire, the fact that kippers are cold-smoked means that they have to be cooked. 'You can grill them, fry them, bake them or poach them,' Neil said as he pulled a pair of kippers from the smoker for me to examine. A freshly smoked kipper is one of the most glorious sights in British food, burnished with a deep bronze hue, the eyes staring up at you on both sides as if they were auditioning as models for Picasso. The smell too was unmistakable, a delicate combination of light smoke and fishiness.

I am well aware, however, that what appeals to me about kippers – the look, the smell, the bones and the taste – is what repels others. In particular, I know it is the smell that people find most challenging, which can linger in the house like an unwelcome guest at the tail end of a party. I asked Neil how he prepared his to avoid the criticism. 'I like mine jugged,' he replied, telling me that the simplest way to prepare kippers was to put them in a large jug and cover them with boiling water. 'It cooks the fish very gently and also prevents too much of the smell escaping.'

I left Neil to get on with his work, which no doubt involved filling in more forms in the long-winded search to attain his PGI status. I collected a couple of pairs of kippers to take with me on the journey back to London. They were wrapped first in brown paper and then in plastic before being sealed in a freezer box in the boot of my car. Yet despite this formidable packaging, the tang from the freshly smoked fish managed to permeate its way through its rear tomb to fill the car and tantalize my nostrils in the driver's seat all the way home.

The next morning I prepared one of the kippers for breakfast just as Neil had instructed. I did not have a wide enough jug, so I placed it in a large deep-sided frying pan and poured over the contents of a boiled kettle. Four minutes later, I removed the lid, allowing a deep fishy aroma to escape into the kitchen, and lifted the kipper out carefully with a fish slice so it did not fall apart. I topped it with a knob of butter, which began to melt immediately, and then finished it with a soft poached egg whose yolk I speared with my fork so it could ooze out over the salty flesh. The fish broke in meaty flakes to reveal a gleaming white bone at its centre. It was delicious; how could anything that has been smoked for eighteen hours not be?

But every bite reminded me why kippers have fallen out of favour. Victorian gentlefolk may have had plenty of time to spend a morning removing kipper bones from their teeth and servants to waft away the lingering pong. But back in the real world of the twenty-first century, kippers simply no longer fit into the notion most people have of the perfect breakfast. Cooking something that will make your home smell like a small animal has crawled under your sofa and quietly died is never going to have huge popular appeal.

It is a great shame, but as I ate my kipper and reached for the dental floss, I couldn't help thinking that Neil Robson has far more serious challenges ahead of him than where he buys his fish.

# 5
## The King's Liver

I had just been to Costco and I was loading my car with bulk quantities of life's little essentials when my mobile phone buzzed in the back pocket of my jeans. I reached for it, managing at the same time to scatter piles of toilet rolls, Radox shower gel and washing-up liquid across the car park. It probably explains why my tone was a little less courteous than it perhaps should have been as I punched the answer button.

'Is that Simon?' the voice on the other end of the line echoed through the tinny earpiece. 'This is Mike Robinson.'

My strewn shopping was forgotten immediately. It takes a lot to impress me, but Mike is the chef/owner of the Pot Kiln, near Yattendon, which is one of my all-time favourite restaurants and his approach to cooking is one I have admired for many years. To hear his voice on the other end of the line was a more than pleasant surprise, even if his call had made me drop my shopping.

'I heard about your journey around the UK,' he added, 'and wondered if you had ever eaten the king's liver? Why don't you come up and see me at the Pot Kiln? We can go hunting and then, if we bag a deer, I will make you a hunter's breakfast.' It was too good an offer to turn down and, after agreeing a time and date, I returned to retrieving my purchases and loading the car with considerably more enthusiasm than would normally have been the case.

The Pot Kiln is set in acres of Berkshire countryside. As well as retaining its position as a pub for locals from the nearby village, it has become a destination for diners all over the country, not least because the majority of what is offered on the menu comes from ingredients that Mike has caught, foraged for on nearby estates or grown in the impressive kitchen garden to the rear of the pub. When it comes to hunting, Mike Robinson is the real deal.

I should probably make it clear that I am not talking about fox hunting, what Oscar Wilde famously referred to as 'the unspeakable in pursuit of the inedible'. What I was about to experience was the acceptable face of hunting, which, Mike told me, as far as he was concerned, had two main purposes.

The first was pretty obvious. What we shot would provide food for the restaurant. What we killed, if indeed we killed anything, would be for the pot and not slaughtered as a trophy. The second reason was just as important: efficient animal husbandry. Mike explained that the surrounding land had a vast population of roe, fallow and muntjac deer, which were capable of doing huge amounts of damage to crops if the growth of the herds was left unchecked. By killing a number of the smaller, weaker animals, Mike would not only frighten the rest away from the crops, but he would also improve the quality of the herd.

It made sense, and its logic was reinforced later while doing some wider reading about the history of hunting. As far back as the twelfth century, papal edicts allowed monks to hunt, but only when the numbers of the animals had become such that they threatened to damage the crops. In that respect, it was apparent, very little had changed in nearly a thousand years, even if the courtly ritual that surrounded the art of hunting had long since been lost.

Excited as I was by the prospect of seeing a deer being prepared in the field, Mike warned me that hunting was not like a computer game where deer popped up obligingly at regular intervals so you could dispatch them with little or no effort. This was to be real stalking where Mike's skill with a gun and knowledge of the animals, their habits and habitats would be pitted against their own cunning and strong survival instincts. 'There is no guarantee of catching anything,' Mike added as we drove through thick fog that was just beginning to lift, to the edge of one of the estates on which he had a licence to hunt. 'I have been hunting these fields pretty hard in the last few weeks, so they are learning to keep away.'

He retrieved his rifle from a locked case in the rear of the pick-up, and slung it over one shoulder as he walked towards the trail.

'Are you ready then?' he said in a loud whisper.

'Absolutely,' I replied, trotting after him trying to keep up.

'Er, I was talking to the dog,' he sniffed, as Sassy, his black Labrador retriever, ambled up alongside him already in hunting mode. She sniffed the air and loped gently from one side of the trail to the other in search of a scent. I fell back, face reddening as much from embarrassment as from the rapid pace he was setting. It had not been the most auspicious start to my hunting career.

A gentle breeze meant that the only noise we heard was the rustle of the leaves in the trees and, as the sun continued its ascent and burned away the fog, the trail was marbled by the light dappling through the curtain of branches above our heads. The stunning landscape of the Berkshire countryside was slowly coming into focus around us.

Mike and Sassy worked in harmony, he whispering orders and encouragement, she waiting for his commands before scampering ahead of us to sniff for a trail. I ambled along behind them, taking Mike's hand signals to mean I should follow directly in his footsteps so as not to make two objects for the deer to spot. It was tiring work, not just from the physical requirements of walking, but also because of the concentration required as we scanned the land for telltale signs of deer. This was stalking as I had imagined it and I was beginning to see why so many hunters talk of their addiction not just to the end result but to the means to the end result.

'There,' Mike hissed suddenly, pointing into the distance where I could see nothing but a clump of trees. He pointed again and moved forward more rapidly, crouching down so he did not alert his quarry. Sassy too kept low, scurrying along behind Mike. I followed in their wake. At a small clearing, Mike flung himself on the ground, bringing his rifle around quickly to stand on a two-legged rest so his eyes were level with a telescopic sight. He motioned for me to lie flat too, handing me a pair of binoculars.

'He'll do,' he said, as I saw the furry creature in the distance come into focus against a copse of trees. 'He's a fallow deer, a year or so old, not a particularly great specimen for the herd, but good eating.'

I sucked in a breath and waited for what was only a few seconds but seemed like an eternity. The rifle let out a single loud 'crack' as Mike squeezed the trigger and a split second later the small animal gave a start, and staggered towards the woods. Mike was up instantly and walking at a rapid march to cover the distance, while Sassy was way ahead of us running into the bushes to see where the deer had fallen, a few feet away from where it was hit.

'It's a perfect kill,' Mike said with some pride, pointing to where the bullet had entered the animal's body just under the haunch.

Mike dragged the carcass on to the nearby field, then produced a large hunting knife from his trouser pocket. He began the operation of gralloching or field dressing the animal, slitting it along the belly from tail to throat and pulling out the intestines and the rest of the innards, checking for signs of reportable disease as he went. He discarded most of the guts of the catch but pulled aside the kidneys, heart and liver.

'This,' he said, waving them at me, 'is what we want for breakfast.' And with that, he placed them back in the chest cavity of the animal for safe keeping and tied the deer to a leather harness which he hooked over his shoulders, allowing him to drag its dead weight back to his waiting pick-up truck.

Back at the Pot Kiln, the kitchen staff had already been hard at work for the lunchtime service for some hours and barely looked up as Mike wandered in clutching the entrails of a dead deer. It was obviously so regular an occurrence that it needed no comment.

I left him there and headed out into the garden to enjoy the warmth of the sun, which by now was dominating a cloudless sky. Fifteen minutes later, Mike joined me, carrying two large white plates on which our hunter's breakfasts had been artfully laid out. The kidneys had been quickly 'devilled' in Tabasco, English mustard and tomato sauce and were layered on top of a toasted slice of excellent bread. The sauce was soaking in to the slice and dribbling down the sides to form an unctuous pool on the plate. A small Barnsley chop of roe deer had been added to our contribution and had been cooked rare so the meat had to be gnawed from the bones to release its sweetness. On top of the chop, Mike had added a taste new to me, two pheasant's eggs, which have a very short season, only a matter of weeks. They are halfway between a quail's egg and a hen's egg, and had been fried so their whites were creamy and soft, the yolks bright yellow.

Given pride of place on the plate, and quite rightly so, was the liver; it was barely an hour since the animal had been killed and the fresh liver had been sliced thinly and seared in a hot pan until the outside was cooked and the inside remained beautifully pink. It had been fanned on the plate and I cut off a small piece and began to chew as Mike explained why he had called it the king's liver. 'In medieval times,' he told me, 'by law, the liver of a fallow deer was considered the finest part of the animal and the property of the king. To eat it without paying tribute was punishable by death.'

Since the liver was so fresh it had none of the high, gamey flavour that many people find so challenging. The texture of the flesh was almost silky and although it definitely revealed its offal origins, the taste was deeply meaty and savoury.

This is real food, I thought as I cleaned my plate, and then drained the last drops from a small glass of crisp dry cider, the perfect accompaniment to the richness of the game. Karl Marx talked of man being alienated from the means of production and nowhere is that more obvious than in what we eat. Most of us in Britain are so far removed from the origins of our food that we have lost all respect for the animals that are slaughtered for our benefit. The slabs of protein on our plates are, for many, entirely unconnected with animals that once drew breath.

While I knew that the visceral nature of how we spent our morning would blunt as many appetites as it whetted, I also knew that the animal Mike shot had led a free, if short existence. It had eaten well and died quickly and painlessly, free from the stress of queuing for oblivion at the abattoir. It had been killed for a purpose and every scrap of it would be put to good use by Mike Robinson, a man who had total respect for the animals he hunted.

At a time when sourcing and provenance have become such buzzwords for what we buy and when we are so uncertain of what happens in the production of our food, to eat a dish this fresh and full of flavour in these stunning surroundings was a true privilege.

'So, are you a convert to hunting?' Mike asked me and, thanks to him and, of course, the king's liver, yes, I was.

# 6
## The Arbroath Smokie

We use the term 'food hero' far too much in Britain. I hate it. I really do. It implies that something so many nations take for granted, the desire to produce and sell amazing food, is still so rare in our country that, when we do find someone offering anything even vaguely worthwhile, we have to fete them as if they were the second coming of Christ. None of this, of course, is to say that these producers don't deserve respect or that what they do is unimportant but, as far as I am aware, no cheese maker has yet found a cure for cancer, no farmer offered up a solution to Sudden Infant Death Syndrome nor butcher negotiated a lasting peace treaty between Palestine and Israel.

They make food. Er, that's it. It's an artisan craft worthy of praise but not of fawning adulation and yet turn the pages of any one of the myriad colour supplements of our Sunday newspapers or switch your television set to the cookery channels and you will find the latest 'next big thing', which only goes to confirm that our relationship with food in Britain is still so fractured that we attach ourselves to the slightest evidence of talent as if it were a piece of driftwood in a stormy ocean after a shipwreck.

Nor does it help that some producers play up to the slightest bit of attention they receive. We now live in the age of the celebrity farmer, where parading around on television in tweeds and a silly hat and speaking with an almost indecipherable broad regional accent is equated with being any good, when often the opposite is true. The quality usually declines in direct proportion to the number of appearances the farmer makes on television.

I am guilty as charged too and can be found getting all giddy and excitable when I find someone selling something sensational. However, most decent producers are rather embarrassed by it all. Not just by the slavish devotion of some of their peers to the glare of publicity, but by any attention that comes their way from just about anybody, being more concerned just to keep doing what they know and love to the best of their ability.

Iain R. Spink is the perfect example.

Iain lives and works in Arbroath, a small town on the east coast of Scotland now primarily famous for having a lowly placed football team that still holds the record for the highest losing score in senior football (36–0 against the mighty Bon Accord, in case you were wondering) if it were not also responsible for the glory that is the Arbroath smokie.

At its most basic, the smokie is a smoked haddock, but that does not even begin to do justice to the magical transformation that occurs when the fish is gutted, salted and smoked over oak chips to be eaten hot off the fire. Iain R. Spink, a quiet and unassuming man in his forties, can lay claim to being its true guardian and along with his father has done more to protect and promote this fishy wonder than anyone else, even managing in 2004 to gain PGI protection which ensures that only those fish smoked within a given distance of the town itself can use the coveted appellation.

I arrived in Arbroath after a long and tortuous drive along single roads and in torrential rain that had me crouching forward in my seat so I could peer through the windscreen that my wipers were making a valiant but ultimately futile attempt to keep clean. I found my way to the harbour front and, having parked on a small side street, went in search of the processing plant where Iain had arranged to meet me. It was not as easy as it sounded, primarily because there were a number of fishmongers on the street and the majority of them seemed to belong to people named Spink. No relation, Iain told me later.

Iain was bent over a machine straight out of Heath Robinson, with whirring brushes and water gushing through a tank at the front. It filled the air with a loud piercing noise as he operated it with his knee. He waved me over when he noticed me enter the workshop.

'Hi, I'm just cleaning ma fish,' he called out above the noise. A slightly redundant comment as he had a large dead haddock in both hands. He was taking each fish, already gutted and head removed, and after dipping it in water, holding it against the brushes until the insides were cleaned of any remaining detritus, rinsing it and tossing it into a plastic tray. He worked at a bewildering speed and before I had even had a chance to throw some questions at him, he had emptied a tray of fish and moved on to the next part of the process, tying them in pairs with cord, just below the tail.

'It's a tricky job,' he explained. 'Too tight and you cut through the bone, not tight enough and they can loosen over the smoke. Either way, they end up in the fire and cost you money.' Again, he worked with such speed it was almost impossible to catch the action as he selected two similarly sized fish, tied them with one motion and flipped them into another clean container. Finally, when faced with 200 pairs gutted, cleaned and neatly tied, we moved on to the last part of the pre-smoking process. He laid the fish in yet one more container and covered them with salt 'for about six hours', he told me, spreading the salt evenly so that every part of each fish was covered. Hard work and, although undoubtedly repetitive, demanding attention because at any point in the process the fish could be spoiled by lack of care.

I thought that Iain at least deserved some lunch and we decamped to a nearby pub. Inevitably, I ordered an Arbroath smokie from the menu. Iain appraised it with a professional eye. 'It's no bad,' he admitted. 'But wait until you try the ones I give you hot from the fire at the market,' he added, turning back to his own bowl of warming soup.

There are romantic stories about the origins of the Arbroath smokie, which involve haddock being hung up to dry over a smouldering fire in the shack of a Nordic settler or a Victorian housewife depending on which version you hear. In either case their cottage subsequently burned down and the 'smoked' fish is discovered in the rubble and found to be delicious, thus giving birth to the tradition. All complete and utter nonsense of course and a story I was to find being promoted wherever I encountered a smokehouse. The Nordics, it would appear, were great invaders but bloody useless at fire prevention.

The real history of the Arbroath smokie, as told by Iain R. Spink, did indeed date back to the time of the Nordic invaders who first came to pillage and then to settle. They brought with them their own methods of preserving food for the harsh winters and modified them to use local ingredients, in this case taking advantage of the plentiful shoals of haddock off the east coast of Scotland to replace herring.

The first records of smokies themselves being made came in the 1800s a few miles north of Arbroath in the small fishing village of Auchmithie. After lunch, Iain drove me to the site and expertly managed to navigate his van right down on to the beach. He took out an album containing a selection of old photographs he had collected of the fishermen and women of the region in the nineteenth century. I laid it across my lap and turned the pages of sepia photographs as Iain gave me a running commentary. In the pictures, the men were lean and wiry, the women broad and powerful, both testament to their respective roles in life and the conditions under which they lived.

The Arbroath smokie is a perfect example of how the conditions and resources of an area conspire to create a dish. As we sat inside while the wind and the spray from the waves lashed at the windows, Iain explained that it was on this spot and in these conditions that the women of the village would smoke the fish, more to preserve them than for the flavour. They would use as their containers unwanted barrels from local whisky distilleries, half buried in the sand to protect them from the winds. The smoke would come from oak chips made from more barrels and the fish would be hung across the fire over staves, which had been soaked in water to prevent burning. Showing even more ingenuity, the barrels would be covered in sacks scavenged from the local jute mills and the fish would be left in the hot smoke to cook for just under an hour.

Getting a glimpse at the expressive looks on the hard faces in the pictures of the men and women made me appreciate exactly what a harsh, uncompromising existence they had led and the efforts that had gone into a dish it would be easy to dismiss as simply a smoked fish. Like so many of the best British dishes, the Arbroath smokie was born as much out of necessity as culinary creativity.

I agreed to meet Iain two days later at the Kirkcaldy Farmers' Market and after spending the night in Arbroath, I spent a day hiking before driving the short distance down the coast. It was already dark when I arrived, but I was tired and ravenously hungry. Inspired by my conversations with Iain, I headed out in search perhaps of some local food to eat.

After leaving my bags at a B&B, I walked along the high street weighing up my possible choices. They were legion but none looked as if it might provide something edible and all confirmed my theory that of all the places in Britain, Scotland had the biggest fracture between the wonderful food that it is capable of producing and finding any bugger who wanted to eat it. Kirkcaldy, it has to be said, ranks up there as one of the most depressing towns in the whole of the UK, and I was brought up in Rotherham.

There were fish shops, of course, offering the inevitable deep-fried option. There were a handful of curry houses, a Thai restaurant, even a Polish deli recognizing more recent immigration to the UK and a handful of pubs packed with young people enjoying the offer of a cheap journey to oblivion. But nowhere was there any sign of food any sane person might actually want to eat. Not even in one local hotel offering of 'set menu of Indian-Scottish Fusion' which I suspect meant they delivered your chicken jalfrezi to your table with a headbutt rather than a naan bread. I slunk back to my B&B with nothing more than a chocolate bar to keep me from starvation.

Early the next morning, when I arrived as the farmers' market was being set up in one of the town squares, Iain and his helpers were already well ahead of schedule. To replicate the conditions of the original smoking barrels, Iain had purchased a portable planting bed from a garden centre and half buried his barrels in the soil. Oak chips were already glowing in the base of the barrels and smoke swirled from them into the morning air as Iain laid the staves of fish across the top and covered them with jute sacks, which he had sprinkled with water to make sure they did not burn. By now an acceptable queue had formed, consisting mainly of older people ordering pairs to take home. The ones I spoke to confirmed that they had been eating smokies all their lives and they would drive from all over Fife to come and buy some from Iain Spink. As for the new generation, one small child approached the barrels curiously, peering inside to see the fish. Iain offered her a flake of smokie to taste. Just as she was about to pop it in her mouth, her mother snatched it away saying, 'You'll no like the taste of that. It's fish,' in one fell swoop condemning fish in general as something to be avoided. Iain shook his head. It was obviously something he had seen many times before, but the image of parents foisting their own dislikes on their children was a depressing one.

When it came to my turn, Iain picked a particularly plump example fresh off the fire for me and let it cool for a second before laying it on brown paper. He removed the central bone with a practised precision. Unlike the kipper I had tried so recently, the smokie was not laced with sharp pin bones and was much more pleasant to eat. 'Have it now, while it's hot. You'll no have tried anything quite like it,' Iain said, handing it to me to balance in one hand as I tried not to let the fish juices dribble down my jacket. He was right. The oils of the fish were still bubbling on the surface from the hot smoke. The colour of the skin had turned from a drab grey to a golden bronze, which penetrated the fish for a few millimetres before it returned to a pristine white flake that pulled away from the skin with little effort. 'It needs nothing on it,' Iain continued, 'no butter, no salt. Nothing.'

He was right. Although smoking was originally a method of preservation, now it was all about the flavour and the flesh had definitely taken on a strong, but not unpleasant taste of smoke. I imagined it tasted much as it would have done when prepared by the tough, leather-faced women in the photographs Iain had shown me back in Auchmithie and I appreciated that without him and the few other producers who still cling to the old traditions in Arbroath, I would never have had the chance to try this wonderful dish.

I may hate the term with a passion, but if I were pressed to name a real 'food hero' it would be Iain R. Spink.

# 7

# Staffordshire Oatcakes

He was a big lad was Chris Bates.

His upper arms were the size of beer barrels and protruded from the armholes of a string vest, which struggled to cover the vast expanse of his chest. Even when he smiled or laughed, which he did often, he looked like he could have crushed me to an even crumb with a flicker of his eyelids. If I hadn't liked the plate of food he had just plopped in front of me, I would still have made loud and exaggerated yummy noises as I ate. I am vain, I am greedy, but I am not stupid.

As it was, the sausages, bacon, eggs and cheese wrapped in a sturdy pancake were just what I needed after an early morning start. I was on my way to Lancashire. I had not made time for breakfast and the munchies had hit me as I turned off the M1 on to the dreaded M6 at a little before 7 a.m. I pulled into the first service station I encountered, parked up and threaded my way through the rep-mobiles and delivery vans that were already filling the car park at this ungodly hour. As soon as the automatic doors opened my nose was assailed by the hideous smell of old fat. The décor may have changed but that rancid smell remained the same as it had done when sausage, egg and chips at a local motorway stop were a weekend treat for the Majumdar clan.

In the 1960s, my father's status as an immigrant doctor

from India had limited his opportunities and his income as he was passed over time and again for jobs for which he was more than well qualified in favour of someone of the correct hue. Finally, as much in desperation as desire, he ended up at a hospital in Rotherham and at the bottom of the pecking order, which meant long hours and relatively low income, until by sheer hard graft he clawed his way up the greasy pole of the abjectly racist health service of the time.

With a family of four kids, dining out was a rare treat. Uncle Sam's Chuck Wagon in Sheffield was a cheap and reliable favourite, much requested by us all for their fried chicken and chips in a basket (still available I am told). The Sujon Indian restaurant was another, although I always disliked the fact that the staff insisted on seating our family at a table by the window to be viewed like menagerie animals by passers-by, as if to say, 'Indians eat here, we must be good.' Every few months, my parents would cram all four of us into the back of my father's car and drive the fifteen miles down the M1 to the Woodhall Services and treat us to the luxury of a plate of sausages and chips in their waitress-service restaurant. Memories of these humble but enjoyable beginnings to my eating career serve as useful reminders not to be a pompous jerk when I am about to complain about some minor griev-ance when dining out. Inside, I am still the kid who clamoured for chicken in a basket and I suspect I always shall be.

However fond I was of these family meals, the service stations of the 1960s and '70s were undoubtedly grim places and although the horror-comedy of grime and grease may have been replaced by modern, sleekly designed arrivals, filled with coffee shops and super-markets, that smell of old fat remained with me as if it had been ingrained into the very fibre of the motorway service station to be released when I entered. As I wandered around I recoiled in horror at the sight of the 'All Day Breakfast' whose components already looked like they had been around since my childhood days and, after purchasing a hot chocolate to perk up my sugar levels, I returned to my car to figure out other possible options.

I flicked through the pages of my road atlas and realized that, once I had navigated the bottleneck of Birmingham, it would take me only another twenty minutes to reach the outskirts of Stoke-on-Trent and the possibility of sampling one of Britain's truly local dishes. I punched the required words into my mobile phone's internet browser and came up with the name and address of the Oatcake Kitchen and pulled out of the car park with that Proustian smell of stale grease still in my nostrils.

Staffordshire oatcakes are unlike their Scottish cousins. They are soft, pancake-like and cooked on a griddle rather than crisp and baked in the oven. They were developed, like so many of the dishes in Britain, to deliver carbohydrates and slow-released energy over the period of a long day's hard labour. Their origins are the subject of argument and many even claim a link to returning soldiers recreating the breads of their time in colonial India. The more persuasive notion, however, is that they were created in Derbyshire in the 1800s as a fortifying breakfast for the county's coal miners, using the oats that were the abundant winter crop in the area since they were more hardy than wheat.

As families migrated west from Derbyshire towards the five Staffordshire towns that make up the Potteries in search of work in the burgeoning ceramics industry, they took with them their staple meal. Although they were originally made at home and served spread with dripping, the wives of the pottery workers soon began to sell them on street corners and then from market stalls to men rushing on their way to the factories. Eventually they began to open bakeries and oatcake shops, which at the turn of the twentieth century could be found on most street corners offering 'oatcake flannels' for sale. Their popularity continued throughout the early part of the twentieth century and two world wars when they were appreciated as cheap and readily available sustenance.

The last fifty years saw a marked worsening of their fortunes. The decline of the ceramics industry, which recently saw the bankruptcy of famous names like Wedgwood and Royal Doulton, took away the captive market of customers. The children of retiring bakers were less inclined to continue the business and the challenge from other fast foods and the rise of supermarkets meant that by 2009 there were only forty oatcake bakeries left in the whole region. Between them, they still manage to make 350,000 oatcakes a year and as they sell almost entirely within the Stoke region, it was hard not to imagine the bakers as akin to some remote Amazonian tribe waiting for extinction, unnoticed by the rest of the world. Since he bought his bakery after being made redundant, ex-ceramics worker Chris Bates has set out his stall to protect and promote one of Britain's great regional food secrets.

A little over an hour after leaving the smells of the service station, I pulled up outside the Oatcake Kitchen. It was an unassuming old school café, situated on a narrow side road a few hundred yards from the Britannia Stadium, the home of Stoke City, one of the city's two perennially underachieving football teams.

The place was empty, apart from one old dear draining the dregs from her cup of tea. I walked to the back of a small split-level dining room and found a seat. Picking up the laminated menu, I could see that on one side it listed the usual standard breakfast offerings, but on the reverse was a long list of the possible fillings to have with the oatcakes. 'What's the best way to have them?' I asked the young waitress who appeared at my side.

'Well,' she replied, her accent a classic Potteries burr, 'most people round here like them with cheese, because that's traditional, but you can have them filled with egg, sausages and bacon too.'

My hunger was unabated and I ordered one with everything they had to offer and sat back with a large mug of builder's tea to take in the smells of my breakfast being prepared. It was delivered to the table a few minutes later by the chef in person, already puffing and an alarming shade of red from his exertions over a hot griddle, which he told me had begun at five in the morning. He placed a laden plate in front of me and took a seat at an adjacent table, watching me intently as I began to eat. As I worked on my breakfast, Chris explained to me how he was working to bring all the other bakers together into an association. It would be, he hoped, not only an organization that would codify what an oatcake was for future generations, but also protect it by way of gaining the European PGI status I had already heard mentioned around the country.

As he talked, I carried on eating. If truth be told, the sausages and bacon were by Chris's own admission unremarkable 'greasy spoon' fodder, but the oatcake itself was an interesting new taste to me. It was more dense than a traditional pancake, with a grainy texture that came from the use of oats in the batter and allowed it to soak up the yolk of a perfectly fried egg. 'It's certainly not fine dining,' Chris added, 'but there's not a lot better for setting you up in the morning.' He was right, it had certainly filled a hole in my corporeal temple better than any motorway service station all day breakfast could ever have done.

Although the numbers of bakeries was on the decline, Chris told me that his sales were on the increase. He had begun to use the internet to promulgate the glories of the oatcake, with the result that expatriates had begun to e-mail requests for his oatcake batter mix to be sent to far-flung corners of the globe. 'We send packages regularly to Canada, Australia and New Zealand,' he said, pinpointing places where former ceramics workers might have headed in search of new career opportunities. 'We receive dozens of e-mails a week from Stokies longing for a taste of home.'

After I finished my breakfast, wiping the plate clean with the last of my oatcake, Chris invited me back into his small kitchen to help him make the last few batches of the day. The batter was a secret recipe he bought from the previous owner when he took over the bakery and he would not reveal its exact details. But he would at least share with me that it consisted of three different types of flour and the coarse milled oatmeal from which the pancake took its name. With a fresh mug of tea in hand, I perched myself on a kitchen counter and watched Chris as he began cooking. The hotplate, seasoned by years of constant use, was given a thin film of cooking oil. Then ladles of batter were poured in rows by Chris with a well-practised flip of the wrist until there were ten oatcakes bubbling away at one time. By the time the last one had dripped from the ladle, the first was ready to be turned to cook for a few seconds on the other side and then flipped on to a wire rack to cool.

It looked easy enough and Chris motioned me over to have a go. When Chris handed over the ladle to me I wondered just why his wife and the young waitress had stopped work and were peering into the kitchen to watch. I soon found out as my attempts to pour the batter in the same way as Chris had saw them leak across the hotplate and begin to form one enormous and hideously misshapen pancake on the griddle while the excess batter made a run for it over the edge and dripped to the freedom of the floor.

Chris let out a loud sigh, took the ladle from me and added, 'I can make 1,000 a day if I have to.' He was soon back in control, giving me one more demonstration of the oatcake maker's art before he allowed me to try again. This time I attacked the griddle with more confidence and although they weren't perfect by any means, they were mine and when Chris placed them in one of his Oatcake Kitchen bags for me, I carried them proudly out to my car and placed them carefully in a freezer box in the boot.

Despite the fun of spending a morning making

misshapen oatcakes and my first experience of eating them in the company of Chris Bates, my time in the Oatcake Kitchen was tinged with a degree of sadness. Chris may be working hard to preserve the Staffordshire oatcake, but in truth all he is doing is preserving the memory of them for future generations. When he retires, it is unlikely that anyone will rush to take his place. It is, quite simply, too much for a new generation less inclined to work so hard or rise so early. The same is probably true of the other bakeries and I can believe that in a generation they will all be gone, the Staffordshire oatcake being consigned to the pages of a history book or occasional demonstrations at a Potteries folk museum.

It's a great shame. They may not be haute cuisine, and I can't begin to imagine them finding their way on to even the most ironic of gastropub menus. However, they are a living link to our past industrial heritage and damn delicious to boot. So try one while you can or get what you deserve, which could well be a motorway service station, all day breakfast. Don't say I didn't warn you.

# 8
## The Bacon Butty

As I mentioned earlier, the breakfast at the Little Chef in Popham was very nasty indeed. But at least one thing Heston Blumenthal had done was to source decent ingredients. He had revamped the 'All New Olympian Breakfast' to include the results of his search. The bacon was superb. It tasted, well, ridiculous as it sounds, of bacon. I immediately scrawled in my notebook and promised myself I would contact the producer if only to congratulate them on surviving the Little Chef makeover experiment. The bacon came from Denhay Farm, one of the largest producers in the country and was part of a new range of Wiltshire cured bacon they had perfected and submitted to Heston just in time to be considered for the Little Chef menu.

George Streatfeild, the owner, invited me down to join him, his wife and daughter at their farm in deepest, darkest Dorset so I could see how it was produced. Denhay Farm is a large estate and has been in the Streatfeild family for generations. Bacon, what they are now most famous for, was not originally the farm's main business. It was, as I had seen on other dairy farms, a by-product of cheese-making. They also produced considerable quantities of West Country Farmhouse Cheddar, which utilized milk from their own dairy herds. As I was to find out on my visit to Leagram Dairy in Lancashire, it had traditionally been a regular part of the cheese-making cycle to sell the by-product of high-protein whey created during the process to pig farmers in return for cuts of pork, sausages and joints of bacon and ham. Here at Denhay Farm they had moved to a much larger scale by rearing their own pigs and so successful had their bacon become that George had recently made the decision to move production from the farm itself to a dedicated unit a few miles away.

It's an impressive facility, although I must admit that I would find it hard to criticize any place dedicated to the production of pork goods. Making bacon is a painstaking process and one that cannot be hurried along if you want an end result as fine as that produced by Denhay. This is real old-school bacon production and, while the facility itself is modern and well equipped, the attention to detail paid to each joint is a testament to their farmhouse origins. Many producers, however, are not so scrupulous, both skipping some parts of the process and hurrying along others in a rush to get their bacon on the supermarket shelves. Many, too, inject their bacon with brine to build up the weight, weight that all comes out in the pan as that all too recognizable sticky, white sludge as the bacon is cooked. Like so many other food products, the debasement of our nation's bacon can be traced back to rationing and the period immediately after the Second World War, when volume was as important, if not more important than quality. As a nation we became used to our daily rashers shrivelling in the pan and as a child I remember scraping away a pool of noxious gunk from my plate as part of the daily breakfast routine.

But great bacon is one of Britain's real treasures and I

am told by a number of recovering vegetarians that it was the smell of bacon frying that finally brought them from the dark side back into the holy light of the carnivorous. It was not hard to understand and, after our tour, as George pulled up in the courtyard of the farm, the smell of bacon being prepared wafted towards us and made me slobber before I had even taken off my seat belt.

Inside the farmhouse kitchen, George's wife, Amanda, and daughter, Ellen, were already laying the table for lunch. They produced four different types of bacon and, to aid me in my quest for the perfect bacon sandwich, had placed plates laden down with each type on the wooden table. There was smoked and unsmoked and different cuts and cures including the Wiltshire cure that had managed to overcome being prepared by the staff at the Little Chef. Alongside the plates of bacon were thick slices of white bread and some brown in case I wanted to go off-piste. There was butter made with milk from their own dairy herd and a large slab of their excellent West Country Farmhouse Cheddar.

I took little prompting to begin my attempt to construct the perfect bacon butty.

Of course, any right-minded person in Britain will confirm that the bacon sandwich is the greatest of all 'between bread' creations. If anyone doesn't they should, quite frankly, be run out of the country on a rail after we re-establish the fine art of tarring and feathering. However, I will concede that there are many different routes to the perfect bacon sandwich. Mine, obviously, is the best, so here it is.

# *Bacon Butty*

## (SERVES 1)

*5, yes, count 'em, 5 thick-cut rashers of good bacon (I prefer
  smoked with a good ribbon of fat)*
*2 thick, hand-cut slices of white farmhouse bread with a hard
  crust*
*a good thick spread of unsalted butter*
*tomato ketchup*
*HP sauce*
*white pepper*

Fry the bacon over a low heat for 5 minutes on each side
until the fat begins to crisp up (a bacon sandwich without
crisp bacon fat is not a bacon sandwich).

Spread both slices of bread with enough butter to
alarm your cardiologist. Apply tomato ketchup to one
piece of bread and then layer your rashers of bacon on
that slice in a criss-cross pattern. Apply HP sauce to taste
and sprinkle with white pepper.

Top with the other slice and leave to sit for 1 minute
so that the heat from the bacon can melt the butter and
the juices can run into the bread.

Then, and only then, cut the sandwich.

NB: NEVER cut your bacon sandwich diagonally, as
you allow the flavours to escape.

Serve with a cup of strong builder's tea.

— *Elevenses* —

Even in these tough economic times when many employers seem hell-bent on sucking any and all vestiges of pleasure out of the daily existence of the average working stiff, some things remain sacrosanct. Chief among them is the partaking of elevenses. Even if we spend the majority of our lives glued to a desk, staring at a computer screen or in meetings pretending we care about the interpretation of a spreadsheet, the break for a hot drink and a little snackette halfway between breakfast and lunch is a covenant between Britain and God. It can never be broken. Not by war, not by economic crisis and certainly not by namby-pamby middle managers who dare not make a comment but will peer across the room as if to ask 'Do you not have anything better to do with your time?'

Elevenses really begins around 10.30 a.m. with a slight rumbling of the stomach, which if you are lucky will go unnoticed by colleagues. The rushed breakfast of cereal and toast happened in another lifetime and the appropriate point at which to open the chicken salad sandwich you bought on your way in to the office is an awfully long way away. This is where elevenses comes into its element. It is the perfect pick-me-up, a great British institution, which goes some way to explaining why, even when I was a little boy, my school still owned maps that were at least a quarter covered in empire pink. Let's not beat around the bush, elevenses helped Britain rule the world. I am not the only one in this country who believes that if President Obama offered the G20 summit 'a nice cup of tea and a slice of Battenberg' at 11 a.m., the troubles of the world would be dealt with so much more easily. Conversely, if Hitler had decided to time Operation Sea Lion attacks to 11 a.m. and 4 p.m., this book would probably be called *Ich Esse Für Großbritannien*.

Simple as it may seem, however, elevenses is not a task to be taken lightly. It takes planning and thought. Do you just make your morning cup of tea or coffee for yourself? Or, in the best traditions of British fairness, should you offer to make it for all your colleagues, miming your intentions with that familiar 'cup to mouth' action that any fool can recognize as meaning 'fancy a cuppa?'?

Once you have decided on your level of generosity, you are then faced with the hard decision as to what today's elevenses will consist of. Do you raid the company's box of 'Executive Selection' chocolate biscuits normally saved for visits by the bank manager or VAT man? Do you use your own stash, secreted in your desk drawer from where you covertly sneak rich tea biscuits and suck on them quietly because you only have six left and don't want to share them? Or do you go the whole hog and pop across the road to your local supermarket for a box of doughnuts, which you offer to everyone, making sure that the fat bloke in Accounts (yes, there is always a fat bloke in Accounts) does not take more than his fair share.

Even if you have to rush through your elevenses before getting back to the drudgery of your normal day, there is no doubt that this all too short break makes the world a better place.

# 9
## Tea and Biscuits

*Well I think we should all sit down and have a nice cup of tea, and some biscuits, nice ones mind you. Oh and some cake would be nice as well. Lovely.*

www.nicecupofteaandasitdown.com

I could not agree more with this mission statement from one of my all-time favourite websites. For those of you who don't know www.nicecupofteaandasitdown.com I recommend you take a few moments, make yourself a nice cup of tea and find a comfortable place to place your ample rear. Then spend half an hour away from the pain and misery of the world while you sip and read about the joys of the Fig Newton, the horrors of Nice biscuits and why Jaffa Cakes are not biscuits at all (the clue's in the name, stupid). You won't regret it.

It goes to prove that I am not alone with my slight obsession for tea and biscuits. Surprisingly, Britain rates just behind the Republic of Ireland as the country that drinks the most tea in the world. Even so, the majority of us sip our way through a staggering, wait for it, 75,000 cups in a lifetime. I am guessing I am at well over 50,000 right now and, as soon as the kettle comes to a boil, will be adding to that number by one in a few minutes. It is a passion that can be traced back to the very early years of the eighteenth century when Queen Anne began to take black tea with her meals, although green tea is known to have been introduced by Catherine of Braganza, in the mid seventeenth century, when she married Charles II. The desire to ape royalty led to tea becoming fashionable in London's coffee houses, the most famous of which was Tom's Coffee House, run by a man whose surname is forever associated with top-quality brews, Thomas Twining.

It wasn't the British who first brought tea to Europe. Dutch missionaries discovered that in China and Japan leaves were infused with boiling water to create a liquid considered to have mystical powers of healing. Dutch traders began returning with boxes of tea leaves for their patrons and it became fashionable to serve it at parties where the guests would sing the praises of its health-giving properties and its appearance would confirm the wealth and standing of the hosts. Its popularity as a tonic grew rapidly among people at the top end of society, replacing ale as the staple drink for those who could afford the enormous expense. Although science later proved the benefits of drinking tea, it is probably as likely that any positive effect on health at that time came from the fact that water, which was heavily contaminated, became purified as it was boiled to make the tea.

By the end of the eighteenth century Britain alone was importing over 11 million pounds of tea a year, nearly all of it from China. However, the real growth in the popularity of tea and its move from being a drink for the elite to an everyday brew for the working man did not take place until the middle of the nineteenth century. In 1835 the East India Company lost its monopoly on importing tea from China and in response cultivated its first plantations in India, at first in Assam and then later in Darjeeling. Perhaps the most pivotal point in bringing tea to a wider audience came in the final decade of the century when Thomas Lipton, owner of over 300 grocery stores throughout the country, called Lipton's Markets, bought vast tracts of land in what was then Ceylon to produce cheap, uniform quality tea for his shops. It was an interesting precursor to the way modern supermarkets work today to maintain their supply of wines, the key being to ensure quality at a price and consistency of supply.

However, just as it does now, consistency of quality often equated to mediocrity and although the British began to develop an insatiable taste for tea, it was for what one Calcutta tea merchant once described to me as 'any old rubbish, as long as it is brown and wet'. While there is now a growing market for fine teas and teas grown on single estates, well over 90 per cent of the tea we drink in this country is still prepared using tea bags and a large proportion of that by dunking a bag in a cup of boiling water.

I have been fortunate enough to taste some of the best teas in the world. I have spent time at the Goomtee Estate in India as the first flush was harvested in the shadows of the hills of Darjeeling and sat in the guesthouse gardens drinking tea made from leaves processed less than twenty-four hours before. I have spent a great deal of time in the company of my friend Henrietta Lovell who runs the Rare Tea Company. She is the winner of so many awards for her loose-leaf teas that she should rent a separate flat just to keep them in. She has tried, God knows she has tried, to inculcate in me the pleasures of legendary teas from China, teas from small farms in Malawi and teas from the great estates of Assam, Darjeeling and Sri Lanka but all to no avail. It is still, despite this exposure to the very best, a box of my favourite tea bags that is the first thing in my suitcase whenever I travel. When entering the US I am often asked by curious customs officials why I am muleing such readily available items into their country.

THEM (holding up a Ziploc bag containing the evidence): What is this?

ME: Er, it's tea bags. I bring them with me when I travel.

THEM: You can get tea bags here, you know.

ME (thinking of the disgusting examples I have had to suffer when I forget to bring my own): No, no really, you can't.

There is usually a quick shrug of the shoulders and I am allowed through carrying my prized stash of 'proper' tea bags. All I need to do now is mule around a 'proper' electric kettle and I shall be all set.

My own personal preference is for Yorkshire Gold, the superb tea bags produced by Taylors of Harrogate. I was fortunate enough to meet Ian Brabbin, the tea buyer of this famous old company. I have to admit that the last time I was as excited was when I went to see Graceland in Memphis, sad but all too true. He told me, with a gloomy shake of his head, that although as a nation we still turn to tea bags, we are losing the art of making tea with them properly. The average length of time a person leaves a tea bag immersed in boiling water is usually no more than a mere eighteen seconds. According to Ian, it should be left to brew for at least four minutes to get the right strength and colour.

The importance of tea to British culture comes not just in the taste of tea but in the process of making it. It is a procedure that, if it is done correctly, allows you the chance to take at least a ten-minute respite from your cares while the kettle boils and the tea brews. But it must be done properly. It requires a pot in preference to a cup, an electric kettle to boil the water correctly and enough time to allow the tea to sit and wait until it is a deep, rich brown as it dribbles from spout to cup. I don't bother to warm the pot. People will give you all sorts of bunkum about that, but it is a tradition that originated in working-class homes where poor quality china and unglazed pots could crack if they were not warmed through. The same is true of the perennial 'milk first/tea first' debate. Again, working-class families would add milk to reduce the temperature of the tea as it hit the cup in the hope of preventing breakage. Although the quality of mass-produced chinaware soon made this unnecessary, the tradition survived and carries on today. I always put my milk in first, but it is more from habit than because of any proof that it makes a better cup of tea. The final result should achieve what tea experts call 'brightness' and, in a perfect world, be the colour of a polished two pence coin. So now you know.

The decision to 'put the kettle on' is not just an invitation to have a hot drink but also an invitation to stand back from whatever situation precipitated such a thought and use the time to take stock and make a rational judgement. In real life it could be anything from pondering on what to have for supper to dealing with the emotional trauma of a break-up. If the soap world is to be believed it can also clear the mind wonderfully before and after the murder of a spouse, an illicit affair or even a barney in the pub. Little wonder that a cup of tea is known as 'British penicillin'.

With a cup of tea, of course, come biscuits. I am eating one as I write this chapter. Well, of course I am; there are few pleasures in my life that come close to a large mug of builder's tea and a plateful of biscuits. It is a pleasure that began when I was a small child and treated by my mother to sole ownership of a packet of chocolate digestives after a particularly protracted bout of aggravation by my older brother, Robin, known to one and all as The Great Salami (and hereafter referred to as TGS), a food related title he bestowed upon himself while torturing the rest of the Majumdar siblings during a particularly malevolent babysitting stint. I scoffed half immediately and secreted the rest in the drawer of my bedside cabinet, where I promptly forgot about them. Two weeks later, I discovered them again while looking for a copy of *Whizzer and Chips*. They were by now, of course, totally soft, but I ate them all anyway. Not just because they were there, my usual excuse with food I find by accident, but because they were mine, a sign that I was becoming a person in my own right and with my own tastes, likes and dislikes. I learned another valuable life lesson that day. A whole packet of biscuits is to be consumed in one sitting. Any other course of action is hideously un-British and very probably means you are a puppy strangler.

For the same reasons of personal growth I gravitated

towards my own biscuit of choice; we all have one. Mine was the custard cream. Two slices of biscuit with a detailed filigree on the outside, sandwiching a thin filling of rich butter cream. I liked them for two reasons. The first one was that no one else in the family seemed to like them much, or, if they did, they placed them below the chocolate-covered biscuits my mother would buy in a tinned assortment from Fine Fare, so leaving plenty of them in the tin for me. Possibly more important was that no biscuit on earth is better suited to the serious task of being dunked in a hot cup of tea. Don't ask me to explain the science, although I am perfectly sure there are people, presumably single, who have done very detailed research. The density of the custard cream is unbeatable at with-standing the hot liquid, so most of it does not end up at the bottom of the mug. Yet at the same time, by some almost magical process it retains enough of the tea to create a soft, sweet mix, a *mélange*, if you will allow me, that is hard to beat.

The custard cream also contributed to my acquisition of a degree in theology. I was not the most hard-working of students and would always leave a string of essays, due to be turned in at the end of term, to be scrabbled through in little more than the remaining week before the deadline. My strategy would be to skip all lectures and lock myself away in my small room and not let myself leave until they were completed. In case you are wondering, yes, I used the sink. I am not proud of it, but there you go. For sustenance, I would buy bags of broken custard creams available for pennies at a low-rent super-market on Camberwell High Street and eat them in a perpetual motion of 'dip and munch' until the work was done. I usually emerged on a sugar high from which I would not come down for days. On more than one occasion, I was summoned by the college librarian to come and explain away some interesting brown stains on a book detailing the exegesis of the Synoptic Gospels.

The name biscuit comes from the Latin *panis biscotus*, which means 'twice-baked bread', and Alan Davidson, in his superb *Oxford Companion to Food*, tells of Roman chef Apicius making a paste of wheat flour and water, baking it and then cutting it into slices to be fried before being served with honey. Although biscuits were produced throughout the Middle Ages, they had more in common with cakes than the biscuits we know today and in the southern states of the USA a request for a biscuit will find you being presented with something more akin to a scone than anything you might care to dunk in your tea. Hardtack biscuits were developed for the British navy. They were baked and allowed to dry and often baked again so they could survive long sea voyages. The end result was so hard that they had to be dunked in hot liquid or ale to make them palatable, no doubt the beginning of the tradition that is so much a part of Britain's culture today.

Given the cost of sugar and the labour-intensive manufacture, sweet or 'fancy' biscuits were usually only for the rich, and it was not until the rapid growth of the British Empire at the beginning of the nineteenth century, the technology of producing sugar from local beets and the development of machines for mass production that prices began to come down and these biscuits were made available to a wider audience. They soon became hugely fashionable and new varieties were created all the time so that by 1903 Huntley & Palmers, which by then had already been in existence for over eighty years, was offering over 400 varieties of biscuits. These were sold, much as they are now, either in packages of a single variety or in attractive boxes to be opened on special occasions such as Christmas. Many of our current favourites stem from this time and our luxury bourbon with its layer of chocolate cream filling, the Garibaldi 'squashed fly' biscuit with its chewy dried fruit centre, the humble yet versatile rich tea and the mighty digestive have long and noble histories. Chocolate biscuits are more modern, appearing only in the 1950s, but they have rapidly established themselves at the top of the dunking table.

We need to be very clear that we are talking about biscuits here, not cookies. Cookies are the cuckoo in the nest, they are interlopers. They are the outward and visible sign of the inward and rotten permeation of American culture into our society. Like the proliferation of the cupcake, which threatens our own perfectly good fairy cake, cookies are overly sweet slices of nothingness, which should quake in terror before the solid John Bull stoicism of our own home-grown biscuits. We need to protect them in the face of those pieces of flavourless cardboard that are offered to us in chain coffee shops up and down the country. I apologize for the rant, but I take such matters very seriously, perhaps too seriously.

I think what I need is to put the kettle on and have a nice cup of tea and a sit down.

Lovely.

# 10
## Yorkshire Parkin

There is something about Bettys of Harrogate that seems from another time. As you walk into the grand tearoom of their original branch, uniformed staff appear to float from one end to the other carrying trays of cakes and polished teapots with steam twisting from their spouts. On one side of the room you may see a whole family celebrating, their table laden down with sandwiches, while on the other you will see a young girl, dressed up to the nines, being treated to high tea by a loving but overpowering grandmother who keeps telling her to sit up straight while she butters her Fat Rascal. The clothes of the diners may have changed over the ninety years since Bettys opened, but precious little else has and it holds a very dear place in the heart of anyone who has ever been taken there.

The lack of change is no bad thing and tea at Bettys is enough to bring back memories of a simpler age that seems to have been forgotten in the rush to modernize, process and mass-produce. At Bettys, however, thankfully it would appear that it has not been forgotten at all and even though, over the years, it has developed from the single famous tearoom in Harrogate to six dotted all over Yorkshire, the same family values have been maintained since it was opened by Swiss confectioner Frederick Belmont in 1919.

The first thing I noticed on entering the production area of Bettys' craft bakery just outside Harrogate was the quiet. Of course there was the odd clatter of mixing machines and the occasional bang from a metal tray being replaced in a rack, but that was about it. There was none of the whirring and buzzing I expected from large machines capable of dealing with the output Bettys' tearooms and mail order now demand. Instead there was a small brigade of people, each at their own position, quietly getting on with their allotted task. At one station, a young woman mixed the ingredients for florentines, mixtures of nuts and candied fruits ready to be dipped in chocolate. At another, a man in his middle age was portioning out quantities of dough to be combined to create the signature Fat Rascal, Bettys' famed hybrid between a scone and a rock cake, and at a third, preparation was under way to create the reason I had travelled all the way from London to arrive at the craft bakery as instructed by 7.30 a.m. It was a pleasure to see all the other cakes and breads being made and I happily accepted a feather-light vanilla slice and a restorative mug of tea as I sat with bakery manager Caroline Grant in the staff canteen. But I was there for one reason: I wanted to learn how to make proper Yorkshire parkin.

Parkin (or perkin if you listen to the folks nearer the Midlands) actually derives its name from a diminutive for the name Peter popular in the eighteenth century and, like its name, the roots of the dish can be traced back to the same period. Ginger and treacle, produced by slave labour in the Caribbean, would be shipped into the west coast ports, particularly Liverpool, and would be transported across country to the east coast ports of England for sale to Europe and beyond, much of it shipped from the east coast port of Grimsby. Oats were an abundant and hardy crop in Yorkshire and, at some point, the ingredients were combined to make parkin, a cake that provided energy for working men and was capable of being stored for a number of weeks, both properties that were something of a blessing for the women who ran the household.

For those unlucky enough never to have tried it, parkin is one of Britain's great cake creations and its dense, rich combination of treacle, oats and ginger has an effect as Proustian as any madeleine on any Yorkshireman. For me, parkin will always be associated with bonfire night, in my case, witnessed on the corporation playing fields across from our house in Rotherham. The occasion would be as much a chance to eat some of our favourite once-a-year foods as it would to watch Catherine wheels whirring sparks or to play with sparklers. There would be dense cinder toffee, which managed both to dissolve on the tongue and stick to the teeth at the same time. There would be tinned frankfurters served in soft milk rolls with fried onions, baked potatoes with no other toppings than salt and butter unwrapped from a small foil packet and, of course, at the end of it all there would be a big slab of gloriously sticky parkin.

The moment it was portioned out was the moment I had been waiting for all night and I would carry away my prized piece of cake in a paper napkin to a quiet corner where I would pick small crumbs from it to make it last. If it was a good example of the parkin genre, it would have been left to sit for at least a couple of weeks. Consequently it would be dense enough to retain a print when I poked it with my finger. The treacle and the chewy oats would be offset by a huge hit of powdered ginger and the end result would be a slight but pleasing burn at the back of my throat.

At Bettys, after a quick search to find a white coat that would fit me, I joined baker James Proudfoot as he prepared their own famous version of parkin. With the possible exception of the addition of a small amount of invert sugar to keep the cake moist, the ingredients James poured into the super-sized bowl were identical to the ones you might use at home, only in quantities enough to make 120 cakes at a time rather than a couple of loaf tins. Tubs of black treacle glistening like an oil slick as they were poured on top of rolled oats, wholemeal flour, butter and a hefty amount of that powdered ginger were mixed together before being portioned by hand into the same sort of cake tins you or I might use. While the cakes were taken away to the ovens, I took the chance to see the rest of the bakery. There are constant reminders of the origins of Frederick Belmont, not least in the fact that the craft bakery also houses a superb chocolate department, where two members of staff were painstakingly dipping flower petals in rich, dark chocolate to decorate a specially ordered wedding cake.

A little under an hour later, I was summoned back to the staff canteen to taste the reason for my visit, the finished parkin. It was certainly delicious, good enough at least for me to have three slices and an extra cup of tea. However, there was something missing, something that did not quite tally with my vivid childhood memories of parkin. Perhaps it lacked the powerful hit of ginger I remembered? Perhaps it was my memory that was at fault and not Bettys' parkin? It may, after all, just have been a mildly gingery squishy cake and the pleasure I derived from it was as much from the context in which it was eaten as it was skilled baking.

After saying my goodbyes to the lovely people of Bettys, I drove back down the A1, making a short detour to pick up the necessary ingredients to find out for myself. It was an unlikely decision for me to pull on an apron, because although I like to cook, another result of my Yorkshire upbringing is that I have always considered baking to be, well, ever so slightly suspect.

The staff of Bettys were very secretive about their recipe, so, early the next morning, I began to scour the internet and my old cookbooks to come up with one of my own. Both sources offered up dozens of suggestions, some of which seemed likely candidates and some of which were decidedly odd, sounding like no parkin I had ever eaten and making me want to wail with their suggestions of adding dried peel and honey. In the end, I decided that the only way I was going to come up with the perfect recipe was to create one myself and I spent a frustrating day in the kitchen making batch after batch until both I and most of the work surfaces were caked in flour.

In the end, however, I cracked it and the resulting recipe was enough to transport me back to my childhood.

## — *Parkin* —

### (MAKES 1 LARGE OR 2 SMALL LOAF TINS)

*200g butter (at room temperature)*
*200g muscovado sugar*
*200g black treacle*
*100g golden syrup*
*200g self-raising flour (or plain flour with 1 teaspoon*
  *bicarbonate of soda)*
*200g medium oatmeal*
*½ level teaspoon salt*
*2½ level teaspoons ground ginger*
*8 tablespoons milk (warmed through)*
*2 eggs, beaten*

Melt the butter, sugar, treacle and syrup in a pan, heating gently until they form a syrup. Allow to cool.

Mix all the dry ingredients in a bowl and make a well in the centre. Pour in the syrup mixture. Add the milk and mix all the ingredients well. Then stir in the beaten eggs.

Pour the mixture into one large or two small cake loaf tins, lined with baking parchment, and bake in the centre of a preheated oven at 325°F/160°C/gas mark 3 for about 1 hour.

To test if the parkin is ready, insert a metal skewer. If it comes out clean, it is done. If not, then the cake will need 5 minutes more.

Allow to cool in the tin for 15 minutes and then turn out on to a wire rack.

The general consensus is that parkin is best left for at least a couple of days before it is eaten, but that was never going to happen and, once the cake had cooled sufficiently, I hacked off a thick slice to sample. There it was, the perfect parkin of my childhood, gloriously gooey, messy fun with the unapologetic kick of ginger I had been looking for all along. If I closed my eyes for a moment, I could have been back on the council playing fields. All I needed now was a sparkler.

# 11
## Welsh Cakes and Pikelets

Pat Maddocks reminded me of my grandmother. She wasn't nearly old enough to be, but it was her manner as she worked in her narrow kitchen with quiet efficiency that reminded me so much of my own grandmother. Added to which, the gentle accent with which she spoke as she went about her business transported me back to my days as a child watching Eva John bake for Wales in her own small kitchen.

If I pestered enough (and believe me, I could and still can pester at an international level when the need arises), Nana would break out the mixing bowl and I would sit with her as she mixed the ingredients for her perfect Welsh cakes, rolling out the perfect dough, and cutting them into perfect rounds ready to be cooked on her traditional and ancient flat griddle. My mother too made Welsh cakes, wonderful ones, and every time I paid a visit to my home in Rotherham I would come away with a biscuit tin filled with them to bring back to London. Most of my college friends had never encountered them before, but would gather at my hall of residence bedroom door minutes after I returned, asking me if I had brought any of those 'squashed scones' down with me. Being the good sort that I was, I always shared and within a couple of hours they would all be devoured.

Now both my mother and grandmother are gone and it had been well over a decade since I had last sampled the results of their baking skills.

Once I had decided to head to Wales for a few fleeting days of eating, I scoured the internet to find who might be able to help me rediscover another of the great tastes of my childhood. I came across a tiny company called Cakes of Wales, the husband and wife team of Tony and Pat Maddocks, based in Southgate overlooking the cliffs of the Gower Peninsula. A quick call and they readily agreed for me to pay them a visit.

I wasn't at all sure I had come to the right place as I pulled up in front of their house. It looked like a building site, but Tony appeared almost immediately at the front door, reassuring me that they were just in the process of adding an extension for a small tearoom to the front of the house. Every summer the town plays host to thousands of walkers and Tony was keen that they should have the chance to come and sample Pat's baking hot out of the oven.

The scent in the air as he led me to the kitchen was already transporting me back over forty years. The smell of Welsh cakes on the griddle is unmistakable and Pat had been hard at work in the kitchen for the last few hours preparing the sweet dough. 'They are getting really popular now,' Pat sang at me as she carried on working. 'I make nearly 1,000 a day,' she added as she began to roll out the dough to a half-inch thickness on a floured work surface. Then, using an ancient-looking steel cutter, she separated them into rounds with one deft twist of her hands.

'The dough is very simple,' she said in the same sing-song accent, 'just flour, butter, water, eggs, baking powder, currants and a little bit of salt. But you have to know what you are doing or they misbehave themselves on the griddle.' I took up position on a stool near the stove to watch her in action, just as I had done as a small child with my grandmother. The griddle looked as if it had been put to plenty of good use. Pat told me it had belonged to her own grandmother, which must have made it well over a hundred years old. It was well seasoned with age, needing no oil to stop the dough sticking as they were placed on to its smoking-hot surface. Within seconds the smell of griddle cakes began to fill the air and I took in a deep sniff of one of the favourite scents of my childhood as Pat monitored the latest batch, flipping them over expertly just as one side had become a beautiful golden brown.

Satisfied that they were evenly cooked, Pat moved them to a wire rack to cool a little before she coated them with a sprinkling of sugar. She turned to me and nodded. 'Try one while they're hot? Just don't burn your fingers.' They were the exact words Nana and my mother would have used as I stood up on tiptoes peering over the edge of the stove. Of course I wanted to try one and I peeled a particularly lovely looking example gingerly from the wire rack, tossing it until it became cool enough not to burn my hands or my tongue. I broke off a small piece, releasing crumbs on to Pat's spotlessly clean floor, and popped it in my mouth. Some things never taste as wonderful as you remember them, but the hot Welsh cakes fresh from the griddle here in Southgate were every bit as lovely as I hoped they would be.

Buttery and filled with fruit, they were the perfect example of why Welsh women are so renowned for their baking prowess.

Pat asked me if I wanted to have a go and, despite my reservations about baking, I wrapped myself in an apron and grabbed at a ball of dough she had already made. Rolling it out was easy enough, so too was the cutting to shape but the griddle was angry at being handed over to my novice hands and once I placed my attempts on the hot surface, instead of gently turning golden brown they went from raw to charred in a matter of seconds. 'It does take some getting used to.' Pat smiled, flipping my feeble attempts on to a plate and returning to her day's work. I decided it was best to leave the cooking in the hands of an expert and instead returned to my stool with a second cup of tea as we talked about my own Welsh roots.

'Did your nan make pikelets?' she asked.

Of course she did; they are another classic example of simple yet delicious Welsh baking and, like the Welsh cakes, it had been well over a decade since I had last tried one.

'Let's make a batch then,' she said, adding, 'they're easy enough.' And she reached across the counter for a clean mixing bowl into which she tipped enough flour, eggs and milk together with the essential ingredient, a spoonful of baking powder, to make a thick batter. Using a metal ladle, she poured small amounts of the batter on to the griddle, watching carefully as they bubbled up on the hot surface then turned them over to cook for a few seconds on the other side. That was all the cooking required and Pat flipped one on to a plate and covered the surface with a thick smear of butter, the only way they should be eaten.

Few things can bring back memories like the smell and taste of favourite foods and my few short hours with Pat Maddocks had whisked me back to my own childhood days. Sitting on the stool by the stove as Pat passed me pikelets and Welsh cakes made me feel like I was five years old once more and I sat chatting happily to her until it was time for me to leave and drive to my next destination.

Pat wrapped up a parcel for me to take away, including my own rather foul, misshapen efforts and gave me a final huge hug before placing the package in my hands. 'Take care now and make sure to come back and see us soon,' she said and she seemed to mean it. Just as I did when I said I would be sure to return. Tony guided me out of my parking spot and the pair of them stood in front of the house, waving at me, only stopping as I turned the corner and vanished from sight.

I drove for a short while and then parked the car in a secluded spot overlooking the ocean, pushing my seat back to give me a little more room. I reached over to the passenger seat for the package, opened it carefully and began to eat one of the cakes, which was still warm. It immediately melted into a pleasing sugary memory in my mouth. I smiled to myself. Time may have robbed me of my mother and grandmother, but it had not robbed me of my memories and all it took to bring them back to me was a simple yet delicious Welsh cake.

— *Lunch* —

I get confused when people start talking about lunch, because as far as I can remember from my northern childhood, lunch was always called dinner. Even though I came from an affluent family and my mother would shiver at the words, 'Can I have some money for my school dinner tickets?' pressure from my peers would always ensure that I used this slightly old-fashioned term for the midday meal. Lunch wasn't 'only for wimps' it was for 'softies', 'benders' and 'rich bastards' whose days would almost invariably end with their heads stuffed down the grimy school lavatories as some of the bigger lads practised their many and varied flushing techniques.

The distinction still remains. In part it is based on geography, with the use of the term 'dinner' for the second meal of the day confirming in many people's eyes that you are a cloth-cap-wearing whippet fondler whose meal will consist mainly of dripping. Lunch, on the other hand, conjures up images of hard-working southern professionals grabbing a quick bite at their desk or concluding multimillion-pound deals while poking at a salad (dressing on the side, of course).

It can be many things to many people. It can be a snack, very much in line with its original definition as 'As much food as one's hand can hold' in Dr Johnson's 1755 *Dictionary*, or it can be the multi-course, three-martini blow-out lasting until the late afternoon which was still clinging on to existence when I entered publishing in the mid-1980s. It can be a solitary meal taken while eating a sandwich, sitting on a park bench and people-watching or it can be a festive occasion bringing busy family members and friends together on Sunday as they marvel at the size of a slab of dead animal and its accompanying surround of vegetables.

Whatever lunch means to people now, meals all still have their roots in the dining cycles of pre-Industrial Revolutionary Britain. In part they were influenced by monastic orders whose days, including times of eating, were scheduled according to the changes in the seasonal sunrise and meals were taken at the end of the different sessions of prayer. Even more influential would be the need to take sustenance to provide energy for long days in the fields, particularly during harvest times. For rural workers, a light breakfast would be snatched the moment they awoke and before they trudged out for their day's labour. By 11 a.m., reserves would be depleted and they would take a second, more substantial meal. This 'dinner' would be their major intake of food for the day and would be supplemented by a lighter meal at the nones or noon hour, which was nine hours after sunrise. This would be followed, at the end of the day, by supper, which was often almost identical to breakfast.

The Industrial Revolution and urbanization, which was an inevitable consequence, saw vast numbers of people moving from rural areas to the ever growing cities. These had enormous impact on how and when we ate, as people's meals moved from being governed by the natural cycles of the day to being decided upon by the demands of factory owners. The rights of the labour force were almost non-existent and factory shifts could stretch to as long as fifteen hours with little or no time allowed for food. Breakfast was taken on the move, snatched from street stalls and costermongers on the way to the factory. The next meal, often carried with them, would be taken just as quickly during a down time when machines were being serviced, and the last meal of the day became the most important. The same impact was felt by members of the fast-growing middle class, whose days as administrators and bureaucrats were just as long if nowhere near as arduous and who also made the last meal their main one of the day. It was only the wealthy, with time on their hands, who continued to make lunch their main meal. By the end of the nineteenth century, although the terms for daily meals were pretty much as we know them today, geographical and class distinctions remained with both 'lunch' and 'dinner' being used for the midday meal depending on who and where you were.

Whatever its origins and whatever you may call it, lunch is a meal that still deserves our respect despite the pressures on our time. So here are eight of the best the country has to offer.

# 12
# *Lancashire Hot Pot*

What do you think of when you hear the words hot pot?

If you didn't immediately say '*Coronation Street*' go and stand in the corner, or as they say in Lancashire at 'the foot of our stairs'. The Rovers Return is, of course, the spiritual home of the hot pot, particularly when doled out by octogenarian barmaid Betty Turpin and served alongside a foaming pint of Newton & Ridley's bitter.

For such a relatively small nation, Britain's attachment to its regional dishes is something to be admired and nurtured and few dishes can be more associated with a place than the simple, savoury and delicious combination of slow-cooked meat and potatoes that is the Lancashire hot pot. Although arguably having the same roots as Welsh cawl, Irish stew and the lobscouse, which gave the people of Liverpool their nickname, hot pot is as firmly identified with the red rose county as any dish is to any region of the country.

It developed as a nourishing meal that could be left to its own devices while men, women and children worked long hours in harsh conditions in the mills, factories, ports and mines that fuelled Britain's economic growth. There are some claims, usually citing the price of expensive ingredients such as lamb and the absence of domestic ovens in working homes, that the hot pot is actually a dish of considerably higher status and was sampled by the working classes only when donated by wealthy benefactors in times of hardship. However, during my research, I found enough references to dishes of hot pot being cooked in the dying embers of the local baker's oven and to cheap cuts of meat, such as neck end, being used that the former idea still strikes me as the more plausible. Whatever the case, there is little doubt that everybody now associates hot pot with the Lancastrian working classes as a filling dish, which eked out expensive protein with cheaper and more abundant carbohydrate.

By the middle of the nineteenth century, Lancashire was the centre of the world's cotton textile industry, a business that was at the time responsible for almost half of Britain's home-produced exports. Hours for the workers in towns like Rochdale, Oldham, Bury, Burnley and Preston were long, with the day regularly beginning at 5 a.m. or earlier and stretching on until seven in the evening, with only a short break for a grabbed lunch when machines were serviced. Every member of the family would be expected to work in some form or another and there would be little time or energy to prepare meals on the return home at the end of a long day.

The hot pot was the perfect solution not only to the constraints of time but also to the need to provide sustenance and fuel for the next day's work using relatively cheap and readily available ingredients. Even though by comparison to others mill workers were among the better paid of the working classes, a hot pot was still not a regular occurrence, with carbohydrate-providing vegetables, oatmeal and potatoes bulking out the majority of the daily diet. When it was prepared it was, no doubt, as it remains today, a real treat as the brown earthenware pot that gives the dish its name was opened to reveal layers of meat and vegetables in a gravy produced by the slow cooking.

The recipe has several variants, but all are based around the same theme: lamb, but also sometimes beef, baked in the oven with potatoes and possibly other root vegetables in water or stock until the meat is cooked and the potatoes have softened. That's it. It shouldn't be too hard, I thought, to find the best examples and the best people to show me how it was made.

I had numerous options. Should I find an elderly housewife who has been making it all her life, or a pub where the landlady, like the sainted Betty, has been ladling out steaming plates of it to grateful customers for as long as she can remember? Perhaps there was a fine dining version where the hot pot had been transformed from rustic peasant dish to a dainty mouthful served on fine white china, or a modern version where the traditional ingredients had been replaced by new and unusual combinations (ostrich hot pot anyone?). I had the opportunity to do all of the above, but was intrigued when I was contacted by the Hastings restaurant in Lytham St Annes and offered the chance to watch this dish and another on my list, the Eccles cake, being made for me by a former UK Young Chef of the Year, Warrick Dodds. It would be interesting, I thought, to see what a new generation of young cooks made of one of the region's most famous dishes.

Warrick Dodds is a quietly spoken chef in his early

thirties who received most of his cookery training under the tutelage of Nigel Haworth, owner of Northcote Manor, one of Lancashire's few Michelin-starred restaurants. Haworth is renowned for his promotion of Lancastrian dishes and for his energetic support of local producers. As I travelled around the region, it was noticeable how much respect he was afforded by everyone I met in the food business and how much of an impact he had on helping to make the great ingredients produced in the region available to the local population. So much so that I could make a strong case for Lancashire as the prime model for many of the more gastronomically challenged regions of the country to follow.

After a number of years working with Haworth, Warrick Dodds had moved to pastures new and was now heading up the kitchen at the Hastings, bringing with him the same passion for local producers and dishes that had been drummed into him at Northcote Manor. The Hastings was a light, airy pub with comfortable seating and friendly staff and packed to the rafters with chattering diners when I arrived. As I walked through the swing doors to the kitchen, Warrick wandered over from the stove in his chef's whites. He had been hard at work for some time, but was ready to take a break from his service with the ingredients for our Lancashire hot pot laid out ready and waiting for our attention.

His recipe was a traditional one, but viewed through the prism of his starred chef's training. Rather than a large family-sized dish, he was making it in individual portions. It's not a complex process. He began by sweating sliced white onions with a little sugar until they were soft and sweet. Then he layered them in a dish with some thinly sliced potatoes and carrots, which he had tossed in a little melted butter with some finely chopped rosemary. He finally added the main ingredient: lamb neck and shoulder which he told me were the perfect cuts to give richness to the end dish as their fat content released delicious meaty flavours during the cooking process.

Seasoning each layer with salt and pepper as he went, Warrick topped off the dish with more sliced carrots, another layer of potatoes and finished with some fresh chicken stock and then covered the dish. It looked deceptively simple, but I could see the attention to detail Warrick gave was as great as if he had been preparing a Michelin-starred dish with the most costly of ingredients.

I had time to kill before my meal would be ready so set off for a brisk walk along the seafront to pass the time and work up an appetite. Lytham St Annes turned out to be a sleepy but rather engaging town. The trees along its streets of imposing houses confirmed its nickname of 'leafy Lytham' and the lack of amusement arcades were proof that it was the genteel equivalent for those people who were too 'naice' ever to consider going to Blackpool for a holiday.

An hour and a half later, as scheduled, I returned famished and chilled to the bone by the brisk breeze along the shoreline. I sat myself down in the Hastings' dining room to be presented with the finished Lancashire hot pot. For the last ten or so minutes of cooking time the cover had been removed to allow the layer of thin potato slices to crisp to a crackling crunch and the top was brown and golden with the few gaps between the slices of potato allowing the hot juices to bubble through like an orchestrated meat dance.

Some parts of Lancashire will serve hot pot alongside a plate of crumbly Lancashire cheese. Warrick had chosen to present me with another traditional accompaniment: a plate of pickled red cabbage, whose texture and sharp juices were the perfect contrast to the unctuous stew.

The layers of potato beneath the crisp topping of the hot pot had poached in the chicken stock, to create what the French would call *boulangère* potatoes, which melted on the tongue as soon as I put them in my mouth. The two different cuts of lamb had released their fat as Warrick said they would and cooked down slowly to a succulent perfection in the simple gravy.

It was an altogether fabulous dish, as good as anything I had eaten on the journey so far. It confirmed that when made with care and attention, using great ingredients, simple British dishes have absolutely nothing to apologize for. Within ten minutes of my dish being placed before me, I was scraping the bowl clean with a large serving spoon and using the same to transfer the last chunks of meat to my mouth.

Warrick popped his head around the kitchen door more than once as I ate, nervous of his visitor's reaction to such an uncomplicated dish. He need not have been concerned; his hot pot was the perfect example of a traditional dish being transformed into a modern classic without losing sight of what made it so wonderful in the first place and I suspect that St Betty of Weatherfield might well have approved.

I certainly did and Warrick has been kind enough to share his recipe so you can too.

# — *Lancashire Hot Pot* —
## (SERVES 4)

850g white onions, peeled
   and sliced
2 tablespoons vegetable oil
salt to taste
30g sugar to caramelize the
   onions and give them a
   sweetness
1kg lamb (shoulder and neck)
white pepper to taste
30g flour
45g butter (unsalted)
1kg King Edward potatoes,
   peeled and sliced

4 large carrots, peeled and
   sliced
1 sprig of fresh rosemary,
   finely chopped
1 garlic clove, crushed
200ml good chicken stock

4 hot pot dishes, 21cm in
   diameter by 9cm in height
4 cartouches or circles of
   greaseproof paper, cut to
   the diameter of your pots
foil

Sweat the sliced onions down in the oil with a little salt and the sugar until they are caramelized.

Dice the lamb into 2.5cm cubes and season with salt and white pepper. Coat lightly with flour then arrange neatly in the bottom of the hot pot dishes. Add a layer of caramelized onions.

Melt the butter and, in a separate bowl, pour over the sliced potatoes. Add the sliced carrots, the chopped rosemary and the garlic clove, stirring them around with your hands so they are all well coated with the butter. Add salt and pepper to taste.

Layer the potatoes and carrots on top of the onions in the hot pot dishes. Pour over the chicken stock until it reaches the level of the potatoes. Cover with a grease-proof paper circle then foil.

Bake in a preheated oven at 160°C/325°F/gas mark 3 for 1½ hours.

Remove the tin foil and greaseproof paper and brush the top layer with melted butter. Return the dish to the oven until the potatoes are a crunchy and beautiful golden brown, which should take about another ten minutes, and serve with a bowl of pickled red cabbage and some crusty bread.

## — *Pickled Red Cabbage* —

(SHOULD BE MADE AT LEAST A DAY IN ADVANCE TO TAKE ON ALL THE FLAVOURS)

*1 red cabbage, shredded*
*1 teaspoon salt*
*500ml malt vinegar*
*250ml white wine vinegar*
*400ml balsamic vinegar*
*300g sugar*
*8 cloves*
*4 star anise*
*4 whole dried chillies*
*2 bay leaves*
*2 cinnamon sticks*

Mix all the ingredients in a large bowl and cover with clingfilm. Allow to sit in the fridge for at least 24 hours. You can keep the cabbage for around two weeks if you store it in sterilized Kilner jars.

## 13
# Fish and Chips

This is a daunting chapter for me to write, not only because there is probably no dish more quintessentially British than fish and chips, but also because there is no dish in the whole wide world that I adore as much as a plate of fish protected in a coating of perfectly fried batter served with a scattering of finger-thick chips and sprinkled liberally with salt and vinegar. If I am particularly fortunate there may be a pickled onion or two involved, but even without the pleasure of crunching into these sharp little accompaniments it would still be my final meal of choice if I knew I was on my way to the electric chair.

I am not alone, of course; there are still nearly 12,000 chippies in the United Kingdom and despite rumours of their demise the queues outside local chippies on a Friday and Saturday night appear to be as long as they have ever been. However, they are certainly facing a continual barrage of threats from a number of sources. In part there are the squeals of protest from the health brigade whose sole task seems to be to remove every last ounce of joy from our relationship with food.

Then there is the well-documented dwindling of fish stocks, which makes anyone who admits to a liking for a nice piece of cod receive a reaction as if they were carrying a sign around their necks reading 'Kiddie Fiddler and proud of it'. Finally, and possibly most challenging of all, there is the very real threat from the growing popularity of alternative takeaways (is it just me or does that sound like a great name for an Indie band?) representing the relatively recent arrival of immigrants from India, China and other countries to the UK.

It is ironic that the status of our national dish is under threat from new arrivals as its very existence in the first place depended on the same. The origins of fish and chips are subject to much debate, but like so many dishes in Britain have their roots in immigration, in this case with the arrival of Jewish refugees from Portugal and Spain who brought with them the art of frying fish in a light coating of flour and the arrival of Huguenots from Belgium and France who brought with them the tradition of serving potatoes fried in fat. Charles Dickens's reference to a 'fried fish warehouse' in *Oliver Twist* is usually credited with being the first mention of the art of fish frying in Britain, but where the two main constituents first came together is more disputed.

London's claim comes from the opening of a shop by Joseph Malin selling a combination of fried fish and potatoes on Cleveland Street, east London in the 1860s. In Lancashire, there was already a tradition of selling fried potatoes, and in 1863 John Lees opened a shop in Mossley near Oldham, the first recorded fish and chip shop outside the capital.

Wherever and whenever they first began serving fried fish with chips, it was a huge success and by the turn of the twentieth century there were more than 25,000 shops in the country, many little more than the front room of a terraced house and fish and chips was firmly in place as

Britain's national dish. So much so, in fact, that during the Second World War fish and chips was one of the few things that was never rationed, so worried was Churchill's government about the impact it would have on the nation's morale to lose their regular fix wrapped in the daily newspaper.

As for the Majumdar household, fish and chips has always played a part in our search for a balanced and varied diet. No childhood Saturday would have been complete without polishing off a plate of haddock and chips from a tray perched on my lap while watching Frank Bough on *Grandstand*. Even now on my all too infrequent returns to my home town, the same will always be on the menu at least once as the male members of the clan take part in a long-standing ritual of a Saturday lunch in front of the telly constructed from the lengthy menu of one of the many nearby chip shops.

By midday the trays, which retain the labels with our names on which my mother gave them back in the 1970s, will have been laid out ready and waiting by my younger brother Jeremy. Although well into his forties he still languishes in his position as sibling 'bitch' to his two older brothers and so must quite rightly do most of the grunt work. By 1.00 p.m., when the family's pangs of hunger cannot be assuaged by pork scratchings alone, the journey to collect lunch gets under way and my older brother, TGS, and I leap into, well, squeeze into, Jeremy's Toyota Yaris for the short journey to the chip shop.

There will, of course, always be a line waiting to order or for their meal to be prepared. It is the unwritten law that a chip shop without a queue is one to be avoided at all costs. Inside, the young women at the counter are already exuding a perfume scented with the beef fat in which the chips have been cooked. Can there be any better fulfilment of a northern teenage boy's dreams than a girl who smells of chips?

They are eager as we arrive and place our order, following our own tradition of ordering haddock, which must be cooked to order. Within seconds of our fish being ready the girls have placed them gently on a triple sheet of paper and are shovelling what equates to an entire Russian harvest worth of potatoes to accompany them. Looking up from their work, they ask, 'Do you want salt and vinegar, love?'

They douse our meal liberally with both before we have even issued a reply, the very idea that a sane person may not want the classic accompaniments being too odd to consider. They wrap everything expertly in two more layers of paper, then close the outer bag with a final practised twist of the hands. It is a thing of beauty to watch and as important a part of the fish and chip experience as eating them.

Then begins the journey home. It resembles a frantic emergency run by ambulance carrying a precious donated organ, TGS driving at speed to prevent our lunch getting cold, I, mobile phone pressed to my ear, relaying important information about our status to HQ.

'We are just around the Stag roundabout.'

'We are turning on to Broom Lane.'

'We are at the bottom of the drive.'

'We are walking in the door.'

All these important updates allow Jeremy and my father to coordinate the buttering of thick slices of white bread and the twisting of lids from jars of gherkins and pickled onions whose sharp vinegar we will add to that already applied at the chip shop.

Within minutes of us walking through the door carrying our spoils aloft in triumph, we are lifting the fish gingerly and placing it so the battered ends hang over the side of the plate and surrounding it with chips manhandled from their wrapping in great fistfuls. Pickles will be plopped decoratively on the side of the plate and a small carton filled to the brim with perfectly lurid green mushy peas will be placed on each tray. Finally, beer, wine or sometimes even champagne in hand, we will balance our trays on our laps, focus only on our plates and tear into our lunch until the plates are emptied. The only sound bar that of the television is of batter snapping, pickles crunching and drinks slurping until we are done. We deposit the trays on the coffee table for 'bitch' sibling Jeremy to clear away as it is his joy and duty so to do. Who says families don't still know how to eat together?

For my own experience of eating fish and chips, I had to undertake considerable research, which involved eating in nearly fifty chip shops in the London area as well as trying fish and chips just about everywhere I stayed around the country. In truth, I am sad to say, the results were pretty disappointing and I came to the conclusion that our national dish is under threat, not from the increased popularity of the curry or the Chinese takeaway, but from the fact that so many chip shops in the UK are just so bloody horrible.

The fish used is often frozen rather than fresh. Whatever anyone tells you, it makes a vast difference to the end result. Fish, cod in particular, is rarely cooked to order and sits in heated cabinets until required, by which time the batter has become soft and oily, sticking to the paper in which it is wrapped. Don't even get me started on the chips, usually undercooked and stained with Dry-White, an additive used to protect the pale colour people expect from a chip-shop chip.

I like to think I am something of an expert on matters fish and chipular, but even at the lowest estimate I have a strong claim to have eaten in more fish and chip shops than just about anyone else in the country. I can say with some certainty that the current state of our national treasure is dispiriting to say the least and that the numbers of shops are dwindling comes as little surprise. However, when well prepared fish and chips remains a dish of considerable beauty and I consider it a worthy task to report on the best of them.

Finally, after all my eating efforts both good and bad, I decided to offer one lucky shop the chance to show me how to make fish and chips. It could easily have been one of the more famous places that I visited during my journey, such as the legendary Magpie Café in Whitby, with its equally legendary queues for a table, or the Anstruther Fish Shop, which in 2009 was awarded the prize as 'Seafresh Best Fish & Chip Shop in Britain'. Both were very enjoyable and definitely worth my hard-earned cash and the honour of showing me how they achieve such high standards. However, when I heard the background story of one particular shop I changed my plans and headed not to the coast of east Scotland, nor to join the long lines in North Yorkshire but to a newly opened chip shop in the unlikely setting of a slightly grim shopping plaza in Britain's second city, Birmingham.

The Great British Eatery was opened in 2008 by Andrew Insley and Conrad Brunton, two Brummies who combined their determination to start up a business of their own with the lack of a decent chip shop in the city. I have to admit to having my doubts when I first heard about it. Primarily because whenever young people – Andy and Conrad are both barely thirty – get involved with one of Britain's great traditions, they often bring with their enthusiasm lashings of irony, which might give them a chuckle but does little to add to the quality of the end result.

As I walked into their chippie, I fully expected to see those small round tomato sauce dispensers shaped like a tomato. Had I been correct, I would have turned around and walked straight out. Instead, I was greeted with the meaty beef-scented breeze from their impressive frying machine. Glory to God, they were using dripping, the only medium in which good fish and chips should be prepared. It was a sign that I had chosen well and I decided to stay.

The young man behind the counter took my order and shouted it out to his colleague who was hard at work behind the fryer: 'One haddock, chips and mushy peas, please.' It confirmed that they were cooking to order, another good sign. While it was being prepared, I took in the small room. This was primarily a takeaway. There were a few stools, where I could sit and have my lunch, but other than that and a few posters of British icons on the wall to back up their choice of name, they had thankfully remained very close to the great tradition of British chippies.

When my meal arrived in a fluted cardboard tray, it

certainly wasn't flawless, but showed enough promise to make me believe that the Great British Eatery could become a very decent chip shop indeed. The batter around the fish had puffed up and bubbled as it should, separating itself from the fish to provide a protective cover under which the haddock could steam to a perfect flake. The chips were the correct size and colour, with sufficient little crisp bits of potato in the tray to add to the excitement, and there were peas, a great big messy sludge of glorious mushy peas, the right colour, the right texture and the right flavour. For two newcomers to the profession, Andy and Conrad had every right to be proud of the fish and chips they were serving.

After my meal, they granted my request to step behind the counter so I could get a close-up of their nascent operation. It was impressive. So clean even my late mother would have given it her highest accolade of 'spotless', with large chill cabinets filled with pre-filleted fresh fish and finger-thick chips that had been cut that morning. In the back kitchen the hot oven was filled to bursting with steak and kidney and chicken and mushroom pies and a cauldron of mushy peas was gurgling to itself happily on a small electric ring. A state-of-the-art fryer was filled with melted beef dripping. A piece of cod had just risen to the surface, a sign that it was ready, and was lifted out to sit in the heated glass cabinet to drain for two minutes before being served. In a heated drawer next to the fryer, a mound of freshly cooked chips waited ready to be piled on top of the fish in the way that would give any nutritionist the screaming abdabs. The Great British Eatery may have been a new chip shop, but there was enough here to suggest that it could become a serious contender for my favourite in the country.

Given some of the indifferent and downright lousy fish and chips I had eaten on my travels around the UK, it made my fatty heart particularly joyous to see two young guys cooking up our national treasure with such passion, using great ingredients from sustainable sources and without apology to over-zealous health nuts and, judging by the queues, putting up quite a fight against more recent takeaway arrivals. Like so many of our traditions in Britain, fish and chips may be under attack on many fronts, but with places like the Great British Eatery, one thing is for certain: it ain't done yet.

# 14
# Cawl

The rain came down in a constant drizzle, the sort of rain that slowly soaks through supposedly waterproof clothing and seeps into your very bones so you feel as if you may never be dry ever again. Rain like this is a fairly typical occurrence in Wales and, as I stood in a small cemetery in Pont-y-Gwaith looking over the rolling green hills in the distance, the raindrops slid off my uncovered and freshly shaved head until they merged with the tears I was beginning to shed. The name of Pont-y-Gwaith may not mean much to anyone bar the few people who live there, but it means a lot to our family. It is the place where my mother was born, but also the place where her ashes were scattered in 2005, after she lost her life to that most vile disease leukaemia. The Welsh side of my heritage often receives scant attention, swamped by the exuberance of my father's Indian background, but it still forms a vital part of my life. Although I don't discuss it as much, I remain hugely proud of that part of my character that was forged in the deep, dank mines of South Wales.

I had no plans to linger in the small village. Indeed, since the mines closed in the 1980s, there is very little reason to linger in any of the small towns that dot the sides of the famous Rhondda Valley. But I needed to pay my respects and remember my mother, so vibrant in life and so missed in death. Having done so, I wiped my eyes and gathered my thoughts. I returned to my car and pointed it in the direction of my original destination, Saundersfoot on the Pembrokeshire coast of Wales, where I had been invited to take part in the small town's annual cawl festival.

I can imagine that many people reading this book will never have heard of cawl. Like its cousin, Irish stew, it has its roots in trade and invasion from Scandinavia and in particular in a dish called labscasse, still popular in Sweden. In Liverpool it became lobscouse, and it simultaneously made its way to Wales and across the sea to Ireland. In each case it is the same dish, a simple stew made with root vegetables and meat, slow-cooked in a low oven until it creates its own thin gravy. It doesn't sound like much, but to anyone like me, part of the wider Welsh diaspora, the very sound of the word cawl is enough to drag happy memories from the back of the brain and raise that smile that only nostalgia can produce.

My Welsh grandparents were ever present as I grew up. My grandfather, Arthur, was quite frankly a bit of a rogue. Not a bad man, by any stretch of the imagination, but more fond of the beer and bookies than he ever was of work. By the time I was old enough to realize what he did for a living, he was close to retirement and biding his time as a message runner at the Scottish Office (which probably explains the fact that all my childhood drawings are on government-headed notepaper). Before that he seems to have had hundreds of jobs, mostly behind the bars of West End pubs from which he was habitually fired for dishing out free drinks to all his many friends along with £10 change for the £5 they had given him in payment.

I worshipped him and, on our frequent visits to London, where he moved after the Second World War, the four Majumdar grandchildren would pester him to take us out for the day. Our mode of transport was always the impossibly romantic London bus and until the age of seven, when I had a growth spurt and could not get away with it any more, he firmly instructed me to tell the inspector, 'I will not be five until September.'

His greatest passion was practical jokes and I would happily follow along as his foil while he caused chaos wherever he went. In the 1960s when each bus had a driver and conductor, communication between the two often took the form of a coded series of foot stamps to let the driver know that all the passengers were aboard and it was safe to pull away. This was mother's milk to Arthur John who would sit at the front of the bus, whenever possible, and wait until crowds of people were beginning to clamber aboard before giving a practised stamp, causing the driver to pull away leaving most of the passengers stranded at the bus stop and a good number splayed on the ground as we sped off. Shameless and dangerous, of course, and I loved him for it, even when we were inevitably ejected on to the pavement ourselves by a furious conductor and had to wait for the next bus.

As you can imagine, my grandmother, Eva Florence, was a woman of huge patience and would react to Grandpa's fiery Welsh temper with a calm equanimity that made him even more furious. Whatever he did outside the house, she ruled within and, being Welsh, that meant she spent most of her time cooking. Whenever we visited, dish after dish of food would emerge from her tiny kitchen, covering the dining table until its wood veneer top was barely visible beneath an assortment of ill-matched plates and trays.

None of her dishes would ever be described as haute cuisine; my grandmother was what some people describe disparagingly as a 'good, plain cook'. She was definitely frugal, used to squeezing out a diet from a meagre ration book and then, in later life, a pension book. Like so many of her generation, she was able to stretch these limited resources into filling and delicious meals, memories of which stay with me still.

She baked, lord, how she baked: buttery biscuits, Welsh cakes studded with currants, sponge cakes filled with cream and seemingly unending trays of buns and biscuits. There appeared to be nothing she could not instinctively turn her hand to. Savoury baking was a must too, with golden crust-topped pies filled with slow-cooked beef and lamb's kidneys or, my favourite, sausage meat. There were pastry straws flecked with sharp Cheddar cheese and the dishes of offal she learned to cook at a time when poverty meant using every part of the animal. Stuffed lambs' hearts and braised brains may sound like horror stories to many, but these are the dishes I grew up on and would give anything to taste again.

Finest of all was her cawl, where cheap cuts of lamb were slow-cooked with lots of root vegetables in a pot on the stove. When the stew was ready, the contents were ladled into bowls and spooned into the mouth with the help of doorstops of fresh baked white bread, often still warm from the oven. It is remarkable how odd little

memories stay with you and I can still see my grandmother buttering and slicing the bread in a way I have
only ever seen in Wales. Holding it under one arm, she
would spread butter on the exposed piece of the whole
loaf and only then slice it by drawing the kitchen knife
towards her in a sawing motion.

She died in 1984, ten years almost to the day after my
grandfather, and I had not tasted cawl since. When I read
about the festival in Saundersfoot, I got in touch and was
soon invited to join chairman of the festival committee
and cawl enthusiast Andrew Evans as he walked the trail
apportioning marks to each of the town's bars and
restaurants and pubs taking part. Saundersfoot fashions
itself as a 'Padstow of Wales' and is building a reputation
as a food destination, in no small part thanks to Andrew
who owns three restaurants in the town and the hugely
impressive St Brides Hotel which overlooks the harbour
and is smart and discreet enough to attract a regular
celebrity clientele.

The morning of the festival, I arranged to meet him in
the large marquee that had been set up in the harbour car
park and, after a stroll around the seafront to walk off an
excellent breakfast at my B&B, I arrived to find it was
already filled with people enjoying a small farmers'
market the organizers had arranged as an added draw. In
the corner of the marquee was a stand for those who
wanted to take part in the Cawl Trail, staffed by a gaggle
of blue-rinsed elderly ladies, each one of whom reminded
me of my grandmother as they fussed about keeping their
stall tidy. In front there was a display of the specially
made earthenware bowls which participants had to buy
and into which each restaurant would dispense their

version for tasting. To the side of these were cellophane-wrapped 'Cawl Kits', complete with a recipe card for people to buy if they wanted to try making it for themselves at home. They were rather optimistically priced at £4 given that the contents were mostly root vegetables available from the supermarket for about 50p.

Andrew Evans was every inch the prosperous Welsh businessman, with a pleasant manner and a gently rounded figure that was a testament to his own admitted love of Welsh baking. After purchasing a bowl each, we set out on the trail around the town clutching a scorecard on which was also printed a map showing the location of each of the restaurants taking part. Andrew knew everybody in the town and word soon spread that he was on his rounds and bringing with him a 'journalist from London'. Since the ingredients were more or less identical, the fact that the twelve small bowls we sampled varied considerably shows how even the simplest dish is open to interpretation. Some chose to use beef brisket instead of lamb, some used potatoes and leeks, others just the classic turnips and carrots. Some laced theirs with an eye-watering amount of white pepper, others with enough salt to send your systolic levels crashing off the scale. Some made lots of effort, serving theirs with slices of warm bread and another classic accompaniment, slivers of crumbly Caerphilly cheese. Others, according to Andrew, made no effort at all and he dismissed one particular participant out of hand for 'doing no more than opening a bloody tin of Irish stew'. A damning indictment.

Andrew knew his cawl and, after sampling each one, he would ponder for a moment before committing pencil to paper with his marks. In each location we were joined by dozens more cawl enthusiasts, ranging from young children with their parents to teenage couples attempting to slurp from the bowls with one hand as they tried to remain entwined. It was a good-humoured event with lots of banter and although three of Andrew's restaurants were taking part, he didn't take it too seriously, and after sampling our twelfth bowl he wiped his clean and we ambled back to the marquee to hand in our scorecards. Andrew invited me to join him for lunch at one of his restaurants, but although I love cawl, twelve bowls was enough food for any man for a day, even me, so I declined and instead went for a long stroll to walk off all the slow-cooked lamb.

Andrew e-mailed me the following day to tell me that one of his own restaurants, the Mermaid, had come out as the top choice from over 400 scorecards received during the festival and, looking at my own notes, I could see I had agreed with the consensus. A triumph indeed and it certainly was excellent cawl, although family loyalty means it was obviously not up to the standard of my grandmother's recipe, which I am happy to share with you now. I hope it brings you as much happiness as thinking about it again did to me.

# ~ *Cawl* ~

## (SERVES 4–6)

*900g lamb ring chops (from the lamb neck). Do not use beef.*
  *People who use beef in a cawl should be made to sit through*
  *an entire Eisteddfod as punishment.*
*1 teaspoon salt*
*1 teaspoon white pepper*
*3 large carrots, peeled and chopped into large chunks*
*3 turnips, peeled and chopped into large chunks*
*1.2 litres water*
*3 large potatoes, peeled and chopped into large chunks*
*1 leek, cleaned and sliced into thin strips*

Season the meat with the salt and pepper and place in a large saucepan or slow cooker. Add the carrots and turnips to the pot along with the water and bring the temperature up until the water reaches a gentle simmer and leave to cook for 3 hours. Remove from the heat and allow to cool.

Once cool, the fat that has been released by the lamb will have collected on the surface and can be removed with a slotted spoon.

When ready to serve, bring the pan back to a gentle simmer and add the potatoes. Cook for a further 20 minutes or until the potatoes become soft.

Before serving toss in the leek and check for seasoning, adding more salt and pepper if necessary.

Serve with large chunks of warm bread and a block of good Caerphilly cheese.

# 15
## Lancashire Cheese

That we have any cheese in this country for me to write about is remarkable. Had it not been for one or two determined individuals, cheese, which in Britain is currently experiencing something of a boom, might now have been all but extinct. Prior to the First World War Britain's cheese-making industry was a thriving, but mainly localized business consisting of farmers using excess milk to make cheese for their own use or to sell at nearby markets. Every region had its own style of cheese-making that reflected the size of the farms, the types of cattle they reared and, obviously, the tastes of the locals. Even though there are records of cheeses from all over the country being sold in London as far back as the 1600s, most cheeses would have been consumed within a few miles of where they had been made.

The Second World War and our old friend, rationing, changed all that when the government decided that all milk should be directed to the production of one single type of cheese. Government Cheddar, as it was called, was the Crossroads Motel of dairy products. It stayed around for a long time, but I have never met anyone who admitted liking it. Flavour was low down on the agenda when it came to making decisions during the war years. More important was the need to keep the nation fed on staples without which health and morale might suffer. Government Cheddar ticked all the boxes. It could be produced easily in vast quantities, it could be stored for a long time without going off and it could be kept centrally and distributed easily both at home and to the various fronts of battle. Milk was collected locally and then taken to central production facilities where the Cheddar was produced ready for shipping.

While Government Cheddar may have served the war effort well, its impact on Britain's cheese makers was catastrophic. Before the First World War, records show that there were over 3,500 dairies in the UK who reported making cheese. It's fair to assume that there were many more who were never on the list because they made cheese just for their own use. By the time rationing was ended in 1954, there were fewer than 100 dairies recorded making cheese and many of the regional cheeses had all but disappeared.

If you have a conversation about the current state of cheese in the UK, it can't be more than a matter of moments before someone mentions the name Randolph Hodgson and then the name of his company, Neal's Yard Dairy. It would be little or, indeed, any exaggeration to suggest that, without the single-minded determination of Randolph, there would be few cheeses of any note being prepared in the UK at all. Randolph joined Neal's Yard in 1979 not long after it opened. He was looking for a job to tide him over after completing a food science degree, but soon found himself fascinated by cheese although dispirited by the lack of provenance of many of the cheeses on offer. He realized that they were anonymous and bore little or no stamp of their maker's personality. A chance sample from a cheese maker in Dorset changed matters and Randolph soon began working with new producers as they rediscovered Britain's lost craft of cheese-making.

I know from my many conversations with the people of Neal's Yard that it has not been an easy task. However, over the last twenty years, he and his growing team of enthusiasts have helped build up not only the reputation of British cheeses at home and abroad, but also the number of people making cheese to the extent that they now number in the hundreds, more than in France I have been told on more than one occasion. There can rarely be a dinner gathering of food fans in the UK that does not end with a plate containing at least some slabs of superb British cheese.

There were some obvious contenders when it came to selecting a cheese maker to visit for my trip. There was Cheddar, of course, which, because it is a method of making cheese as well as a place, is allowed to be replicated all over the world. However, it is never made better than it is in the golden valleys of Somerset. There was Wensleydale, first made by Cistercian monks and now famous the world over for being the favourite snack of a Plasticene Yorkshireman and his daredevil dog. There was one of my all-time favourites in the shape of a barrel-sized round of sharp blue Stilton made only a few miles from my other 'go to' food, the Melton Mowbray pork pie. Finally, there was Lancashire cheese, that sharp, white crumbly cheese that goes perfectly with pickles and a piece of crusty bread torn off a hot loaf.

I made one of my all too regular visits to Neal's Yard's shop at Borough Market and returned with slabs of each of the contenders so I could conduct my own taste test. I laid them out on a board and took small slivers from each. They were all in prime condition. Cheddar from the incomparable Jamie Montgomery, Stilton from Colston Bassett and a Hawes Wensleydale, but it was the Lancashire cheese that really caught my attention. This particular example was from one of its most famous makers, Kirkham's Farm. I had eaten it many times, most notably when used in a famous dessert combination at St John Restaurant close to London's Smithfield Market, where it was used alongside a dense Eccles cake. I was sure that a visit to Kirkham's Farm would give me all the information I needed about the making of one of my favourite cheeses and prepared to fire off an e-mail requesting an audience.

Then I paused for a moment; these were all fine cheeses, made by dedicated farmers but was there anything new to say about any of them? They had all received plenty of coverage. Perhaps, I considered, there were some other dairies who were equally as passionate about the cheeses they made, but who were less known and just as deserving of attention. I turned to my e-mail, recalling that I had received one from the British Cheese Board detailing a cheese-making course that was to be given by Bob Kitchen of the Leagram Organic Dairy in Chipping, near Preston.

Bob has been a cheese maker for over thirty years and with his daughter, Faye, has been running Leagram Dairy for a little over a decade. They were a perfect choice, a small-scale operation that had a great reputation both for the quality of their cheese and the passion they showed for promoting it and Lancashire. One short phone call later and Bob had invited me to spend a day with them learning how to make not only Lancashire cheese but also a stunning young curd cheese, which restaurants in the area had been discovering.

I may not have been born there, but at heart I remain very much a Yorkshire lad. And, being a good Yorkshireman, I have an inbuilt wariness of all people, places and things from the other side of the Pennines.

This enmity between the two counties had its bitter roots in bloodshed stretching back to the Wars of the Roses between the House of Lancaster and the House of York to secure the crown of England in the fifteenth century. Now, however, it tends to be expressed in fiercely competitive but relatively cheery sporting rivalry. In my own youth, friends and I took it in turn to take our battered first cars (red Fiat 127 for the record), stuffed beyond legal capacity, over the Snake Pass to the other side of the Pennines to support our beloved football team, Rotherham United. The matches were against opponents with names like Preston North End, Bolton Wanderers, Burnley or Bury and we would taunt the opposing fans with our Shavian wit, belting out head-shakingly offensive songs at the top of our voices.

*In your Wanderers slums, in your Wanderers slums*
*You look in the dustbin for something to eat*
*You find a dead rat and you think it's a treat*
*In your Wanderers slums.*
(To the tune of 'In Your Liverpool Home')

At least I can say that my insults even then were always about food.

Despite the fact that we would always travel in hope

and usually return in silent misery after a heavy defeat, those days were some of the happiest of my life. We would congregate in front of a chosen pub at 10 a.m., pile into the back of the car and have heated arguments all the way to our destination about the best formation, the injury of a key player and the security of the manager's job as we shouted to be heard against the sound of the Human League's first album blaring out of the tinny speakers. On arrival, just after opening time if we had judged it correctly, we found a pub that didn't look too full of intimidating opposition fans and continued our arguments over pints of the local brew. Shortly before kick-off we would make our way to the ground, stopping only for the prerequisite football match snack of a steak and kidney pie.

Most of the football matches are long forgotten. So too, if I am honest, are most of the people who made the journey with me. But these trips were an important part of my upbringing and looking back on them contributed hugely towards my passage to manhood. Probably the most important lesson was the importance of buying rounds. It may seem odd to suggest that buying a drink can give you a life lesson, but the way I judge people now is influenced in no small part by the time I spent sitting around a table with my friends in a pub in my formative years. More than any other aspect, I judge people and indeed restaurants by their generosity of spirit. The buying of rounds soon tells you all you need to know about a person. Those who always bought their round are the people I would still want to spend time with and those who mysteriously always had a call of nature just before it got to their turn are the sort I still avoid.

If you are looking for generosity of spirit, then you don't have to look too much further than at Bob Kitchen. My day with Bob and Faye was one of the most enjoyable of the entire trip. Bob was generous with his time as a guide as I learned to make cheese and even more generous as he piled my car high with samples as I set off for home later in the day.

Bob and his two colleagues were already in white coats and hats ready for work by the time I pulled up outside Leagram Dairy. A large container was parked in the yard pumping the organic milk Bob buys from local farms through a wide pipe into the tanks within the dairy. Inside, Bob was monitoring the latest batch of cheese production. I quickly donned my own coat and hat and guided my feet into an oversized pair of wellington boots, which I dipped in disinfectant as I made my way into the cheese-making room.

'The first thing you should know,' Bob instructed, 'is that there are three types of Lancashire cheese, creamy, tasty and crumbly.' It was certainly news to me and, if I took nothing else away with me from my day's visit, I would still have a piece of trivia that could help me in my long-term goal of being able to bore at an international level.

Mentions of cheese-making in Lancashire date back to the twelfth century. There are even records of King John granting Preston the right to hold a cheese fair in 1199. However, it was not until towards the end of the nineteenth century that the standards for making what we now know as Lancashire cheese became codified. In the last decade of the century, Joseph Gornall, a local civil servant and well-respected cheese maker, was tasked by the county council with visiting all the farms in Lancashire to offer advice and to standardize the producers' methods, so worried were they that the cheeses were being made in so many disparate ways. He was, it appears, also a savvy businessman as he took the opportunity to sell many of the cheese makers his own brand of tools including curd knives and his own invention, the Gornall Patent Cheesemaker, a device for churning milk.

His standard recipe is the one that is still adhered to today and turned the disadvantages of running a small farm into a selling point of Lancashire cheese. Most of the farms in Lancashire before the First World War were smallholdings, which could not produce enough milk each day to make a complete batch. To stop it from going sour, the milk was turned into curds, which would then be blended with the curds from the following day's production. It was this unique method, resulting in a particularly creamy taste, that made Lancashire such a popular cheese and before the onset of the Second World War there were dozens of farms in the county making it. Unfortunately, this method of cheese-making also meant it was designated as a soft cheese and its production was prohibited during the period of rationing. By the time the restrictions were lifted, there were only a little over twenty farmers who still knew the traditional methods. Fortunately, both the taste and the versatility of Lancashire cheese in cooking have seen its popularity increase, although even now there remain only fifteen or so makers in the county.

Bob continued to instruct as he stirred a vat of milk. 'Creamy and tasty Lancashire are the original cheeses. Creamy is aged for anything up to twelve weeks before we sell it, tasty can be aged for up to two years.' He gave the milk in the vat another turn. He had already added rennet and a starter to the milk and the formation of curds was already in evidence in the large steel vat.

He went on: 'Crumbly is a modern invention, because cheese makers wanted a way to get a product out to the market more quickly and to make a cheese that was not quite so powerful that would appeal to those outside Lancashire.' He didn't look desperately convinced by this new addition to the Lancashire cheese canon, which he explained was first made in the early 1970s.

By now, the curds had formed and had separated from the whey. Bob asked for my help as he began to drain the tank. 'It's piped off to a tanker and is shipped to a local pig farmer.' Bob explained a symbiotic relationship between farmers I had encountered in other parts of the country.

Once the curds had been totally drained, I was handed an implement resembling a rectangular harp as Bob instructed me in the fine art of curd cutting. 'You don't want to overwork it.' He demonstrated with a practised sweep of his hand, cutting a wide arc through the soft curds. 'Just cut one way and then the next until you have curds about the size of a penny piece.' I did as I was instructed, moving up and down the tank making sure that there were no large pieces of curd left in the corners of the tank.

When it was cut to Bob's satisfaction, we began to mix the curds from this vat with those that had been pro-duced the day before, blending them gently together until they were fully combined. 'Now we can press them.' Bob pointed towards a large, ancient-looking horizontal press in the corner of the cheese-making room. 'You can use an electronic machine, but you don't get the same control you have when you do it by hand,' he argued, adding, 'Some curds behave differently to others, and with this old machine you can give it an extra half twist every now and again to get it just right.' He slapped the press affectionately as he spoke. It had obviously given him good service over the years.

He began by decanting the curds into large moulds, lined with cheesecloth. I stood to one side and watched with appreciation a process that had remained unchanged since its method was laid down by Joseph Gornall well over one hundred years ago. Once the moulds were filled Bob covered the tops with more cheesecloth and lifted three of them on to the press, giving the screw mechanism a quick turn to make sure they were properly secured. Small amounts of residual whey began to escape from the sides and dribble on to the floor.

'That's it.' Bob grinned. 'Now we just wait.' After twenty-four hours, the cheeses would be removed from the press and left to age. He led me through to the chilled ageing room of the dairy where large rounds of all the different varieties of cheese they made sat on wooden shelves waiting for his expert opinion on their ripeness. He selected some examples of each, smelling them first and then cutting samples with a well-used cheese steel.

'These will do the job,' he said, packing them into a polystyrene cool box for me to take with me. There were small versions of each of the Lancashire cheeses, creamy, tasty and crumbly, which had been dipped in red wax to protect them. There were also samples of the renowned young curd cheese I had tasted as we worked and at least a dozen other cheeses in all shapes and sizes. As I said, Bob Kitchen is a generous man, despite being from the wrong side of the Pennines.

He helped me carry them out to the car and placed them on the passenger seat for me, making certain that the pungent aroma of a dairy man's labours accompanied me on my drive back to the capital. Once home, I carried Bob's package up three flights of stairs to my flat and as I unpacked it the smell made me realize just how hungry I was after such an early start, a long day and a tortuous drive home. I picked up one of the tasty Lancashires Bob had marked as ready for eating, breaking open the wax, releasing even more aromas of perfect cheese. I already knew exactly how I was going to be sampling it. In fact, I had been dreaming about it all the way home.

I opened the fridge and took out a fresh loaf of sourdough bread (yes, yes, I keep my bread in the fridge, get over it) and cut myself a thick slice. I had already turned the grill on and placed the doorstop of bread beneath it to toast one side. As it began to turn a golden brown, I carved wafer-thin slices of tasty Lancashire, lots of them. This was going to be the best cheese on toast ever. Removing my toast from under the grill, I smeared the other side with a thin layer of hot English mustard and then layered the cheese on top of it, slice after thin slice until there was a little hillock of it rising in the centre. I sprinkled it with Henderson's Relish and placed it back under the grill.

Sad though it may be to admit that this is how I get my kicks, I pulled up a chair and sat to watch as the cheese began to react with the heat. It melted quickly, covering the toast and then began to bubble. I watched closely. For it to be proper cheese on toast, I needed a few charred bits on top, but I didn't want it to burn, which would be a waste of all Bob's efforts. Turning off the grill at the precise moment when it would have turned from midnight snack to a piece of *CSI* evidence, I tossed my cheese on toast on to a waiting plate. My first bite was perfection, gooey and delicious as the sharp cheese gave way to the crunch of the toast and the heat of the mustard. I polished the slice off in a few short bites and lifted the plate so I could lick it clean of the crumbs from the bread and oil from the cheese.

A simple, yet perfect snack which made me appreciate all the more the efforts of people like Randolph Hodgson who has almost single-handedly pulled the British cheese-making industry back from the brink and Bob Kitchen who is making sure that it has a bright future, be it crumbly, tasty or creamy.

# 16
## Roast Beef and Yorkshire Pudding

It's time to get serious and talk about the Roast Beef of Old England, and because it is what separates us from the beasts of the fields, some Yorkshire puddings as well.

The part played by beef in British culture has always been significant and has found its way into legend, literature and song. James I is reputed to have dubbed a particularly worthy piece of meat 'Sir Loin' when he visited Hoghton Tower, near Preston, Lancashire, in 1617.

Shakespeare recognized the importance of beef to the fighting man in *Henry V*, where the Duke of Orleans and his constable gloat that victory will belong to the French at Agincourt because the British soldiers had not had their ration of beef, acknowledging that if the soldiers had been well fed on cow, they would 'eat like wolves and fight like devils'.

By the eighteenth century, such was the importance of beef to the British that Henry Fielding constructed the following verse for his *Grub-Street Opera* in 1731.

*When mighty Roast Beef was the Englishman's food,*
*It ennobled our brains and enriched our blood.*
*Our soldiers were brave and our courtiers were good*
*Oh! the Roast Beef of old England,*
*And old English Roast Beef!*

So great was our obsession that foreigners began to parody our love of beef, most famously of all with the French sobriquet 'les rosbifs', in part suggesting that our dining tables had precious little else to offer, but also, one can't help feeling, in grudging admiration of the quality of British animal husbandry, which meant that beef was available to all but the very poorest in society and of sufficient quality that it did not need to hide its light under a bushel of sauces.

It was this abundance that made possible the great British tradition, the Sunday lunch, which originated when landowners would reward farm workers for their hard labours by providing them with a meal of roast meats after church services on a Sunday. It is a tradition that thrived during the move from a rural to an industrial economy, where many factories were owned by devoutly religious men who would allow workers a day of rest on the Sabbath. Sunday was often the only day a whole family could dine together and because of that, the Sunday lunch soon became the focal point of the week and deeply rooted in the British psyche as one of our important meals.

Sunday lunch would not only serve to bring the family together but would be the basis of the meals for much of the following week. Lunch itself would be centred on a chicken or a large joint of roast meat supplemented by lots of filling vegetables. The remains would be eked out during the rest of the week to justify the expense. A joint of beef could become the base for beef stew and dumplings or be minced finely to make cottage pie, covered with a thick layer of mashed potato. Chicken would become soup, lamb turned to hot pot, and pork, with the addition of a few cheap cuts of offal, to deliciously rich faggots to be served warm with a dousing of vinegar.

The great British tradition of Sunday lunch has survived assaults on many fronts from wartime rationing, the horrors of foot and mouth and variant CJD to the hectic pace of modern life and, with it, the decline of the traditional family model. None the less, despite all of these, the Sunday lunch remains one of Britain's great dining events, primarily for its ability to bring people together and remind us that the art of feasting is not yet totally forgotten.

There can be few more thrilling sights than a huge, perfectly cooked joint of beef surrounded by roast potatoes and a mound of Yorkshire puddings being carried to the table, and if you are planning a book on British food then matters pertaining to the classic combination of beef and batter puddings should really come at the very top of the list.

Sunday lunch is also the meal that brings with it such wonderful nostalgia. Memories of meals with grandparents, arguments over the number of potatoes served to a sibling or the portioning of pork crackling and the communal happy groan as chairs were pushed back from tables at the end of the meal. Majumdar family Sunday lunches involved a regular rotation of chicken, lamb, pork and beef. Deviation from the order was never considered by my mother and would never have been tolerated by the clan. Now, in my adult years, beef plays an even more central role in my eating habits and I am fortunate that in my brother, TGS, I have one of the best cooks of beef in the country.

If you care to check out his many cow-related posts on

our blog, Dos Hermanos, you will see what I mean. He has taken the preparation of beef to a whole new level, discovering butchers who will prepare cuts from Argentina and Brazil as well as the classic home-grown cuts that we grew up arguing over. He pores over books and videos about its preparation and more times than I can count has arrived home waving an enormous piece of rib-eye steak on the bone in front of me and proclaimed, 'One point five kilos, forty-day-aged, grass-fed.'

That, for the record, is never, ever a bad thing.

His Yorkshire puddings aren't half bad either, they too being the subject of years of nerdish research and experimentation. But, when it came to *Eating for Britain*, there was only one person's roast beef and Yorkshire pudding I wanted to get up close and personal with and that was Andrew Porter's.

You probably won't have heard about Andrew Porter, but I can say hand on heart that he is one of my favourite chefs in the UK. I first encountered him when he ran the kitchen of an excellent pub restaurant in Yorkshire. It wasn't just the fact that he could cook up a storm. It was the unapologetic enthusiasm he showed for the ingredients he was using that made his food so memorable. He was slightly less enthusiastic about other aspects of the pub and in particular its customers. During my weekend stay, I was subjected to numerous and hilarious five-minute rants where Andy, barely drawing breath, turned the air blue about any of the dozens of subjects that made him very angry indeed. Particular ire was reserved for those who enjoyed a bit of a walk.

'Fookin' ramblers. I fookin' hate them,' he told me over one superb breakfast, which included the best black pudding I had ever tasted, made to his own specification with veal sweetbreads added for extra richness. 'They coom in 'ere after their walk wi' their muddy boots and backpacks and they complain if they can't get a meal for under a fookin' fiver. Then they sit there moaning about it while they compare their new fookin' £100 cagoules.'

On more than one occasion I sprayed food across the table at my dining companion, laughing out loud as his tirades became more heated and hysterical. Although he could vent his fury on many subjects, ramblers did seem to have a special place in his heart. By the end of the weekend, I was convinced his mother must have been frightened by a backpacker during pregnancy.

'What is a cagoule anyway?' he asked me as I was leaving. 'I'll tell ya, it's a fooking Pakamac for wankers. That's what it is.'

If I ruled the world, Andy Porter would have his own daily TV show where he would be given one subject on which to opine until he ran out of breath or expletives, whichever came first. It would be a sure-fire ratings smash.

But, bloody hell, could he cook and during that weekend I tasted plate after plate of the sort of food that makes me really, really happy. Great ingredients not messed around with, prepared by a chef who wanted people to enjoy rather than be impressed by his food. The memory of the final meal, a Sunday lunch, stayed with me in particular. Before taking my seat in the dining room, I visited Andy who was hard at work in the kitchen. He was standing, arms folded, staring proudly at two colossal pieces of meat. One, a joint of pork, was covered with a layer of crackling, which had bubbled up in the high heat of the oven so it made a sound like footsteps on gravel when one of the other cooks cut into it with a long knife. The other, a huge rib of beef, had a thick covering of golden, crisp fat and glistened as it dribbled beefy juices on to the meat board while it rested after cooking.

I was torn. Pork with crackling or roast beef with the Yorkshire puddings I had seen rising like miniature bouncy castles in the oven? These are the real decisions that affect your life, for whichever I chose, the other would obviously look better as it was carried out to other diners and my failure would come back to haunt me later when I grew hungry again. 'Why don't you 'ave a bit o' both?' Andy said, slapping me on the knuckles with a spoon as I reached out to stroke the crackling on the pork. 'I'll give you a side order of Yorkshires as well,' he added. At this point, we both looked down at the ground slightly shamefully. Yorkshire puddings should only ever be served with beef. Anything else could end up at the very least in a sorry shake of the heads from the other diners.

Good to his word, Andy sent out a plate for me laden down with thick slices of each piece of dead animal. Both cuts of meat were as good as you are ever likely to find, succulent and delicious. But it was the Yorkshire puddings that stood out above everything else. They were light and crisp on the outside, slightly doughy on the inside, perfect to sop up the gravy enriched with the meat juices I had seen flowing from the joint earlier. Even I, at that stage going through a slightly extreme 'carbs = death' phase, could not resist them and Andy brought out a towering plateful for our table to share. May my mum forgive me, but I think they were the best Yorkshires I had ever tasted.

Andy later moved on from the pub and I tracked him down to a charming hotel in York called the Pavilion, where he had been offered the position of head chef. Unsurprisingly, when I looked at the hotel menu online, there was no 'Rambler's Special' on offer, but there were some classic Andy dishes and there was, inevitably, the promise of a cracking Sunday lunch. This being Yorkshire, I suspected there would also be some great puddings to be had.

It is unlikely that Yorkshire's claims to have invented the pudding have any merit, since mentions of them go back as far as the early 1700s when a household management guide, *The Whole Duty of a Woman*, made reference to a 'dripping pudding' which made use of the fat from joints of meat roasting on a spit. Eighteenth-century cookery writer Hannah Glasse included a recipe for 'Batter Pudding' in her famous book, *The Art of Cookery*, and so too did Mrs Beeton in the nineteenth century, although her recipe would be frowned upon by anyone from Yorkshire as her pudding was cooked for an hour and the end result was flat and heavy rather than light, with a crisp outside.

The links with Yorkshire probably have more to do with thrift than origin. Traditionally, puddings were made not in the muffin tins we are so familiar with today but in shallow rectangular baking tins. The pudding was cut into squares and served with gravy before the main course as a way of making the expensive protein portion of the meal go further. In some cases it was even served after the meal with jam or cream. Whatever its origins, the name of Yorkshire has over time become firmly associated with batter puddings cooked in beef dripping and there was no question about where I was going to go in search of the perfect Yorkshire.

When I arrived at the hotel, situated on the outskirts of York, Andy shared with me his secret for the perfect Yorkshire pudding. 'Equal parts of egg, flour, milk and water, mixed well, sieved to remove lumps and rested overnight.' It may sound easy, but between mixing bowl and plate there is plenty that can and does go wrong, as the misshapen efforts I have turned out time after time go to prove.

Andy had already prepared the batter the night before and left it to rest. So we headed straight out and jumped in my car as he directed me to his butchers to collect the piece of beef that would be the centrepiece of our efforts. From the outside, M&K Butchers did not look like much. There was a tiny counter behind the entrance with a traditional chain-mail curtain to keep away flies. Inside, there was a short queue, formed entirely of eld-erly women, and behind the counter the master butcher was waiting for us. He'd already selected some large slabs of beef and laid them out in the cutting room for our inspection as we began a detailed debate about which cut would most suit our purpose. A fillet was dismissed for lacking sufficient fat. A piece of topside caught our eye, but it too lost out when our attention was drawn to his final offering, a glorious piece of rib-eye, marbled with a network of connective tissues that we all knew would break down during roasting to release juices and flavour. We nudged the butcher to slice a four-inch-wide piece for us, plenty enough to provide for a few good platefuls.

As we left to drive back to the hotel, we stopped at the counter to collect a packet of fresh beef dripping, the only medium in which both the puddings and the roast potatoes should be cooked.

Back in the kitchen, we began by parboiling the potatoes, then shaking them in the pan after they had been drained to create rough edges that would crisp up during cooking. Andy cut a large slice from the creamy white block of dripping and threw it into a tray on the stove where it began to spit and melt on contact with the hot metal. He did the same with a deep-sided frying pan, seasoned black through years of good use. When the fat was melted in both, he tossed the potatoes in the tray to make sure they were all coated with the dripping and slid the pan on to the middle rack of the oven.

In the frying pan, Andy began to sear our joint of beef on every side until the natural sugars in the meat began to caramelize and turn the outer edge the colour of mahogany. The smell filled the kitchen and the junior chefs gathered around us, giving appreciative sniffs and nodding in approval. Once the beef was sealed, it too was placed in the oven for the relatively short time required to cook it to our mutual preference of serving it rare.

The Yorkshires also depended on vast amounts of God's good dripping and already a muffin tin with a little blob scraped into each compartment was in the oven reaching the required temperature. As the tin began to smoke, Andy opened the oven door and carefully poured batter into each well, making sure not to overfill so there was plenty of room for them to rise. Like a soufflé, once the oven door was closed, it could not be opened until cooking was completed or the puddings were in danger of collapsing in on themselves like a culinary black hole. I peered in through the glass as Andy urged a little bit of patience. 'You can't hurry a good Yorkshire,' and he led me on a quick tour of the hotel to distract me from the purpose of my visit. Finally, he announced they were ready and not before time as the smells filling the kitchen had everyone within sniffing range slobbering drool.

The potatoes were ready for plating first. I stole a small one from the pan, bouncing it up and down in my hands until it was cool enough to eat. They had to all intents and purposes been poached in the dripping in the same way the French might prepare a confit duck leg in its own fat. For the last stage of cooking, the excess had been drained from them to allow the outsides to crisp up to a golden-brown crunch. They were the perfect roast potatoes and while Andy turned his attention to the other elements of our meal, I bit down on my stolen specimen with a loud crunch.

The beef had been removed from the oven and allowed to rest. 'Resting is one of the most important things wi' any roasting,' Andy told me. 'You should rest your joint for almost as long as you cook it,' he explained as he took his large chef's knife and carved a thick slice from the joint. The meat was beautifully rare and the resting had allowed the colour to spread evenly throughout the joint. He overlapped two pink slices on the plate alongside the potatoes.

By now, the puddings were also ready to be removed from their own separate oven. They had risen in the bubbling hot dripping about an inch above the rim of each compartment. The outsides, like the potatoes, were brown and crisp, the insides, as I snapped one in two, revealed their soft doughy underbelly, designed to soak up the gravy Andy was now making with the meat juices the beef had released.

I would have happily eaten my lunch picking from the cooking pans, but, ever the chef, Andy was already plating it up in a more presentable form so I could take a picture. He plucked a prime example from the tray of Yorkshire puddings and laid it next to the beef and the roast potatoes, adding a bunch of peppery watercress, an artful slick of horseradish sauce and, finally, a jug of piping hot juices.

'Tuck into your dinner,' Andy urged, reminding me that in my home county they cling firmly to the old tradition of calling lunch, dinner. I didn't really need much persuading as we both jostled for access to the prime parts of the beef, making sure to take some of the crisp ribbon of fat with each mouthful. Every bite was a perfect example why roast beef and Yorkshire pudding, particularly when accompanied by bowls piled high with vegetables, is a British national treasure.

It is a dish with a traceable history going back over 400 years, a dish that has formed other nations' views about British cuisine for better or for worse and a dish that is still enjoyed by millions every Sunday lunchtime. No dish better sums up Britain's food heritage and perhaps even the British character. It is a dish that speaks not just to the bellies of the British but also to the soul of being British. It eschews culinary flimflammery in favour of classic simplicity, which hides the fact that it actually takes considerable skill to execute well. A typically British approach straight from the 'Oh, just something I threw together' school which covers up the thought and effort that has gone into its preparation, let alone the animal husbandry that has gone into the rearing of the animals.

Like so many of our dishes, the Sunday lunch may be under threat, but I can't believe that its importance will ever be lost to our nation. It is too familiar, comforting and important a meal for it to fall out of favour. As the demographic of our nation changes, so too will the food we serve and Sunday lunch in future, if not already, could just as easily be a meal of Nigerian, Asian or Eastern European origin. But, with each bite of this perfect plate of food produced for me by one of my favourite chefs, I knew that there would always be a place on the dining tables of Britain for the roast beef of Old England.

# 17
## Pie and Mash

As far as journeys for *Eating for Britain* went, this was probably as easy as it was going to get. No 4 a.m. start to drive to the far reaches of the country with only Ken Bruce for company (I am middle-aged, give me a fricking break). No flights on budget airlines where the closest I could get to luxury was purchasing Speedy Boarding and no threading my increasingly creaky old car through narrow country lanes in search of the bed and breakfast accommodation I had booked over the internet. Instead, a good night's sleep in my own bed, a relaxed morning catching up on e-mails with a nice strong mug of builder's tea and a short stroll of less than ten minutes from my flat to the heart of London's most fashionable neighbourhood, Hoxton.

At eleven in the morning, as I walked along Hoxton Market, my nostrils were assaulted by a blast of savoury steam. I was in the right place. F. Cooke Pie & Mash Shop had just opened for business and the waft of meaty air was joined by the clattering of pans as the golden-crusted pies, hot from the oven, were carried out and placed behind the service counter to wait for the first customers of the day. I glanced at the empty dining room. The wooden tables were wiped clean and topped with pots of salt, white pepper and vinegar. The white-tiled walls sparkled in the light that shone through the windows and the floors had been given a thorough sweeping. It was exactly the same sight that had probably greeted eager punters since the shop first opened in the middle of the 1800s and was given added poignancy as my research had shown that it was the last of a dying breed, one of only twenty or fewer pie shops left in London.

The decline of pie and mash shops in London has been dramatic. While doing some background reading at the Guildhall Library, I came across a smashing little book called *Pie 'n' Mash: A Guide to Londoners Traditional Eating Houses*. It listed not only eighty-eight shops in the capital but also a dozen or so more that had been opened in the wider cockney diaspora of Essex towards the coastal towns of Leigh-on-Sea and Southend. Its tone was cele- bratory and convinced that the lot of one of London's traditional foods was on the up and up. It was published in 1995. Fifteen years later and you could probably count the remaining shops on the fingers and toes of a healthy human.

It had not always been like this, of course; the pie and mash shop had been a staple source of nourishment for working-class Londoners for generations. Like jellied eels, often sold from the same establishments, the origins of pie and mash shops lay with the seventeenth-century costermongers. They plied their trade in the East End of London, selling pies filled with hot eels that were shipped into Billingsgate Market from the Thames Estuary and then later from Holland. The first recorded eel and pie shop was opened at 101 Union Street in Southwark by Henry Blanchard who sold meat, fruit and eel pies for a penny. By 1874 more than thirty shops had appeared around the East End, and by the turn of the century the days of pie and mash shop family empires had begun.

Robert Cooke, listed in the 1881 census as an 'Eel Seller', opened his first shop in Bethnal Green in 1889 and soon followed with two more including the branch in Hoxton Market which was run by his wife. Another legendary name in pie and mash history, Michael Manze, an immigrant from Italy, soon had his feet very firmly under the Cookes' table and married Robert's daughter, Ada, before opening his own shop in Bermondsey, where it still stands today. A third family, the Kellys, followed soon afterwards, opening their first shop in 1915, and the rapid expansion continued until by the middle of the twentieth century there were over 130 pie and mash shops in London alone. The popularity of pie and mash shops with the working people of London made them incredibly resilient, particularly in the face of two world wars, which took most of their customer base of adult men off to battle. Even when faced with post-war rationing and a shortage of eels, the shops continued to prosper primarily because of the value they offered. In the end it was simple economics that proved to be the catalyst for their decline and increasing variety that will prove to be the cause of their final demise.

By the early 1960s the economy of the UK began to boom and brought with it massive redevelopment in the Blitz-damaged East End of London. With the rapid growth came huge increases in rent. Traditional businesses simply could not afford to stay where they were and relocated, mainly to the new towns of Essex, and took their workforce and the chief customer base of the pie and mash shops with them. Some pie shops saw an opportunity, opening businesses in some of the satellite towns, but for those in the capital the rot had set in and by the turn of the millennium the numbers put them high up on the endangered species list.

'It's not just the rents,' Joe Cooke told me as we squeezed on to opposite sides of a wooden table. He sipped his tea and waved his hand towards the door. 'It's the fact that people now have so many other options when they want something to eat.' When F. Cooke first opened on Hoxton Market, there were three options if you chose not to eat at home: the pie shop, the fish and chip shop and a greasy spoon 'caff'. That morning as I walked to meet Joe, I counted the alternatives that now littered the same stretch of road. There were over thirty of them ranging from gastropubs, grim chains of bakers selling plastic sandwiches, kebab shops, pizza joints and Indian takeaways.

In the face of all that competition, it is little wonder that the unfashionable pie shops are facing extinction. As we talked, an attractive young woman came over and gave Joe a peck on the cheek. 'That's my daughter,' Joe said proudly as she walked away to meet her friends. He highlighted another reason why the era of the pie and mash shop is coming to an end. 'She wouldn't want to be in this business with her qualifications, so probably there will be no one to take over. It's bloody hard work too,' Joe sighed and he should know.

Joe Cooke, the latest and possibly last in the line of Cooke's Pie Shop owners, had been in the business himself for well over twenty years and was still in the shop every morning at the crack of dawn to make sure the pies were produced to the same traditional recipe and that everything was ready for the day. He worked hard at promoting his product to a modern audience as well and had just returned from delivering pies to offices in the City. I couldn't help picturing him as Canute trying to protect his beloved heritage against the unstoppable tide of modernity. Despite that, he remained enthusiastic about his product.

'There was a period, during and just after rationing, where people made pies from cheaper ingredients, but we never did at Cooke's.' He motioned for me to follow him into the kitchen. 'It doesn't matter what you're making, you always have to use the best ingredients,' he said, pointing towards a wiry colleague he introduced as John, quietly working pastry in the corner.

It had been made at first light and rested. Now it was being rolled out into thin sheets ready to layer into shallow, well-used pie tins, which he did with a rapid dexterity that could only have come from years of practice. 'All our pies are made with Scottish beef, butchered flank steak on the bone and shortcrust pastry. That's it,' John explained.

The pie maker carried over a cauldron-sized pan of rich, dark minced beef that had been cooked earlier in the day and allowed to cool. He ladled the mixture into the pie casings until it was right to the brim. 'People don't just want cheap food, they want value for money,' John argued. 'So we have always overstuffed our pies.' Once the lid was placed on top and crimped to create a seal, they were given a swift swipe with a bristle brush to wash the tops with milk and help create a glaze and were then put on the middle shelf of a blisteringly hot oven.

'It's not just the pies, though.' Joe led me to another

corner of the small kitchen where buckets of freshly peeled Maris Pipers had been boiled in salted water and were being mashed. 'The same way we have been doing for decades.' Joe scooped up a spoonful and passed it to me. The taste of the potatoes made me smile as it reminded me of my mother's own take, which she would supplement with the 'top of the milk' to add extra richness, and which required the table to be laid with a knife, fork and defibrillator. More than that, it proved that, in the world of food, there is nothing new on God's earth.

With the pies cooking and the mash preparation under control, we turned our attention to the liquor. Traditionally, this famously lurid green sauce was made using water in which eels had been cooked and to which little more than salt, and a huge amount of chopped parsley were added. As the eels cooked, they released natural gelatine, which if allowed to cool, would set to create the famous/infamous jellied eels. If the eels were removed from the pot to be eaten hot, alongside mashed potatoes, then the remaining stock was whisked with flour to create the rich, thick gravy, which has become so synonymous with pie and mash. Unfortunately, like pie and mash shops, eels too are now an endangered species and off the menu. So the liquor was being made with stock. The timer on the oven gave a loud 'ping'. The pies were ready and another waft of beefy air hit my nostrils as the door was opened and tray after tray of pies was removed, juices bubbling through the pastry.

Joe led me back into the dining room. On the wall behind the counter was the menu. Ordering pie and mash is all about combinations. Do you want one pie and one scoop of mash? If you are hungrier than that, then try two pies and one mash or one pie and two mash or, well, you get the picture. Decide if you want liquor with your meal and that's it.

I opted for two pies and one blob of mash. The pies were plopped from their silver trays, one, as requested, with a few burn marks where the gravy had fought its way to the surface. The mash was scooped in traditional fashion, the spoon dragged across the edge of the plate leaving a mound of potato and finally a ladleful of liquor was dribbled over the lot, oozing towards the sides and threatening to drip on to the floor. I collected some cutlery and a paper napkin from a plastic tray on the counter, and, balancing that and the plate of hot food in one hand and the obligatory mug of strong tea in the other, made my way to one of the wooden benches.

I know how I like my pies, so before I even tasted those from Joe's kitchen, I sprinkled them and the liquor with malt vinegar and gave the mashed potatoes a liberal shake of white pepper. The piecrust broke under pressure from my spoon, releasing a slick of thick brown gravy, which mixed with the pool of liquor. I lifted it to my mouth with a scraping of potato to help soak up the juices. No one would ever claim that this was pretty food and the combined contents of the pie, liquor and mashed potatoes soon left the plate resembling a slurry pit. But, if it is undeniably messy, it is redeemed by also being very tasty indeed. The long slow cooking of the mince created a deliciously savoury filling and the buttery mashed potatoes were as good as I can remember. There are more reasons that pie and mash shops have been around for over 150 years than just being good value (my meal cost under £5). It's also because, when prepared as well as they are at Cooke's, they are bloody delicious. Well-brought-up boy that I am, after I had cleaned my plate I returned it to the staff behind the counter and collected another mug of tea.

Returning to my bench, I began to make some notes of my conversation with Joe, who had left to make another delivery to the City. Glancing around the room, I could see that while it was reasonably busy it was certainly not full and that most of the customers were elderly. They were possibly the last generation who would consider this an option for lunch.

I gathered my things and stepped back outside into Hoxton Market. As I walked home, I peered inside the rival cafés and sandwich shops along the street. Most were full and some even had queues of people trailing out of their doors on to the street. It was a disheartening sight. A few of them might have had decent food, but most, I knew, would be selling bad food at cheap prices. Yet a few short yards away on the same road was a true piece of London history, offering the same delicious and good value meals it had provided to Londoners for over a century. I suspected that few of the people I passed knew or indeed cared.

One person who did care about pie and mash, however, was arguably the world's most famous chef, Ferran Adria. While attending a conference in London at the end of 2008, he was taken to the Manzes' pie and mash shop on Tower Bridge Road. He claimed to have enjoyed his meal, but the British press treated the whole matter as a huge joke. And therein lies the truth about the future of dishes like these in Britain. We no longer take their survival as a matter for serious concern. Pie and mash won't disappear altogether, of course. Some chef in the not too distant future will put an ersatz version on their menu at an exorbitant price and it will be snapped up by those for whom 'slumming it' adds an extra dimension to their dining as they sit faced by myriad cutlery and crisp napery. But, within my lifetime, I believe that one piece of Britain's food jigsaw will disappear for ever. Its disappearance will be as much a function of time as it will of quality, but it will disappear none the less and people like Joe Cooke will be nothing but a memory or a post on blogs like my own.

It seems almost inevitable, so all I can do is urge you to find one of the last remaining pie and mash shops in London, line up with the remaining customers, order whatever combination of pie, mash, liquor and eels takes your fancy, squeeze yourself into one of those wooden benches and tuck into a genuine piece of British history. While you still can.

## 18
## Jellied Eels

At 6 a.m. Billingsgate Market already looked like it was winding up for the day. I walked from the station, fighting my way through a sea of people heading in the opposite direction, all clutching carrier bags filled with the daily fish requirements for their restaurants and shops. The car park was already beginning to offer up valuable parking spaces as the white vans headed back into London leaving black tarmac behind them like gaps in a row of teeth.

I always find fish markets fascinating places and have made certain to seek them out wherever I travel. I have vivid memories of the smells of the challenging markets of China and India and, of course, of Tokyo's incomparable Tsukiji Market where I saw colossal tuna being sold for the price of a semi-detached in a nice leafy suburb. However, few fish markets could claim a history matching that of Billingsgate. It was one of the very first markets, along with Cheap and Smithfield, to be granted a charter in London by King Edward III in 1327. The charter stated that no rival markets could be set up within six and two-third miles of each other, that being the distance it was considered someone could walk to market. Without competition, Billingsgate flourished.

The original market was called Blynesgate, named, it is thought, after one of the small watergates along the

Thames where goods were loaded and unloaded. Initially its remit stretched beyond the sales of fish to include everything from coal and iron to other foodstuffs like wine and precious salt. By the late 1600s, however, it was already famous as a place to buy and sell fish and an Act of Parliament in 1699 declared that for six days a week and on Sundays before divine service it was a 'free and open market for all sorts of fish whatsoever'. The only people exempt from this free-market economy were Dutch eel fishermen, who were given a monopoly on selling eels in recognition of their bravery during the Great Fire of London when they continued to sail up the Thames to deliver their catch. However, the fact that a Dutch king, William of Orange, was on the throne probably had some impact on the decision too.

Eels were a staple part of the sixteenth- and seventeenth-century Londoner's diet, but records of them being eaten go back even further with the Doomsday Book recording the landing of eels at Twickenham Ayte, which later became known as Eel Pie Island when a tavern was first built there.

The Thames was, of course, the primary source of eels; however with the growth in demand and a sharp decrease in numbers due to over-fishing in London's own river, Dutch eels were soon as readily available in London as the native ones. They were a more hardy species and able to survive the sea journey from the Netherlands. By the late 1800s London's emergence as an industrial super-power led to such pollution in the Thames that the eel population was all but wiped out, leaving the market entirely to the Dutch. The relationship remains and, although the state of the Thames may now be far removed from its murky past, the majority of the eels that cross our tables still come from Holland.

Eels were very much a food of the poor man. They were cheap and nutritious, but they were also full of bones and difficult to eat which made them less popular with the higher classes. They were sold on London's streets by costermongers, the low-life street sellers who would push their carts around the capital singing out the name of the goods they were offering to customers considered not good enough to buy from smart shops. The eels would be cooked by stewing them in water with spices until the fish began to release its natural jellies and then they would be sold hot, in pies, or cold, where the liquor had been allowed to set, sealing in the fish to help preserve them. The traditional accompaniment to the cold eels was a good splash of vinegar spiked through with a dose of chilli, a testament to the status of London as a trading city where goods from all over the world flowed through the Thames ports to the rest of the country.

By the mid-1800s many of the costermongers had amassed sufficient wealth to move from the streets into shops or at least to find permanent sites for their carts, which became famous landmarks, particularly in the East End of London where the majority of them lived. When Henry Blanchard's shop opened in 1844 it was the very first such shop, but by the end of the nineteenth century there were well over a hundred shops and carts in the city selling eels. Up until the Second World War jellied eels were as synonymous with being a Londoner as pie and mash, flat beer and fish and chips in newspaper, and a whole generation of Londoners grew up with the ability to suck the flesh from the bony eel, leaving nothing but a few shards to be discarded on the sawdust-covered floor of the shop.

In 1982 Billingsgate Market left its historical site on the Thames and was relocated to a purpose-built market hall near Canary Wharf. Although smart, clean and modern, there was little sense of history as I made my early morning rounds. That was not all that had changed. Where once there would have been dozens of eel merchants, now there was only one, Nick's Eels, and they looked like they were already getting ready to finish for the day. The one fishmonger still on duty was busy cleaning down ready to close and go and have some much deserved breakfast at one of the packed cafés in the market. I was there early, but I had obviously not been early enough to catch the last of a dying breed.

Billingsgate itself also looked like it had seen better times. In the nineteenth century it was the largest fish market in the world. Today, it appeared a much sadder affair, whose prime business seemed to be supplying frozen varieties of unusual fish to London's ever growing ethnic communities. There is nothing wrong with that of course, but there was a dismal air about the place, which suggested that I had not only arrived at the end of the working day but possibly at the end of an era. At the very least the thought struck me that it was only the support of recent immigrants to Britain that was propping up one of its oldest institutions.

The era of the jellied eel, however, ended long before my visit to the market. Where once their number was in the hundreds, now there are only a handful of eel stalls and most of those face closure in the very near future. In part, it is because of increases in rents and rates. In part, it is because the owners are nearing retirement and their children don't consider following in their footsteps a worthy career. In part, it is because eels are becoming increasingly endangered because of overfishing in Europe, but also because of changes to the natural spawning ground in the Sargasso Sea. What is landed usually finds its way to a smokehouse and from there to the tables of fine dining restaurants to be served with horseradish at prices that would make any true cockney keel over.

However, the real reason for their impending extinction is that most people find the notion of jellied eels really very nasty indeed and would rather suck their own brains out with a straw than ever have to sample what they consider to be nothing more than fish-flavoured mucus. With increased affluence, increased travel and increased availability have come wider food choices. We no longer have to eat something because that is all there is.

On the downside this has contributed to the decline of some of our greatest traditional dishes and the disappearance from our tables of interesting ingredients like offal and a true understanding of the notion of seasonal food. On the upside it does also mean that some dishes are dying out with few tears shed by a population who balk at the thought of eating them. Jellied eels are probably top of the list.

I had never sampled jellied eels until 1982. I moved down to London and university and considering myself a culinary adventurer I found my way to Tubby Isaac's stall on the corner of the Whitechapel Road and Goulston Street in London's East End. Tubby Isaac's stall was opened in 1919 by Isaac 'Tubby' Brenner and since 1938, when he handed it over to his assistant, Solomon Gritzman, has been in the same family for over four generations. It's still there and now in the hands of Paul Simpson who can be found behind the counter most days spooning out bowls of eels to a loyal but dwindling clientele.

It was my first sampling of a dish I had only ever really known about from my grandfather, but despite my worst fears, I found myself rather enjoying them. It wasn't just the taste but the whole experience of ordering and eating a famous dish among a group of elderly men and women who told me they had been coming to the stall for most of their lives.

I handed over 50p for my container and following the example of my elders and betters covered it in a good slick of vinegar before spooning the first taste of eels into my mouth. I could certainly understand why they were considered an acquired taste and the texture was certainly challenging, but the combination of meaty fish and spiced jelly appealed to me, as did the crunch of the bones as I scraped the last of the flesh from them. I spent a good half-hour working my way not only through another pot of eels but also an added order of cockles and whelks to complete the experience. I was proud of the nod of approval given to me by my dining companions when I finally headed for home.

After my trip to Billingsgate, I paid Tubby Isaac's another call. As I stood there next to two old boys gumming their fish before spitting the bones on to the floor in the time-honoured fashion, I could not help but think that, like my visit to the pie and mash shop, we were seeing the last chapter in the story of jellied eels. Their days are numbered now, not just by the increasing scarcity of eels, but by the increasing scarcity of anyone who might actually want to eat them. There are still a handful of stalls and a few pie and mash shops that serve eels up both hot and cold when they can get them, but their numbers continue to dwindle as indeed do the numbers of their rapidly ageing clientele.

Jellied eels won't disappear totally. Some young cook will place a cheffy version of them on a menu to be served garnished with huge amounts of irony. But the truth is that, possibly in my lifetime, this link to British history stretching back to 1327 and beyond will disappear from London never to return and that has to be a matter for mourning, whether you like fish in jelly or not.

# 19
## Welsh Faggots and Peas

Okay, let's get it over with. With the possible exception of a spotted dick is there any dish in British cuisine that elicits such an immediate and humorous response as the faggot? Its name is strike one against it. Strike two is the fact that it is made out of bits of the animal that might otherwise have found their way into pet food. The third strike is that, probably because of strikes one and two, most people would never even consider eating one. It's a great shame as these large and savoury meatballs can be delicious and eating them brings back some of my fondest childhood memories.

The term faggot actually comes from the Welsh *ffagod*, meaning little bundle, and refers to the fact that they were originally held together by being wrapped in caul, the stomach lining of the pig. Like their Scottish cousin, the haggis, Welsh faggots were a way of using up every last scrap of the slaughtered animal and were made by mincing belly pork with pig's offal and spices, wrapping in the caul and then baking.

Across the borders in the Midlands you can find something very similar called a savoury duck, but for anyone with even a smidgeon of Welsh in them only the ones from the Principality will do and the thought of a piping-hot savoury faggot with mushy peas and a sprinkle of vinegar is enough to get tears flowing as quick as a rendition of 'Cwm Rhondda'.

Inevitably for me, all thoughts of eating faggots bring with them even more memories of my Welsh grandmother. She had a peculiarly Welsh turn of phrase that when delivered in her singsong accent used to have all our family rolling on the floor in stitches. Pester her too much (nearly always for food) and she would bark, 'Give me some sand and I'll play you "The Desert Song".' Ask her to do too many things at once and she would retort, 'Shove a broom up my bum and I'll clean the floor while I am at it.' Most bemusing of all, if she interrupted an all too regular scene of noisy family in-fighting, she would roll her eyes and exclaim, '*Dieu*, it's like Barney's Fair in here.' Later research showed that Barney's Fair was a travelling circus that had toured Wales in the early part of the twentieth century and had closed down when she herself was a small girl. Bizarrely, the term 'like Barney's Fair' remains in regular use in the Majumdar family nearly a century after it ceased to have any relevance at all. But, like just about everyone else I have met from Wales, her only concern seemed to be to make sure I left my grandparents' home full to bursting and laden down with enough baked treats to keep me going until my next visit.

On my arrival, all four bars of the electric fire in the living room would have been turned to full as a special treat. I would take off my thick coat and stand in front of their orange glow, rubbing my hands until the winter shivers had subsided. My grandmother would appear from her kitchen with a large bowl, instructing me to 'sit down now' in her valleys accent as she ladled faggots on to a plate then covered them with a rich coating of dark, glistening onion gravy. To the side she would have placed a bowl of mushy peas, enough to feed about four people, alongside slices of bread and the only condiments she deemed worthy of an appearance, white pepper and Sarson's malt vinegar. On days when the cold began to eat its way down through to your bones, the sight and smells of a plate of faggots and peas were more welcome than just about anything else I could have asked for.

My grandmother would let out a loud but affectionate 'tut' as I sprinkled the food with pepper and doused it with vinegar before even tasting it. But any consternation she showed would soon turn to a smile as I proceeded to clear the plate, hacking huge chunks off each faggot with the side of a spoon and scooping it to my lips along with some of the peas. When the faggots were all gone, I would clean both my plate and all the bowls of their residual gravy with the slices of bread until you would hardly be aware that they had ever been used. Memories of those meals and my grandmother remain some of my happiest, so when it came to finding the perfect person to show me how to make the perfect faggot, there was only one direction I was going to be looking and that was towards Wales.

Neil James took over the family business in Raglan, Monmouthshire, when his father retired nearly ten years ago. He retained the name and N.S. James & Sons is now considered one of the finest butchers in the country, supplying customers as far away as London and Bristol. When my research told me that Neil had also won a True Taste of Wales award for his faggots in 2008, I called to ask if I could disturb him one morning for a lesson in making this fond memory from my past.

'No problem,' he replied, 'but you will have to come

early as we start making them at eight in the morning.' I made plans to stay the night in Raglan and arrived at the shop on schedule to find Neil and his staff already hard at work cutting meat for the shop displays.

N.S. James & Sons is a proper butcher's shop. A butcher's shop as you remember they used to be. It has its own small abattoir at the rear and most of the animals that come to be slaughtered there travel no more than a few short miles to prevent stress. The meat is stored in a large ageing room and is the real deal. There are thick pork chops layered with a half-inch ribbon of fat, beef brisket rolled ready for slow roasting, lamb kidneys protected by a covering of their own fat and rows of free-range chickens that have spent most of their lives wandering around farmyards rather than looking for floor space in cramped pens.

Alongside the impressive displays of meat there was a chilled cabinet of cooked food prepared in the spotless kitchens of Neil's shop. Hand-raised pork pies, black puddings, sheets of belly pork which he told me had been cooked slowly in his mother's Aga so that the crackling had bubbled to a perfect crunch and, best of all, tray after tray of faggots ready cooked so they could be sold to the small line of locals that had already begun to form the moment he opened his doors.

Neil took me to a small food preparation area at the back of the butchery and pointed to the trays of ingredients he had laid out ready and waiting for us to make faggots. There was a large slab of fatty belly pork, an equal amount of lamb breast, a tray of ruby-red pig's liver, a bowl of fresh peeled onions, fresh breadcrumbs and his own secret spice mix, which smelled strongly of white pepper and transported me immediately to the days spent with my grandmother.

She would have used more cheap cuts of offal in her frugal and hearty versions than Neil did in his own faggots. 'People are better off now, see?' he explained. 'They are not so used to strong tastes like that, so I have had to adapt the recipe.' The lamb breasts and the belly pork would keep the faggots moist while they baked and the pig's liver would add just enough taste without overpowering the rest of the dish.

He began to place all the meat into the deep pan of a commercial mixing machine. 'The key is to use fresh onions,' he added, 'because they give all the juice you will need to make great faggots.' He poured them into the bowl, making sure that every last piece of meat was pushed through the whirring blades. 'My other secret is to double-mince them, this time with the spices. It gives a much smoother texture to the end result.' He poured the spices into the meat and mixed them in thoroughly before pushing the meat once more through the blades of the mincing machine. The end result resembled a rustic pâté and I had to remind myself it was raw meat to stop myself from taking a sample with my finger. Finally, Neil added enough fresh breadcrumbs to help bind everything together and scooped the contents of the pan into another large mixing bowl.

We then began to shape them into specimens of fine faggothood. 'They should be about the size of a cricket ball,' Neil added helpfully as he turned the mince in his hands until it was a perfect round. I tried to keep pace and between us we had soon filled a tray. 'Traditionally, they should be wrapped in caul fat' – Neil mimed covering the faggot – 'but we make so many that the caul is hard to come by. Also, people get a bit squeamish when you tell them what it is. So we use bacon instead.' Not just any bacon however. Neil's bacon comes from pigs slaughtered no more than a matter of yards away from where we were standing. The layer of fat marbled throughout was confirmation that not only had the pigs led a good life, but the bacon they had surrendered would keep the faggots moist and juicy as they cooked as well as providing a crisp outer layer as an extra treat.

Neil had already made a batch of faggots before my arrival and they were baking in the kitchen ovens, the smell filling the room. He pulled a roasting dish from the oven and pierced the largest specimen with a fork. The bacon had cooked to a golden brown, the fat layers crisped up to give a sublime crunch when I broke through them to the meat underneath. The texture of the faggot was softer than I recall from those made by my grandmother and the taste was more of pork than of offal. But the spices were almost exactly as I remembered and the white pepper hit my nose as I lifted my first forkful to take a bite. The second mincing had made the faggots surprisingly light, more like a juicy meatball than the dense traditional versions I had grown up with, but excellent nevertheless.

Neil packed the tray of raw faggots we had made into a freezer box for me to cook at home, waving away any attempts to pay for them. He helped me carry them out to the car before turning back to get on with his real life.

I did not waste any time on my return to my apartment and soon had the entire dozen of them cooking ready for TGS's return home from whatever it is he does for a living. His nostrils were flaring as he walked through the door and when I pulled the ready-to-eat balls of meat from the oven, his eyes lit up. His memories of our grandmother's versions were as vivid as my own.

We sat at the dining table, the faggot-laden dish in front of us along with the prescribed accompaniments of thick gravy and mushy peas. We both tucked in, spearing faggots from serving dish to plate until we had laid waste to the entire dozen. We both raised a glass and gave a toast to our grandmother, Eva John. She would no doubt have rolled her eyes, said, '*Dieu.*' But, deep down, I suspect she would have been rather proud.

This is my own recipe. They may not taste quite like my grandmother's, but they are definitely worth a try.

## — *Faggots* —
### (MAKES 12)

*500g pork belly (trim off the skin and, unless you are a savage, keep to make crackling)*
*250g pig's liver*
*250g lamb breast*
*125g pig heart (optional, but adds real flavour)*
*1 large white onion, finely chopped*
*1 teaspoon salt*
*1 teaspoon white pepper*
*1 teaspoon fresh sage, finely chopped*
*1 teaspoon fresh thyme, finely chopped*
*125g breadcrumbs (made using day-old bread)*

## For wrapping

*If you can find caul fat at your butcher all the better, but, if not, strips of good unsmoked back bacon will do just as well*

Mince all the meats together, mixing to make sure they are combined. Add the onion, the salt, pepper and herbs and mince once more to the texture of a rough pâté. Add the breadcrumbs and mix well.

Form the mixture into cricket-ball-sized balls and wrap in caul fat or in a criss-cross of bacon. Chill in the refrigerator for at least 1 hour to firm.

Bake in a preheated oven at around 180°C/350°F/gas mark 4 for 50 minutes to 1 hour.

Serve with a thick, rich gravy and a bowl of home-made mushy peas doused liberally with malt vinegar.

# 20
# Balti

The balti is a uniquely British dish.

Sits back and waits for the toys to be ejected from prams of pedants all over the country.

Let's start again. The balti, the dish that we now know from the menus of curry houses up and down the land, has its origins not in the subcontinent, in India, Pakistan or Bangladesh, but in Birmingham or more specifically the Balti Triangle area of Sparkbrook, Moseley and the Ladypool Road.

I had my first balti in the late 1980s when I moved from London and spent a rather unhappy year plodding the streets of Birmingham as a publisher's sales representative for Penguin Books. My first wife and I would spin out our meagre budget so that once every week or so we could walk from our small house in Erdington to the nearby neighbourhood of Boldmere, have a couple of drinks and then visit the Kebbabish, a local restaurant, to sit down for a Balti Mix, a huge sizzling bowl of gloriously spicy food that we mopped up with a large naan bread and washed down with bottles of lager.

It was delicious and, more importantly at the time, it was cheap and our night out for two would cost us well under £20 for enough food and drink to make the walk home more of a waddle than a saunter.

After living in London for so many years, the move up to Birmingham proved too difficult. At the time, it was a grey city, which had suffered more than many from the demise of the UK's manufacturing base and had little charm and even less to offer a couple of young newlyweds. Add to this that the newlyweds were already discovering great big fissures in their own relationship which were widened by being so far from most of their friends and it is little wonder that we both scampered back to London at the first opportunity.

I had not thought about Birmingham much in the intervening years. My marriage had not lasted long after my return to London and scarred my memories of the time in the city. However, as I drew up my list of dishes to search for as I looked for the best Britain had to offer, I knew there was nowhere else I could go in search of one particular dish and that an imminent return was on the cards.

Revisiting Birmingham proved to be a pleasant surprise. The city had changed, that much was obvious as I parked my car in the garage of my hotel. The area surrounding Broad Street, with its run-down canals strewn with junk, was pretty much a no-go area when I lived there. Now it had been converted into a busy development of shops and restaurants and the canals cleaned up to provide pleasant walkways between the attractions of the impressive conference centre and concert venue. The city centre had changed too with the building of a sparkly new shopping mall, the main through roads paved over to make them more pedestrian-friendly.

The one thing that had not changed was the people. Brummies always get a raw deal, but they are some of my

*Contemplating* the legalities of marrying a pie. We would be very happy together for about half an hour, but crumbs would be evidence that our union did not end well for one of us

*The perfect* Ulster Fry breakfast prepared by Peter McConkey, owner of the Georgian House, Comber, Northern Ireland

*Lancashire* black puddings fresh from the boilers of R.S. Ireland

*Chef / Hunter* Mike Robinson of the Pot Kiln with loyal companion and hunting dog Sassy, waiting patiently for a sighting of the first deer of the day

*Arbroath* smokies, dripping with hot juices after forty-five minutes cooking over smouldering oak chips. One of the great tastes of the trip around Britain

*The crisp* bubbly batter and crunchy chips cooked in beef dripping tell you that the fish and chips at the Great British Eatery in Birmingham are the real deal

*Bob Kitchen* proudly shows off his 'creamy, tasty and crumbly' Lancashire cheeses at the Leagram Organic Dairy in Chipping

*Rare* roast beef with Yorkshire puddings and horseradish. Could there be any dish more British?

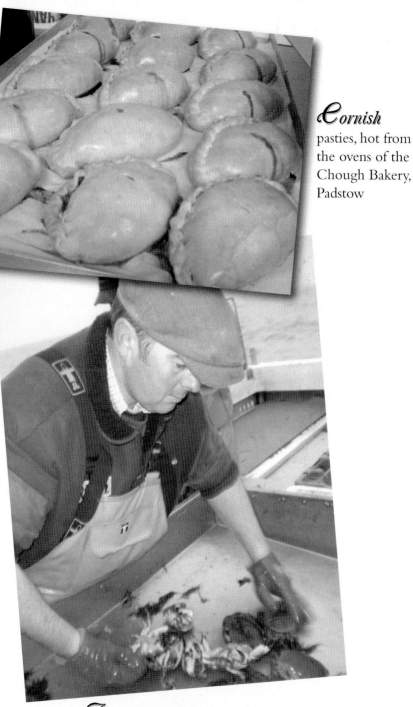

*Cornish* pasties, hot from the ovens of the Chough Bakery, Padstow

*It may* only have been a few hours of misery for me, but for John Davies and his crew braving the seas off the coast of Cromer is a daily event as they work to bring us the best crabs in the country

*Lance Forman* inspects sides of salmon undergoing the London Cure before smoking, a process which has remained unchanged for generations

*Up close* and personal with Brer rabbit. If you are prepared to eat it, you should be prepared to kill it

*'The Shish Mahal Boys'* including (centre) Ahmed Aslam Ali, who lays claim to have invented the Chicken Tikka Masala at his restaurant in Glasgow

*The proud* father of a bouncing baby haggis. Butcher Mark Bowyer just about approves of my attempts to produce Scotland's most famous dish

***Bakewell***, Derbyshire's most famous dish, but don't dare call it a tart or the locals will call you a pudding

***The beautiful*** and hard-working copper spirit stills at the Glenfiddich Distillery in Dufftown, Scotland

favourite people in the whole country. They are not hip like their counterparts in Manchester nor are they knowingly dour like their counterparts in Sheffield. It's true the accent with its nasal rasp doesn't help, but once you get over that and the fact that they seem obliged to say 'tara a bit' instead of goodbye, the Brummies are good people to be around.

Andy Munro was one of the best. In fact, if you looked up the term 'Brummie' in the dictionary they would have a picture of him waving, probably above the words 'Famous people who come from Birmingham: Ozzy Osbourne, Jasper Carrott and that guy from Wizard with the funny-coloured hair who appears every Christmas and then buggers off again'.

Andy worked for Birmingham City Council where his main task was to help redevelop the old Jewellery Quarter by attracting restaurants and bars to replace the diminishing number of goldsmiths and jewellers. His real passion, however, was the balti and in what little spare time he had, he advised the Asian Balti Association on ways to promote the glories of their curry in a bucket.

Andy had agreed to give me a tour of the Balti Triangle and I met him as planned in front of one of his favourite restaurants, the Punjab Paradise on Ladypool Road. He was a wiry man wearing a sharp suit and a thin tie that made him look like a member of an early eighties New Wave band and he talked almost constantly in a thick accent that, at first, I found hard to understand. Everybody in the district seemed to know him and, as we walked people stopped him to say 'hi' and drivers passing by 'parped' their car horns in welcome. I was obviously in the good hands of a local hero.

The history of the balti, or at least Andy's very pro-Brum version of the history of the balti, dates back to the mid-1970s when, looking to offer healthier dishes for their customers than the normal ghee-drenched meals that were available, restaurant owners from Pakistan and Kashmir created a one-pot meal that was cooked very quickly over a high heat with a few ingredients that included tomatoes, onions, ginger and garlic, lamb or chicken and no more than five spices.

The pot used for cooking gave the dish its name, balti literally translating from Punjabi as 'bucket'. It was produced from a special die and made in the city out of very thin steel rather than the normal cast iron, so allowing the food to be prepared and served in the same bowl and it was eaten with large naan breads rather than rice.

Andy's tour included a visit to an Asian hardware store. Heading to the back of the shop, he began rummaging around on the bottom shelf until he emerged with two dusty metal-handled bowls.

'These,' he said with considerable pride, 'are proper balti pans. The man who designed them died a few years ago and the moulds are broken. So unless we can raise some money to make new ones, this is it.' He dusted off the bowls and held them up so I could see how thin the steel had been rolled.

Back at the Punjab Palace, Andy introduced me to the owner, Councillor Tanveer Choudhry who took me into the kitchen where the staff were getting ready for the expected lunchtime rush. A pot of chai tea for the cooks was already simmering on a stove at the rear of the kitchen, one chef was flipping out dough ready to be slapped on the inside of the tandoor oven to make naan and one more was frying a mountain of poppadums to place on the tables as customers arrived.

All this was interesting enough, but Tanveer wanted to show me how a chicken balti desi, their house special, was made. This was a balti with less sauce than most, designed to appeal to their increasing number of Asian customers. The balti pan was already heating up over a powerful flame as one of the chefs added chopped tomatoes and half a chopped onion and allowed them to cook in a small amount of oil until they had softened. The smell of just these two ingredients was enough to make me salivate, but when he then added a spoonful each of garlic and ginger the aroma exploded around the whole kitchen. Spices were added next, less than a teaspoon each of fenugreek, turmeric and garam masala and then, finally, the chicken, cut from the breast and then into small pieces so they could cook through as quickly as the other ingredients.

That was it. No more than five minutes from start to finish and my lunch was ready, to be eaten with a naan that had just been removed from the oven and was gently deflating waiting for my attention.

Andy joined in with as much enthusiasm as I did even though, by his own admission, he had eaten thousands of baltis in his time.

'It may have originated with immigrants to the UK,' he added between mouthfuls, 'but it's a very British dish. In fact, I would go further than that and say that even though you may find it elsewhere in the country, Birmingham is its spiritual home and this street in particular. If it isn't from Birmingham, it's not a balti.'

I was not sure that I totally agreed with his fervour, but as I spooned another mouthful of chicken balti desi into my mouth with another piece of naan bread, in truth, I didn't really care.

# — Afternoon Tea —

A little over ten years ago, a friend who was flying in from New York asked me to create a list of 'must do' food activities for any visitor to London. Activities so important that if the visitor failed to undertake them they could rightfully be accused of not having really visited London at all.

I still have the list. It is very much a record of its time. There is no mention of Borough Market or indeed any farmers' markets, such things being in their infancy and not yet subject to the attention of marketers and television producers. There's a recommendation that they should try Gordon Ramsay's flagship restaurant in Chelsea. Not something that I would ever suggest now that he appears to spend more time in front of a TV camera than he ever does in a kitchen. There are also suggestions for a pie and mash shop to try and dim sum at a Chinese restaurant that I am pretty certain later contributed to three weeks off work with food poisoning.

Most of the suggestions would not be even considered if I were making the same recommendations today. However, at the top of the list I had written:

1) Spend the afternoon taking tea at one of the top London hotels.

Even now, ten years later and with the transformation of the London food scene and the bewildering number of eating opportunities it provides, I am still hard pressed to think of any activity that I could suggest to replace it in top spot. There are few experiences that make you feel quite as pampered or as protected from our increasingly coarse society as taking tea in the luxurious surroundings of a grand hotel.

Afternoon tea may have its spiritual roots in London. Indeed, it is offered here to a level unsurpassed anywhere else in the world, but its origins actually lie further to the north at Belvoir Castle, a stately home within a pork pie's throw of Melton Mowbray. In 1840 Anna Maria Stanhope, the Duchess of Bedfordshire and lady-in-waiting to Queen Victoria, was in residence and at four one afternoon complained of 'a sinking feeling'. The long wait between lunch and supper was obviously too much for her delicate aristocratic constitution and she requested that the kitchen send up a little snack to her room in the form of some bread, butter and a few small cakes and a pot of tea.

It obviously did the trick and the extra meal soon became a regular habit during her time at the castle. On her return to London she decided to continue the tradition, inviting friends to join her for 'tea and walking in the fields'. As is so often the case, the habits of the nobility were aped by the rest of society and the taking of afternoon tea was rapidly adopted by would-be gentlefolk everywhere. It was soon on offer in the better hotels of London and from there made its way around the country and to the rest of the world.

Over 150 years later afternoon tea remains one of the

great attractions for visitors to Britain, but has become neglected by the British themselves as they struggle to deal with the commitments of work, family and finances and dismiss the famous ritual as being 'only for tourists'.

It is a great shame, because afternoon tea is the culinary equivalent of a long soak in a relaxing bath, pampering and decadent. It is an opportunity to forget the cares of normal life for a few hours and to allow oneself to be spoiled in a way that no other meal quite can and it deserves to reclaim its rightful place back in our nation's affections, if only as an occasional treat.

## 21
# Brown's Hotel

Although there are many afternoon teas on offer in London, my own choice has been and shall always remain that served in the English Tea Room at Brown's Hotel on Albemarle Street in London.

Brown's lays claim to be the oldest hotel in London and was opened in 1837 by James Brown, a former butler to Lord Byron. In the nearly 180 years since then, it has played host to presidents of the United States, including both Theodore and Franklin Roosevelt. It has offered peace and quiet to author Rudyard Kipling as he completed *The Jungle Book* and to Agatha Christie who used it as inspiration for her novel *At Bertram's Hotel*. Perhaps most fun of all, it is the site from which Alexander Graham Bell made the very first ever telephone call, although I am pretty certain that he would not have envisaged generations of travellers using his invention to order up a pizza and a high-class transvestite hooker called Desiree when they are far away from home on business.

My own relationship with Brown's Hotel may be nowhere near as noteworthy and certainly does not involve transvestite hookers, no matter what it says on the toilet walls of Oakwood Comprehensive School in Rotherham. However, it brings back memories for me as the first place I ever took a girlfriend for afternoon tea. It was

1983 and our evident gaucheness must have measured off the scale as we entered: my friend, wearing a leather skirt and tottering in on seldom-worn heels; me straining against the ill-fitting three-piece beige suit my mother had bought me when I was seventeen. I may also have had a ponytail and she definitely had a large stud in her nose, but, despite our appearance, the welcome offered was as warm and hospitable as if the Queen's equerry had called up personally and told them to take care of us. The service we received that day made all the difference to two nervous young people and created a magical experience, one that has been added to every time I have visited for the best part of thirty years. If afternoon tea is one of the most civilized ways of spending time, then there can be few more civilized places than Brown's Hotel in which to spend it.

Offering afternoon tea, however, is a serious business. In 2009 it was announced that the English Tea Room at Brown's had received the coveted award for the Top London Afternoon Tea. News of the victory gave me the perfect excuse to plan a revisit and my companion on this occasion was Irene Gorman, head of the Tea Guild whose judges award the prize each year.

Since my previous visit a year or so before, the tea-room at Brown's had been given a makeover. The room was light and airy as the sunshine streamed in through large windows and, in the background, there was the tinkle from the keys of a grand piano as an elderly pianist proved he had been studying the complete Burt Bacharach songbook with enthusiasm. I was, however, given the same warm greeting as I had experienced as a young man and I felt immediately at home as I was ushered to a quiet corner table. Irene was already waiting for me, clutching a thick sheaf of papers and looking around the room with a professional gaze.

'It's not just about the tea and the food,' Irene said, peering over her glasses at me and then at the tea menu she had just been handed as I sank back into a plump luxurious sofa. 'It's about the whole experience from the greeting you are given when you first walk in to the goodbye you receive at the time you leave.'

As she spoke, one of Brown's two dedicated tea sommeliers wandered over to ask if we needed any assistance selecting from their list of seventeen available choices. Neither of us did and as I requested a pot of Brown's own Afternoon Blend, Irene pointed at a First Flush Darjeeling.

'There are over fifty different criteria for judges to look at,' Irene carried on. 'They can range from the choice and quality of the tea and the excellence of the cakes to the state of the furniture and the general ambience.'

A few moments later, our tea was placed before us along with a three-tiered tower containing enough food to feed a platoon. On the bottom tray were small fingers of sandwiches with the crusts removed, the sort of sandwiches that you assume would only ever exist in the pages of an Enid Blyton novel, to be eaten with lemon squash: egg and cress, cucumber, cheese and pickle, and ham with mustard. The next tier up moved from savoury to sweet with a tray of dainty scones. Taking pride of place at the top of the tower were the cakes: light as a feather madeleines, brightly coloured macaroons and even a Lilliputian trifle just big enough to give a single gorgeous mouthful.

As we began our assault on the trays, the tea sommelier appeared to inform us that exactly four minutes had passed and it was now time to pour the tea. 'More bonus points for allowing the tea to brew correctly.' Irene nodded approvingly as her Darjeeling gurgled into a fine china cup, its loose leaves being trapped in the tight mesh of a silver strainer. After another waiter poured my choice and after I had added a spot of milk, I took my first bite from a ham sandwich. It was very good, childhood birthday party good, summer picnic in the park good and Tupperware container filled with lunch for a school trip to York Minster good. Thick hand-carved ham layered between bread coated with 'best' butter as my mother used to call it.

I adore classic British sandwiches, but they are an endangered species. As with so many aspects of our way of life they are under threat from a desperate rush to emulate the American desire for quantity over quality and innovation over provenance. Our traditional sandwiches have been caught in the crossfire. Now, while you might be able to buy a banana, peanut butter, bacon, avocado and raspberry jam sandwich on a multigrain bagel, the chance of ever finding a well-made egg and cress sandwich is about as likely as finding Lord Lucan riding Shergar down the high street of Atlantis. We have not helped our own cause, of course. Generations of children have been put off the great British sandwich by being forced to eat abominably made versions. Eggs mixed with salad cream, hams plumped out with water jets to increase volume, flavourless cucumbers and tomatoes, and chicken that would blink in terror if it ever saw the sunlight. All layered with parsimony between measly slices of bread that bear more in common with a petro-chemical plant than they ever do with anything that came from a farm.

The British sandwich is like a metaphor for so much of our food; generations of bad examples have caused them to be tossed aside with derision and their place taken by interlopers from abroad. You can now find stands all over the UK selling polite versions of burritos, the Mexican classic, but where would you go to buy a proper ham sandwich? You can buy a stuffed paratha or a mutton tandoori roll, but where would you turn in those moments when only a chicken and cucumber sandwich will do?

There is nothing wrong with new arrivals from abroad, of course. Throughout this book you will see just how important I think the arrival of immigrants and their foods is to our country, but we should also not lose sight of how wonderful some of our own traditions are just because they are unfashionable. So do me a favour. Next time you crave something slapped between two slices of bread, go to your local butcher and buy two or three slices of the best ham available. Cut two wedges from a thick farmhouse loaf and spread one with enough butter to make the British Heart Association want to perform an intervention and the other with a thin layer of Colman's English Mustard. Layer the bread with the ham and cut (just as with a bacon sandwich, always across and never diagonally, which is scientifically proven to release all the flavour). Savour it with a handful of crisps and wash it down with a cup of builder's tea. You can then come back and say thank you later.

Where was I before my little rant? Oh yes, Brown's

Hotel. After the sandwiches, I reached for a scone. It was light and sprinkled crumbs on to my crisp linen napkin as I cut it into two halves. I smothered one with raspberry jam and the other with clotted cream, which I'd spooned from a jar on the table, placing the two halves together before lifting it to my mouth and being sent to scone heaven in one bite. Immediately I had taken the first, a waiter appeared and replaced the plate with a fresh one containing warm versions straight from the kitchen. He smiled and said, 'Scones have to be eaten warm.'

Irene nodded her approval once more. 'It's little things like this that make all the difference,' she went on, explaining in detail the other criteria used for judging. Such minutiae might seem trivial, but it was obviously this attention to relatively small matters that had won Brown's the award.

It is also what has made Brown's such a popular destination and every table in the English Tea Room was occupied. 'There is such a wide variety of people who come for afternoon tea,' Irene said, waving her hand in a sweeping motion across the room. In one corner, a group of young Japanese women were laughing at the uniquely alien British spectacle, letting out loud appreciative 'aaahs' every time a tray of cakes was replaced. In another, a young couple, little older than I had been on my first visit, were cautiously getting to know one another. At the table to our right, an elderly lady sat with someone I assumed to be her granddaughter and to our left a whole family, all dressed up in their best, were enjoying a day out.

Afternoon tea at Brown's Hotel is not cheap. At the time of writing it costs £35 a head, a considerable amount, but brought into context by the enjoyment of an unhurried experience and the fact that by the time you leave you will have consumed enough food to make supper and very possibly the next day's meals redundant. After two hugely enjoyable hours in the company of Irene Gorman, I pushed myself away from the table unable to eat one more mouthful except for a whisper-thin sliver of Victoria sponge without which no afternoon tea can be said to be complete. We said our goodbyes and I staggered out on to Albemarle Street with a full stomach and a greater understanding of what it takes to provide a world-class afternoon tea.

I had promised myself that one day I would test the notion of constant replenishment by continuing to eat until the patience of the staff at Brown's wore so thin that they tossed me into the gutter of Albemarle Street or begged me to stop because the chefs had begun to have panic attacks. After nearly twenty attempts, I have never even got close and this day proved to be no exception. I shall be going back for afternoon tea at Brown's Hotel again pretty soon to give it another try.

## 22
# Clotted Cream

On a recent flight back from the USA, I was distracted from watching a feature film starring someone called The Rock by the arrival of the snack service. It comprised a small cardboard box containing a rather tired-looking scone, a miniature pot of raspberry jam and a plastic pot of cream.

It was the little pot that caught my attention and made me pause the film as said Mr Rock was dealing with the on-screen villains using a method that seemed simply to involve raising one eyebrow in a quizzical fashion until they all ran away. On the lid were the words 'Rodda's Cornish Clotted Cream'. This was the real deal and, while the airline looked like they had purchased the scones from Allied Carpets, they had obviously gone to the prime source for their cream.

Next to me, a wiry American man in half-rimmed glasses was studying the pot quizzically, unsure of how to use the contents. He peeled back the cover and stared at the telltale yellow crust then scraped it off with the edge of a spoon and deposited it back into the cardboard box. The rest he dumped in one splodge into a plastic cup of coffee, which had just been poured. It began to curdle nicely, leaving blobs of cream on the surface like the shards of a shattered iceberg. He pushed it away in disgust, no doubt confirming his countrymen's long-held view of British food, and then glanced sideways and watched in fascination as I constructed my own snack. I polished it off in two quick bites, licked my fingers clean of residual cream and jam, then wiped them on a paper napkin and resumed my movie-going experience.

My seat neighbour was intrigued. He called over the air steward and requested another pot of cream and repeated the process with a few glances in my direction to make sure he was getting it right. When he had completed his scone, he cut it in half and took a dainty bite. He raised his eyebrows, Rock-style, turned to me and said, 'Who knew?'

Well, my parochial American friend, I did and so does most of the UK. No attempt at a proper tea would be complete without clotted cream, a bowl of summer berries would seem naked as a newborn without a blob perched on top and even just a sneaked spoonful straight from the pot (yes, you do, admit it) has become an all too regular part of my daily ritual.

There is something about the clotted variety that no other cream can match. The richness of the cream itself is, of course, worthy of praise, but it is that crust that makes all the difference, golden and thick, created as the cream is slowly baked over water. Puncturing that crust, like piercing crunchy batter on fish and chips, taking the first sip of a strong pint of bitter or even just eating a snatched piece of crackling from a joint of pork before it is divvied up, is enough to remind you why you love food and enough to convince that, despite our lack of self-confidence in British food, we have products that can compete with any in the world.

However, like so many of Britain's favourite dishes we

owe our thanks for clotted cream to visitors to our shores. On this occasion to Phoenician merchants who travelled up the coast of Cornwall in the first century BC trading for tin. In return they gave us saffron, which is now found in many Cornish dishes including saffron cake, and they left the slow baking method for turning unpasteurized milk into the rich cream we know today. It is a method and an end result that can be found in very few places around the world including the Lebanon and, as I found on a recent visit, Mongolia, where it is made with horse's milk.

Whatever its origins, the method of production has remained much the same since that time. Originally it would be prepared in the kitchens of Cornish farmhouses in a tin pot placed over a simmering pan of hot water on the hob. The rich butter-coloured milk from Cornish cattle is allowed to separate from the cream by being left to stand for twelve or so hours. Then the cream is removed and 'scalded' to produce the recognizable crust. Once it has cooled, it can be stored. It will keep for a few days, if refrigerated, but seldom lasts that long in my house as I use it not only on scones and desserts but also in many savoury dishes and have even been known to commit the ultimate fusion confusion as I stir a large spoonful of the cream into a bowl of the famous Majumdar 'life-saving dahl'.

The Rodda family, a well-respected collection of Cornish Methodists, have been making clotted cream in Scorrier for 120 years. Fanny Rodda first developed a method of cooking the cream in glass jars so her friends and relatives could take it with them when they returned home. When it became popular, she instructed one of her sons to take the train to London to see if the cream would sell there. He was dispatched with a suitcase full of jars and spent the next days making appointments at the great grocers of the capital. The reaction was positive and they soon began making regular deliveries to hotels and shops including Harrods and Fortnum & Mason's. More recently, their cream won royal approval when HRH The Prince of Wales requested that a half-pound tub be delivered weekly for the pleasure of Queen Elizabeth, The Queen Mother and it was also used at the dinner to celebrate his own engagement to Lady Diana Spencer.

The company is still in family hands and Philip Rodda, grandson of the founder, agreed to let me visit and to give me a tour of the production facility, which is still attached to the original farmhouse buildings. It is much like any other factory with packing lines and lots of steel pipes and workers in white overcoats, but it is the smell, which lingers with the warmed proteins of the cream, giving off a scent not unlike the roasting of beef on a Sunday afternoon. By necessity, the process has been modernized. The company now uses nearly 200,000 litres of milk a week and the cream is separated by the use of a centrifuge rather than allowing it to happen naturally. But the cream produced at the end is almost unchanged from the original recipe and, just in case I needed any proof, Philip pulled back the lid of a large catering pack to reveal the golden contents inside and offered me a spoon to help myself. I pulled the spoon towards me, scraping the crust into a curl, revealing the glistening white cream underneath and ate it in one mouthful. Philip smiled, his pride in the family recipe confirmed by my loud 'yummy' noises.

I questioned him about the Devon/Cornwall divide knowing that, in Cornwall, it is jam that is first spread on the scone then cream, while in Devon the order is reversed. What should take first place on the scone, jam or the cream? He smiled and replied, 'Well, real Cornish people wouldn't have it on a scone anyway. They'd have it on a split.'

I had never heard of a split, but Philip explained that it was a white roll that is made slightly sweet with the addition of caster sugar and he was kind enough to give me the simple recipe Rodda's suggest for making them, which I have adapted here.

## — Split —
### (MAKES 12–15 ROLLS)

*25g fresh yeast*
*1 teaspoon caster sugar*
*300ml warm milk*
*450g strong flour*
*110g plain flour*
*1 teaspoon salt*
*75g lard*

Mix the yeast and sugar and add to the milk. Sieve both flours and salt and rub in the lard until the mixture resembles fine breadcrumbs.

Add enough of the milk mixture to the flour to make a dough and knead well on a floured surface. Cover with a damp tea cloth and allow to prove until doubled in size. Knead again and cut into fist-sized rolls.

Place on a floured baking sheet and allow to prove once more until doubled in size again.

Bake in a preheated oven at 180°C/350°F/gas mark 4 for 20 minutes.

The rolls are best eaten warm.

On my return home, I tried the recipe, adding a glaze of sugar syrup to the rolls for the last five minutes of baking. Taking one of the fresh, sweet rolls from the tray as soon as they were ready, I split it in two and spread the bottom half with a good thick scoop of the clotted cream I had brought back with me from Cornwall. Then, as instructed by Philip, I made a traditional Cornish 'Thunder & Lightning', adding a drizzle of golden syrup in a zigzag pattern over the cream before replacing the top of the split with its crisp, sugary glaze.

It is a glorious and gloriously unhealthy treat. The skill in eating is to prevent the cream from oozing on to you on to the floor. But it is so worth the effort.

As my American friend might have said, 'Who knew?'

— *Snacks* —

My older brother, TGS, gives fantastic snack. Visit the flat we share when there is a big football match to be watched or as the sound of Formula One cars shrieking from their starting grid escapes from the television speakers and you will be faced with some of the very best snacks in snackdom.

You will find a selection ranging from Spanish *jamón Iberico de Bellota*, plump olives, roasted almonds, a whole Melton Mowbray pork pie served with sharp pickled onions and piccalilli, large segments of multiple British cheeses, all in prime condition of course, served on a board with assorted biscuits, and bowls of fruit (fresh and dried). Then, and only then, will the top-up option of crisps and dip be offered. If the cold assortment does not entice, you can press him for a range of piping-hot snacks. Chicken wings crackling in the heat of their own fatty skin as they are pulled from the oven to be tossed in hot sauce, mini samosa filled with potato and fresh green chilli, lamb ribs roasted in herbs and, naturally, British favourites like sausage rolls and bite-sized Cornish pasties. When it comes to snacks, no man can test TGS.

Snacking, as you can see, is very serious business round our way, which makes it all the more depressing that the British seem so unutterably lousy at it. In Britain snacks, literally taken from the Middle Dutch word *snacken*, a small bite eaten on the go, have been reduced by mass production and laziness to objects that inspire few emotions other than extreme terror. One glimpse at the chilled cabinet of a petrol station forecourt will tell you just how low the people of Britain are prepared to stoop when it comes to food taken in a rush. There are industrialized versions of some of our nation's classics like the aforementioned pasties and pork pies. There are crisps in a variety of artificial flavours that make you want to scrawl 'just because you can doesn't mean you should' on the forehead of Walkers Crisps' marketing manager. There are things in pots, to be reconstituted with boiling water, which bring back unhappy memories of times spent in a student bedsit, and there are things that simply beggar belief, evidence for which I offer up using just two words: cheese strings.

We have neither the style of the Spanish with their unbeatable tapas culture nor the exuberance of the flesh-loving Americans and their hamburgers or hot dogs. We don't have the taco trucks of Mexico or the samosa stalls of India. We don't have the snack streets of China offering everything from fluffy *bao* filled with barbecued pork to lizards and scorpions. We don't have the *choripan* of Argentina or the *pane ca meusa* of Sicily. What we have is a pasty warmed up in the microwave of a Texaco garage.

It is not hard to understand why we suck so terribly at snacks and have no street food culture to speak of. It was not always this way and in the nineteenth century food would often be eaten on the go by working men and women who had little time to dedicate to eating during their hideously long working hours and purchased a bite from the thousands of costermongers who were there to fill the demand. The Victorians' astonishing ability to create bureaucracy prompted the decline in costermongers as health and safety issues came to the fore with necessary Acts of Parliament to protect food from being debased by its manufacturers. In the twentieth century rationing too took its toll as the production and distribution of all food was monitored and managed by the government, leaving little room for the spontaneity that is part of any street food culture.

Fortunately, the early years of this century have seen a growth in young, bright entrepreneurs starting their own mobile food businesses, despite the shackles of often ludicrously rigid laws made by civil servants whose sole task, it appears, is to deprive the people of Britain of any eating pleasure at all. These entrepreneurs can be seen popping up at food and music festivals all over the country. However, with so many of the links with traditional British food being lost, they have taken inspiration from their travels and you are more likely to be offered a limp version of a Vietnamese *bahn mi* than you are a delicious savoury pie. It is none the less a good start to our nascent street culture and is being added to by the new generations of immigrants who are bringing food from their own culture to our streets. It would be a shame, though, if there was no longer any room for traditional British snacks.

Unsurprisingly, many of these dishes can still be found in our pubs. The practice of serving a bite to eat with a foaming pint dates back to the time when weak ale or 'small beer' was drunk instead of contaminated water and quick nourishment was required to refuel during days of hard labour. The snacks were filling and cheap and made use of whatever was available locally. Although they underwent the same decline as most British snacks, recent years have seen 'gourmet' versions returning to the menu as they form an essential element of the burgeoning 'gastropub' scene.

Sadly, very few of the chefs who scrawl words like 'scratchings' 'pork pie' or 'Scotch egg' on their pub blackboards with such enthusiasm have ever actually encountered proper versions so ordering them can be like playing snack roulette. Only time will tell if their reappearance is just a trend or if there remains room for these quintessentially British snacks in our multicultural future.

## 23
## Cornish Pasty

It's hard to blame the former restaurant critic of the *New York Times*, otherwise a lover of matters involving meat with a pastry crust, for his jaundiced views on the Cornish pasty. In 1999 he trudged the length and breadth of the Duchy of Cornwall in search of its most famous food offering and came up short, finding only: 'The crust, with its distinctive crimping along the edge, was either soggy or tough. The diced beef, perhaps a table-spoon's worth, had a grayish tinge. The sliced potato and onion filling had weight, and lots of it, but very little taste.'

It would be easy enough to dismiss William Grimes as another bumptious American tourist whose views of the British, usually confined to the poor state of our food and teeth, are as ill-founded as our own about the American lack of dress sense or irony. However, his view of the pasty is one held by many visitors to the UK, usually those who have been unfortunate enough to suffer the dough bombs dished out from the apparently dozens of stalls that seem to have sprouted on our railway forecourts in recent years. They may all claim some provenance in the south-west and have names like Ye Olde Traditional Original Cornish Pasty Shoppe but the mass-produced blobs of stodge they sell in lieu of the real deal are enough to confirm to most visitors that their worst fears about British food have more than a little truth about them.

More alarmingly, however, Grimes's comments were not based on the ersatz versions to be found outside Cornwall, but on those in the county itself that made claim to be the real thing. It left him concluding that the county 'probably offers more bad food per square mile than anywhere else in the civilized world'.

His visit and subsequent report caused sufficient outrage to see locals burning an American flag with the passion of fundamentalist extremists and even requesting a boycott of American food. It had obviously hit a sore point and gave me a good excuse to visit one of the Duchy's award-winning bakeries. Not only to test his opinion that the Cornish pasty was little more than a 'doorstop' but also to see if anything had improved in the last ten years.

The origins of the pasty are disputed, but, whatever its roots, by the early twelfth century the portable snack was already being name-checked in literature with Chrétien de Troyes referencing them in his romantic Arthurian poems and Chaucer in *The Cook's Tale*. Up until the fourteenth century the casing of the pasty, made from thick dough 'paste', would have served the purpose of protecting the contents and was discarded once they had been eaten. It was only with the arrival in Britain of chefs from Italy skilled in the making of edible pastry that the pasties we know began to appear. The first recipe for Cornish pasties appears in the eighteenth century and is made of beef, soaked in claret, with no mention of the potatoes or swede that are common ingredients in today's versions.

By the nineteenth century the tin mining industry in Cornwall was reaching its peak with over 600 mines in the region and thousands of men employed in the mines or in supporting industries. The pasty was well established as the meal of choice, its crimped edge allowing workers to eat their meal without letting the contents come in touch with their hands, covered in grime and metallic toxins from their morning's work. The casing, while by now edible, was still tough enough to protect the dish until ready and thick enough to keep it relatively warm until the workers were allowed a short break. Once lunch was finished, the remaining crust was thrown further into the tin shaft 'for the knockers', the small, impish guardians of the mine whose knocking, in reality the natural creaking of the tin face, was seen as guidance to the next rich seam.

Given that the pasty was 'working man's food' there were no guidelines or set ingredients, with the wives of the miners using whatever leftovers or scraps they had to hand. It could be meat, vegetables, a mixture of the two and sometimes even fruit. There are claims that some pasties contained a complete meal with half comprising the meat course and half containing fruit to be eaten afterwards or saved for later in the day. Unfortunately, I have yet to find anyone who can show me how this can be prepared without its contents resembling the results of the family pet being scared by fireworks.

It was the rapid growth of the railways in the nineteenth century that opened up the beauties of the Cornish scenery to visitors from the big cities. Pasties went from being a working man's staple to a holidaymaker's treat and they became popular outside the county. Local bakeries began to sell them and the ingredients were standardized to include the potatoes, turnips, beef, salt and pepper we know today. The classic Cornish pasty is now so popular that the county produces more than 3 million of them every year. Not everyone, it would appear, agrees with William Grimes.

The Chough Bakery sits on the harbour front of the north Cornish town of Padstow, made famous by TV celebrity chef Rick Stein, whose success has turned the town from quiet fishing village to Cornish theme park in little over a decade. Most of the anger at this transformation seems to come not from the locals who rub their hands together in glee at the rising value of their houses, but from those who have moved there in recent years and entirely fail to see the irony in their complaints of too many tourists blocking the town's streets.

The building housing the Chough Bakery dates back over two centuries and once formed part of the harbourside market. In later years it became a slaughterhouse, then a dairy and, for the last twenty-five years, the bakery which is now owned by Robert and Elaine Ead, makers of award-winning Cornish pasties.

When I arrived to meet Robert at 11 a.m. as requested, the tiny bakery space had been in full swing for hours and the shop was already filled with hungry tourists buying sandwiches, bread and cakes. Mainly, however, their attention was drawn towards the pasties for which Chough's has become so well known. Laid out on baking parchment, they were fresh from the oven and glazed in a golden hue from the egg wash applied before cooking. There were small traces of bubbling 'boil-out', telltale signs of the high heat in which they had been cooked.

In a small room to the rear of the bakery, three staff concentrated all their attention on the preparation of the last batch of the day. The Chough Bakery prepares over 6,000 pasties a week and can barely keep up with demand. While they have a small facility on the outskirts of the town for the production of other baked goods, Robert insists that the pasties themselves are made by hand in the bakery.

Small circles of pastry had been laid out in rows waiting for my arrival. 'It's a type of shortcrust pastry,' Robert explained, 'but we have adapted the recipe so it has more elasticity than normal to allow the bakers to crimp the crust without it breaking.'

The vegetables, in the Chough recipe freshly peeled potatoes and turnips, were cut into thin slices rather than the chunks I had been expecting and the beef was skirt steak taken only from local Cornish cattle and cut into large chunks rather than minced. A good amount of salt and large amounts of both white and black pepper were added. 'Then the secret ingredient to keep the insides nice and moist.' Robert smiled, pointing as one of the young women in the bakery began to spoon a good dollop of Rodda's clotted cream on top of the filling for each pasty.

Then came the most important part, as the young bakers worked quickly at twisting the famous crimp. I wondered if it was the concentration needed to space exactly the required twenty-one twists correctly that meant they paid so little notice to me or my flashing camera. They gave nothing more than a polite smile in return for the insightful line of questioning I was hurling at them.

'They are all Polish,' Robert shouted over the noise of the fan oven. 'They just seem to have a knack for making the crust.' Their rapid twisting hand movements proved him correct and they laid pasty after perfect pasty on to a baking sheet ready to be given an egg wash before baking. Given that in the classic Cornish pasty the ingredients are raw, they have to cook for at least forty minutes. They emerge from the ovens of the Chough Bakery a glorious golden colour with the juices still bubbling furiously through any cracks that may have appeared. They are allowed to cool a little and then carried straight out to the front of the shop where they sell almost as fast as the bakers can make them.

Robert passed me a warm pasty to sample. There is nothing dainty about them; William Grimes was certainly right about that. The casing is thick and needs a healthy set of choppers to penetrate the crust. However, dismissing it as nothing more than a meat-filled doorstop is doing the pasty a disservice. Once that casing is pierced, the steam from the filling billows out, bringing with it the scent from the beef and vegetables within. The meat may not have taken on colour, but had cooked to tenderness in the high heat of the oven. The vegetables retained a bite and had released a few juices as they cooked and the spicing of white pepper was obvious but did not overpower. Hardly a life-changing experience, but why does every dish have to achieve that status?

Pasties may never top anybody's list of the world's fine dining experiences; pasties began as poor man's food and have strayed little from their origins in the succeeding years. They should be judged in that context and if, as at the Chough Bakery, they are made with great care and attention, using decent ingredients, they make an enjoyable and nutritious snack. And, perhaps, just sometimes, that should be enough.

## 24
# Melton Mowbray Pork Pies

It should, given that I have been known to dream about pork pies, have been one of the best days of my life.

My friend Ian Hartland, part of the family behind the making of Mrs King's Pork Pies, had a little surprise for me when I sidled up to his busy stand at Borough Market one cold Saturday morning. He was still peeling a tarpaulin from his counter as I arrived a little after 8.30 a.m., determined to be in and out of the market before the first tourist or baby stroller came into sight.

'Now then, young man' – he began to straighten his butcher's white hat on his head as he addressed me like a lord mayor might a northern town council – 'you quite like pies, don't you?'

The words 'Pope, Woods, Bear' and 'Catholic' came rapidly to mind though not necessarily in that order. Ian had already seen my reaction to savoury baked goods when I had visited the Hartland family two years before to witness the making of their famous Melton Mowbray pork pie. I had spent a day helping him and his brothers create a batch of one of the truly great British products. It is one that is now the recipient of a PGI (Protected Geographical Indication) from the European Union and one that has formed a staple part of my diet for the last two decades as I carry out an experiment to see if it is possible to convert human flesh to pie form through the method of ingestion.

It was a serious question demanding a serious response. 'Yes, I like pies. I like pies a great deal.'

'Well, I've arranged for you to be a judge at the Great British Pie Competition.' He smiled, knowing that the words were quite likely to make me have a small accident right there in the middle of the market. If it were not for the fact that Ian is very much a man's man and would have bludgeoned me to death with a sausage roll for showing such southern softness, I would have given him a great big hug and there might well have been tears.

As I said, it should have been the greatest day of my life, a day when not only was I to be left in a room to eat as many pies as possible but also asked to express an opinion on the efforts of other people, my two favourite pastimes of all. I even created a little countdown clock on my desktop with D-Day (or should that be P-Day?) marked in bold colours and stared at it like a kid waiting for Christmas as I worked at my computer.

When the day finally arrived my eagerness brought me into Melton Mowbray two hours before I was needed. The event was still being set up and a constant stream of liveried vans was making its way through the town's small square as bakers from around the country delivered their prize specimens for consideration. Despite my love of Melton Mowbray pork pies, I had never actually visited the town before and my early arrival gave me the perfect opportunity to go and explore.

Melton Mowbray's pre-eminence in matters pork pie-related has been unquestioned for nearly 200 years and dates back to the Enclosures Act of 1760. The surrounding area was already becoming well known for its making of Stilton cheese and the Act helped to support this by creating an environment in which milk yields could be increased. Where there was cheese there would often be pork production as pigs thrived on the natural by-product of whey created when the curds were separated from the milk.

Another consequence of the Enclosures Act, when added to the perfect landscape, was to make the region the fox-hunting capital of England, with three major hunts operating in a very small area. The Melton Mowbray pork pie was the ideal hunting snack and its hard pastry case and jellied filling ensured that it would survive the rigours of being carried during a long day's hunt.

Although the Melton Mowbray pork pie has always been considered the *ne plus ultra* of pies, it had suffered in recent years as producers from any part of the country could use the name to promote their own inferior products. Now, with the award of PGI status, not only is it protected from that eventuality, the recipe has been set in stone for future generations. As I had learned from Ian Hartland when I visited Mrs King's, there are certain elements that are unique to Melton Mowbray pork pies. They must contain only six ingredients: pork, flour, lard, salt, pepper and hot water; and the jelly is made only from boiling the pig trotters to release the natural gelatine. They must have at least 45 per cent meat content and they must be hand raised to give them their unique shape.

The end result is one of my favourite things to eat in the whole world. The richness of the hot-water pastry gives way to a dense filling of seasoned pork and the silky-smooth texture of the jelly insulates the contents from the pastry. The crunch of a pork pie being divided with a sharp knife is enough to make my mouth water, and when I am on my travels it is a pork pie, served with a chunk of good, sharp cheese, some hot English mustard, a spoonful of piccalilli and a couple of crisp pickled onions, that I miss the most.

I was hoping to get the chance to put all this useful knowledge I had gained over the years to good use. By the time I had made my way back to the venue, Melton Mowbray's parish church, things were just beginning to get under way. My companion judges were milling around chatting amiably and the four Hartland brothers were safely shepherding final deliveries of pies from the car park to the preparation kitchens where some of them would need warming through once more before serving. I entered the church and found my way to a desk under the shadow of the imposing Victorian pulpit to register my arrival. A ruddy-faced man handed me four or five sheets of paper stapled together in one corner. 'These are the rules,' he said, pointing, 'and on the back pages is a list of the judges along with the categories to which you have all been assigned.'

I found a quiet pew at the back of the church and began to read through the document. There was a section laying out the general criteria for marking and to guide the novice judges a note saying that each had been paired with an expert from the baking industry. It made sense, because even though I can easily eat my own body weight in pies in a calendar year, I would still need help with some of the more technical aspects of judging. But, as I worked my way down through the list, I was alarmed not to see my name mentioned.

It was not to be found with the list of those judging pork pies. Well, that was to be expected. Perhaps my association with Mrs King's could have been seen as compromising. I was not listed under 'Savoury Pies' which was disappointing, but I could rationalize that among the other judges in attendance were some celebrity chefs who were more likely to gain media coverage so should be given the top categories. I breathed a sigh of relief when I failed to see my name under 'Hot Fruit Pies', not that I have anything in particular against fruit, but today of all days I had my mind set on a filling of something that had previously 'oinked', 'bleated' or 'mooed'.

Finally, as I was beginning to get a little desperate, I turned to the last page of the list. I blinked and then stared at it for a long while in silent disbelief. I read it again just in case and let out a low, plaintive groan. I looked up to see Ian Hartland at the other end of the church, clutching a copy of the same document, shuffling his feet and trying hard not to catch my eye. It simply read:

JUDGE: SIMON MAJUMDAR
CATEGORY NUMBER: 7
CATEGORY TYPE: SAVOURY VEGETARIAN PIES

This had to be someone's idea of a sick joke. Simon Majumdar, arguably the most carnivorous person since Hannibal Lecter last nibbled on a bit of brain, was going to be in charge of pies filled with the fruits of the earth.

My companion judge, a delightful retired master baker called Tony Spencer, did not seem in the least perturbed by being subjected to meat-free pies for the best part of a day and waved his long baker's knife around with undue enthusiasm as we were led to the judging rooms.

When we reached our destination, we were split up, but not before I caught a glimpse of hundreds of different meaty pies through the windows of the doors to the main judging room. I pressed my nose against the glass panes for a long minute, desperate to be allowed in, but was pulled away by a comforting pat on the shoulder from Ian Hartland. 'No, lad, you're in here,' he said gently as he led me towards a smaller room where the other unfortunate judges of vegetable-based pies were to be found sitting gloomily around their respective tables.

Bizarrely, most of the points to be awarded had been predicated on the technical skill of the baking as opposed to any presence or absence of taste. Tony Spencer carefully carved each pie in half as they were presented to us by the stewards, holding them up so we discussed how well the pastry had been baked and how much filling they contained.

It was just as well for their creators that few marks were allocated for general appearance or taste, as these pies were among the nastiest things I have ever had the misfortune to put in my mouth, and bear in mind I once ate a dried rat in China.

It says much about food in Britain that anyone could even contemplate creating such extreme awfulness in pie form let alone serve it up in the expectation of an award. A pie containing sweet and sour vegetables was bad enough, but it was the appearance of a wholemeal pastry

'Macaroni & Cheese' pie that finally pushed me over the edge and into a storming hissy fit the likes of which have not been seen since Danny La Rue got the second dressing room at the Glasgow Empire. I called it a day, pausing only to give my begrudging vote to one of the least unpleasant pies and left the room in search of a Twix bar to take the taste out of my mouth.

After the judging was completed, there was a presentation ceremony with a nice speech by some posh woman off the radio. Someone with no hair and a dog collar blessed us all and everybody else appeared to be having a good time. However, like a petulant child, I sat at the back of the church sulking at not being included with the popular kids who were raving about all the delicious pies they had tasted. As I wallowed expertly in self-pity, I felt a familiar hand on my shoulder.

'Let's go and have a pint.' It was Ian. Recognizing that beer was one of the few things that could restore my good humour, he led me to the nearest pub and had soon placed a welcome foaming pint of beer in front of me. It worked, it always does and my first few sips of sharp, hoppy bitter were enough to make me forget what had gone before, almost.

'Nicola's making dinner,' Ian added to reinforce my recovery session. 'Cobbler,' he added. There was an obvious reply to that but I held my tongue and followed Ian back to his van for the short journey to his house, where I had been offered a bed for the night. Seeing us pull into the driveway, Nicola had opened the door and was already setting the table for supper. The cork had been pulled from a bottle of red wine and a fabulous meaty aroma filled the air as Nicola carried a large casserole dish to the table. It was the perfect example of a beef cobbler, the juices from the slow-cooked stew leaking through the topping of golden dumplings. It was all I needed to restore fully my good humour and Ian and I sat up chatting until the early hours of the next morning with not a mention of vegetarian pies.

The next day I gave Ian a lift to the Mrs King's kitchens, where his brothers were already working on a batch of pies. The smell of them baking brought back the horrors of the day before. I looked at Ian and said, 'You brought me to Melton Mowbray under false pretences and made me eat forty vegetarian pies including one that contained macaroni and cheese. Give me a pork pie now or I shall kill you and all your family.'

Only half convinced I was joking, Ian presented me with a large pork pie. It was as good an example of the genre as you would ever want to receive and I knew it would last less than twenty-four hours once I got home. It was the very least he could do and I accepted it in good grace, which was the very least I could do.

But, as I left, I looked him squarely in the eye and said, 'Let us never speak of this day again.' And we never have.

## 25
# Pork Scratchings

It was not in Britain that my finest pork scratching-related moment occurred, but in the US, Texas to be precise and, to be even more precise, if my memory serves me correctly, on Highway 31 approaching the college town of Tyler.

TGS and I were approaching the end of one of our food-inspired road trips. On this occasion the trip had taken us from Waco to San Antonio, to Galveston, then to New Orleans, Baton Rouge and was now bringing us back for a final few days of championship dead cow eating in Dallas. We had been driving for well over four hours by the time we reached the outskirts of Tyler. We were exhausted and in as much need of something to eat as our car was in need of a top-up of cheap unleaded fuel.

We pulled off the highway at the sight of a road sign that read 'GAS: FOOD: LODGING' and turned on to a dusty strip of road that led to two dilapidated buildings. One carried a weathered sign reading 'GENERAL STORE' but it was to the other that our attention was drawn; it displayed a huge banner, carrying the information: 'WE SELL GAS, CRACKLIN' & AMMO'.

It could only happen in America. While my brother filled the car with petrol, I wandered inside to check out the other two claims. Behind the counter, which was protected from potential crooks by a wire cage, were boxes of what I assumed was ammunition. They were locked away for safety in metal chests whose labels carried words like 'snub-nosed' and 'hollow point'. They might have meant something to somebody, but not to me and in any case I was there in search of the third element on their boastful sign. Through a small square cut in the wire cage there was a till and seated behind it was a rotund woman with a florid face and a bored expression which I assumed had not changed since she began work that morning. As I approached she managed a thin smile.

'Twenty dollars for the gas; need anything else, honey?'

'Do you have any cracklin'?' Which, given the sign outside, was arguably one of the more redundant questions in history.

She pointed over her right shoulder towards a small stove and deep-fryer. Standing next to it was a large plastic tub containing small, dark, misshapen cubes I hoped came from the skin of a dead pig. She lifted her considerable weight from the stool with a loud 'thwwwwwarp' as her bare legs peeled from the faux leather and moved slowly towards the stove. When she finally made it, she began wearily to shovel the small cubes from the tub into the fryer where they immediately let out loud 'plops' and 'sizzles' as they crackled in dark oil. Two minutes later, she rescued them from their hot bath with a slotted spoon, drained them on a wire rack and sprinkled them with stupid amounts of salt, then scooped them into a brown paper bag which she closed with a surprisingly dainty twist of her pudgy wrists. 'Five dollars, darlin',' she drawled, taking my money before sitting back down, her hardest task of the day completed.

My brother was tapping his fingers impatiently against the steering wheel of the car when I returned, keen to continue with our journey. His eyes lit up at the sight of the package I was carrying. Grease from the contents was already beginning to soak through the paper of the bag and leak on to my fingers. As we hit the road again, pulling out of the gas station on to the freeway, I placed the opened bag between us. We proceeded to play a childish game of pork lucky dip, crowing if the piece we selected was larger than the other's. They remain the best pork scratchings I have ever tasted, hot and crunchy from the deep-frying, salty and with a thick layer of soft, yielding fat which dribbled down our chins as we scooped up handfuls of pork nuggets from the rapidly disintegrating bag.

Back in the UK and ever since then, that cracklin' has set the benchmark for all matters pork scratching-related and we have certainly put every offering we can find to the test. Few weekends will pass without TGS and me downing a pint or three in our local pub, the Artillery Arms. Along with every pint comes a shared side order of pork scratchings contained in a see-through plastic bag, which declares their Black Country origins, a sure sign of quality.

I can't find any strong argument to support any theory as to why the Black Country, to the west of Birmingham, is so synonymous with scratchings other than that, at the turn of the twentieth century, there were a significant number of abattoirs in the region. They slaughtered pigs for Birmingham and from as far away as the Welsh borders. However, the tradition of pig skin being cooked goes back even further to a time when many households in rural areas would keep a 'tunkey' pig. This would be raised during the year and slaughtered by itinerant butchers in the days approaching Christmas. In the days when nose-to-tail eating was a rural way of life rather than a restaurant marketing exercise, no part of the animal would be left unused. The blood was drained off for black puddings, the offal for faggots, poorer cuts for sausages and pies, the head used for brawn and the prime cuts for roasting or preserving to make hams and bacon.

The skin too had its uses and would be removed from the animal soon after slaughter, cut into strips, salted and placed in a low oven until it had rendered all its fat. The by-product of the remaining lumps of skin became dense and crisp and would be served as a perk for the family. Over time, as the rearing of animals became a more commercial business and as butcher's shops began to appear on the high street, scratchings would be sold in large bags for pennies, very much as they still are in any decent butcher's shop today.

Given the levels of salt involved in the making of pork scratchings, it is little wonder that they also began to be sold in pubs, where like other salty snacks they made the punters thirsty for more beer. The combination is a perfect one and biting on the misshapen lumps of crunchy pork skin and fat before washing them down with a pint of mild remains one of the great pleasures in my life.

However, it would seem that the future of the scratching is not a rosy one. The number of pubs stocking them becomes less every year. Health reasons, obviously, play some part, the combination of deep-fried fat and salt not rating high on any sane nutritionist's list of 'go to' foods.

Scratchings also have a serious image problem; like their perfect bedfellows, real ale, the very thought of them shrieks of bearded men in their fifties, wearing Aran sweaters and singing songs about 'leaving Liverpool, never to return'.

Perhaps the biggest reason some people turn up their nose at pork scratchings is their appearance. They are, after all, bits of pig skin and although the producers do their best, the odd strand of pig hair might greet you when you tear open the packet. I reckon it just adds to the nutritional value, but can understand why some people screw up their face at the sight of some deep-fried curly wurly.

I decided, in honour of *Eating for Britain*, to try to make my own pork scratchings. I turned to my chef friend, Yorkshireman Andy Porter, who had given me the lesson in the fine art of Yorkshire pudding-making and he winged through his own simple recipe for the perfect scratching. I visited one of my favourite butchers in London, Theobald's on Theobald's Road near Bloomsbury, and purchased nearly three kilograms of pork belly. A few short years ago, cuts like this were unfashionable and stupidly cheap. Now people have caught on to just how fantastic and versatile they can be and the prices have rocketed accordingly. By at least double, I calculated mournfully, counting my handful of change as I waited for the bus home. Still, this amount of meat would provide at least five meals and, as I returned to my kitchen and pulled an apron across my own plump belly, I knew exactly how I would be making sure the pig from which the belly came did not die in vain.

First of all, I removed the sheet of ribs and cut them into two-inch strips with a wicked-looking cleaver I had purchased in London's Chinatown. They went into a Ziploc bag filled with a marinade I had made earlier from store-cupboard ingredients and then into the freezer to sit until a night when only a bit of rib action would do. I cut half of the slab of pork belly and returned it to the fridge where it too would await its fate, this time as a fine Sunday lunch a couple of days later. Then I stripped the skin off the remaining half of the belly and put it to one side for my scratchings. The remaining meat I cut into cubes and tossed with spices, chilli, palm vinegar and garlic ready to make classic Goan pork vindaloo later that same evening.

According to Andy's instructions, the pig skin needed heavy salting to remove excess moisture. It gave me the perfect opportunity to dig out a blue cardboard cylinder from my spice shelf. It contained jagged crystals of Halen Môn sea salt harvested on the shores of Anglesey.

During my travels through Wales, I made a point of visiting Halen Môn, the Anglesey Sea Salt Company, producers of my favourite salt. The owners, David and Alison Lea-Wilson, had not only agreed to meet me to show how they harvested their product, they also offered a complete stranger a room for the night in their home, a stunning eighteenth-century mansion house.

I arrived exhausted after a four-hour drive from Monmouthshire to find the house empty but open and a text on my phone telling me to make myself at home until they returned from taking their dog to the vet. A few minutes later, David and Alison came bounding through the door with two Jack Russell terriers scampering in behind them. Almost before I had a chance to deposit my bags in one of their comfortable guest rooms, Alison had a cup of tea in my hand and David was putting his coat back on and finding a torch to go rooting around for vegetables in the walled kitchen garden to the side of their house. I joined him, despite the howling wind and sheeting rain and we soon returned with a basketful of lamb's lettuce and kale for Alison to serve with our meal that night.

Few things beat a home-cooked meal when you are on the road for any length of time and as soon as David plopped the cork from a bottle of claret and Alison brought out a plate of locally caught and smoked sprats to snack on, I already knew that they were going to be my kind of people. It was a thought compounded when the main course arrived in the form of a rich stew of lamb shanks with root vegetables, which had been cooking slowly in the Aga all day. I ate more than my fair share and then polished it off with a large slice of treacle tart and a glass of good port to wash down the last crumbs. It was little wonder that my eyes began to close as we sat chatting around the dining table and I had to retire to bed, falling asleep the moment my head hit the pillow.

This was all hugely enjoyable, but I was here for a reason and that reason was salt. Halen Môn literally means Anglesey Salt and David and Alison have been producing one of the finest salts in the world for the last fourteen years, supplying it to some of the best restaurants in the world including the Fat Duck and El Bulli. Given that level of success, it is surprising to find that the notion of producing salt came about as a result of a downturn in their original business, a local sea aquarium.

Owning it had given them a licence to make use of local seawater, which obviously provided a constant supply of raw material. After a few years of trial and error and much research on David's part, they ended up with a process that produces a startlingly pure salt with large flaked crystals and a beautifully clean taste.

The Halen Môn facility is small, but well organized. The seawater is piped straight from a few metres off shore, in the shadows of the Snowdonia mountain range, filtered and then concentrated to increase the saline content; often this is done by allowing the natural evaporation of the water by the sun. But this is North Wales and anyone who has been there will know there is, of course, barely enough sunshine to power a small light bulb let alone dry the salt. So at Halen Môn the water is heated gently until the salt crystals begin to form and they are then removed from the solution, drained, rinsed gently and then dried to around 3 per cent moisture.

It is a simple process, but one that is handled with extreme precision by the small team of salt makers whose pride in the finished product is tangible. They have every right to be proud, as this is a hand-crafted product that requires constant care and attention to reach the standards David demands and the flavour was apparent even to my jaded palate when we did a tasting later in the morning. If David is the boffin and the innovator, Alison is the key to the salt's sales success, getting the product sampled by chefs, stocked on the shelves of supermarkets and even used by manufacturers of snacks and crisps. But they were still keen to do more, and when I was ready to leave they plied me with samples, which I promised to 'tart' around on their behalf.

Back in my London kitchen, I had trimmed the slab of pork skin of excess fat and rubbed it well with the salt to remove the excess moisture, leaving it to sit in the fridge for twenty-four hours. Andy's instructions for the next day were to pat it dry with kitchen towels and then deep-fry twice, once at a lower temperature, which could be done well in advance and then again for a short time in much hotter oil just before serving to make them really crunchy. Finally, his directions said to drain them and sprinkle with more salt to be served hot or allowed to cool and then kept in an airtight container. I split mine into two batches: one I topped with Halen Môn's pure sea salt; and the other with a version they have smoked to order over oak chips at a local smokehouse.

Sticking firmly to my *Eating for Britain* remit, I passed over the half-bottle of fino sherry I had in the fridge. Given the Spanish love of matters porcine, it would have been a superb accompaniment but I needed to stay closer to home. Instead, I reached for a bottle of my favourite IPA, from Thornbridge Brewery in Derbyshire. Its aroma of hops wafted up to my nostrils the moment I clipped the metal cap from the top and I took a long, deep swig from the bottle, not bothering with the glass I had chilling in the freezer cabinet.

I worked in perfect rotation with a 'crunch' as I popped a hot, fresh scratching in my mouth, first letting the porky fat melt on the tongue. Then a long 'swig' as I cooled my mouth down with a glug of beer. I repeated until I had drained the last dregs from the bottle and until there was nothing but a grease mark on the kitchen towel where I had put the scratchings to drain.

I guarantee that if you follow Andy's recipe and put

the end result in front of your guests with a nice cold one, both will be gone in sixty seconds flat. It is impossible to eat just one scratching; they are to all intents and purposes crack cocaine in pig form. It's an addiction I am in no hurry to be cured of.

## *Pork Scratchings*
(MAKES FOUR NORMAL SERVINGS OR, IN MY CASE
ONE SERVING, WHICH EXPLAINS WHY I AM NOW ON
BLOOD-PRESSURE MEDICATION)

*250g pork skin (from the belly)*
*3 tablespoons Halen Môn Anglesey salt (for variation use the*
*    oak-smoked or blend a spoonful of fennel seeds and 4*
*    crushed juniper berries into your salt mix)*
*vegetable oil for frying*

Get rid of the excess fat from the skin, leaving just a thin layer. Rub the salt into the skin and leave in the fridge for 24 hours, to draw out excess water.

When ready to cook, pat the moisture off the skin with kitchen paper and cut it into strips.

Heat the oil to 120°C/250°F and deep-fry the strips until the skin is firm and cooked through. Drain the strips on kitchen paper.

Increase the heat of the oil to 200°C/400°F. Refry the strips for 2–3 minutes until golden brown and crispy. Store in an airtight container when cooled, or serve straight away sprinkled with salt.

— *Supper* —

I hate ready meals. I really, really do. I just don't see the point of making your evening meal by slamming a plastic tray in the microwave or scraping its grim contents into a bowl to be warmed in the oven.

The results are almost always disgusting and leave those who indulge in them spiritually if not physically empty. I am never convinced by the argument that they fill a need when time is short. Give me two minutes and I will present you with a plate of smoked salmon, crème fraîche, capers and sourdough bread. Give me five minutes and I will make you some creamy scrambled eggs as good as you have ever tasted. Give me ten minutes and I could add some crisp smoked bacon to that. Give me the luxury of half an hour and your last meal of the day could be a warming bowl of soup made from whichever vegetables are in season. All this while your depressing 'dinner for two' from the nearest supermarket gurgles away in the dark recesses of the oven.

I know it is hard for many to summon up the enthusiasm and energy for the last major meal of the day. The drudgery of the day's work still weighs heavily upon them and the horrors of the daily commute have sapped their energy. But, supper, dinner, call it what you will, is really something to be treasured, an opportunity at the end of the day to relax over a meal and spend time with family, friends or even in your own company.

Takeaways are an option, of course, but the results are often a bit of a lottery. Instead, I always urge people to treat the preparation of supper as an end in itself, a chance to create and connect in a way that sitting in front of the computer and tapping on the keyboard at work really doesn't achieve. Put on some music, have a cold beer or a glass of wine and indulge in preparing your ingredients however simple they may be. The end results may not win you a place in the *Masterchef* final, but they will almost certainly be better than anything you can get out of a packet.

If the budget allows, why not eat out? It doesn't have to break the bank and few things are more fun than sharing a meal with friends at the end of a long day. It could be the pampering comforts of a fine dining experience or the familiar environs of your local curry house. It could be a bite with a pint at one of the increasing number of gastropubs or a meal at a restaurant owned by some of the more recent immigrants to our country, Thai, Vietnamese or Malaysian.

Whatever it is you decide to do, I hope the following dishes I sampled on your behalf make you want to spend a little more time on your supper and to make me the solemn promise that you will never, ever buy another ready meal.

## STARTER
### 26
## Potted Shrimps

I have a soft spot for places and brands that are often overlooked because they have been around so long that they become over-familiar and people forget how good they can be. Ask me which gin I like and I will wave a bottle of Beefeater at you and ask me about my favourite restaurant in London and I shall more than likely lead you towards the south side of Covent Garden and into the picture-clad rooms of Rules.

The desire of this famous old restaurant to stick resolutely to what it does well may seem terribly old-fashioned in these days when fusion confusion and molecular gastronomy are the order of the day, but there is something hugely comforting about sitting in one of its cosseting booths and tucking into the classic dishes it makes so very well. Likewise its agreeably formal but unfussy style of service may seem out of step with the modern restaurant styles where waiters hunker down at your table or feel they have to introduce themselves by their first name before they are ready to take an order, but it brings with it a feeling that this is how things used to be and, perhaps, how they should be again.

I adore Rules. I always have, through its considerable ups and its handful of downs. It is one of the first real restaurants I was taken to when I came down to London in the early 1980s and I have returned to it on a regular basis every year since. Even as a callow youth, nearly thirty years ago, its history never failed to impress me and I would linger on my way to the bathroom to look at the hunting pictures, photographs and portraits and peer into what was then a private dining room trying to imagine just exactly what it was that King Edward VII had done to Lillie Langtry.

Thomas Rule opened his eponymous oyster house in Covent Garden in 1798. It was a last-ditch attempt to prove to his family that what is euphemistically referred to as a 'wayward' past was truly behind him. To the astonishment of everyone, including himself, his new venture became a huge success and carried on to be so for well over a hundred years after his death. Just before the Great War of 1914, the then owner, his grandson Charles Rule, decided to up sticks to Paris and swapped his business with Thomas Bell who owned a similar restaurant in the French capital. I can't find any record of how well Charles fared, but Thomas Bell did well enough for Rules to remain in the Bell family's hands until 1984 when it was purchased by its current owner, John Mayhew.

In the 212 years since it opened, Rules has been the dining room of royalty, the meeting place of great literary minds and the scene of much ribaldry as actors and artists argued over their collective muses. However, by the mid-1980s when John took over and into the 1990s when it was finally, but sensitively, refurbished, it was fair to say that Rules had seen better days. Even I was aware that the food coming out of the kitchen was as tired-looking as the waiting staff serving it. There seemed to be every possibility that Rules would be consigned to the history books to be replaced by a tapas bar or a Thai restaurant. To his considerable credit, however, John Mayhew did not cut and run and, after significant investment, Rules slowly began to return to its former glories until the turn of the millennium saw it as popular as it had been in the days of its founder.

The menu is littered with the sort of food that we in Britain should be proud of, but are more often than not horrified by as the ghastly versions offered to visitors add weight to their condemnations of Britain's crimes against the culinary gods. Here at Rules they are made with the best ingredients in the country. Many are sourced from land owned by the company and dishes such as dressed crab, potted shrimp, steak and kidney pie and summer pudding are treated with an attention to detail that gives you some inkling as to why they became classics in the first place. When I turned my attention to two of the most British of dishes, potted shrimp and steak and kidney pudding, it was almost inevitable that I would also turn to Rules to find out how they should be made properly.

Potting as a method of preservation dates back to the fourteenth century and at its simplest consisted of warming prepared meat or fish through with spices and butter and then placing or 'potting' in ramekins, knocking the air out and allowing to set so it could be stored in a cool place to keep for up to a week. Potted shrimps were traditionally found in Lancashire and in particular around Morecambe Bay in the towns of Ulverston and Flookburgh, where to this day 'shrimpers' still set out at dawn on spring and summer mornings to harvest the small brown shrimps that made the towns famous.

Brown Morecambe Bay shrimps are the real deal, sweet with a taste of the sea that remains with them despite peeling and cooking. Their flesh also has a porous texture that can soak up spiced melted butter, making them perfect for potting. But fishing for them is hard and dangerous work. Even now that the traditional horse and carts are long gone and tractors are used to haul the nets in to land it still takes years of experience to harvest them safely. Tides can change rapidly and even those with local knowledge can find themselves trapped by quicksand.

As I was to find out in Norfolk when fishing for crabs, it is also a declining industry as new generations decide not to follow in the footsteps of their forefathers and the tractors and nets begin to lie idle on the shore. Increasingly the shrimps you find being used in British kitchens are just as likely to come from Dutch fishermen as they are to come from our own coasts, perhaps a nod to the importance of fish imports from Holland over the last few centuries which date back to the seventeenth century and deliveries of eels to Billingsgate Market. At Rules, the sheer volume sold of their most popular starter means that they have to use a mix of both local and imported shrimp to meet demand.

In principle, it is a simple dish to prepare. Isabella Beeton's *Book of Household Management* uses only five ingredients in her recipe: shrimps, mace, butter, cayenne and nutmeg and recommends the household cook simply to 'Have ready a pint of picked shrimps, and put them, with the other ingredients, into a stewpan; let them heat gradually in the butter, but do not let it boil. Pour into small pots, and when cold, cover with melted butter, and carefully exclude the air.'

At Rules, they do things a little differently, using a lobster oil that takes five hours to prepare and contains nearly thirty ingredients, which should tell you all you need to know about the differences between what we prepare at home and what is served from a professional kitchen. The potted shrimp at Rules is a dish I have tried on just about every occasion I have eaten there, and I persuaded John Mayhew to allow me access to his venerable kitchens so I could spend a day in the company of their excellent head chef, Richard Sawyer.

Richard is a classically trained chef who learned his trade through the apprentice scheme at the Savoy Hotel. He told me how he spent the first six months of his career in the meat lockers at the hotel learning how to cut meat by trimming carcasses, after which he was moved to the fish storage areas to do the same on cheap fish. It was nearly a year until he was allowed to get near anyone's supper and, even then, it took years more experience before he or anyone else considered him worthy of the name chef. He completed his training under the tutelage of the legendary master of French gastronomy and head chef of the Connaught Hotel, Michel Bourdin, and then an enviable career saw him arrive at Rules, just when they needed him most.

The loss of such apprentice schemes seems to have arrived at the same time as the explosion of new eateries in the 1980s and '90s. More cooks needed, less time spent training them. Like First World War pilots who averaged about twenty minutes' flying time before being sent to their slaughter, so desperate was the need that young people were churned out of our catering colleges with few basic skills and the idea in their head that they emerged as fully trained chefs. I have been told many horror stories of trainees who could not tell the difference between a melon and an avocado, even more who thought that Bisto was a good base for a sauce and, most frightening of all, ones who had never seen a whole fresh fish or an animal that had not already been pre-butchered into the required joints for them. While dining styles may have changed from the formal to the casual, the same basic skills are still required and are apparently sorely lacking. Imagine, if you will, listening to the smooth jazz stylings of someone who has never actually learned how to play the piano and you get an understanding of what it is like to eat in many modern British restaurants.

When I arrived at 8 a.m. Richard, as usual, had already been at work for over an hour. He had completed his paperwork for the day and was turning his attention to the fabulous ingredients that were being delivered in a constant stream as lorries squeezed along Maiden Lane. I stood observing him as he watched them slide down a silver chute from street level to kitchen to await his appraisal. In a society where so many, myself included, can be blinded by celebrity, to see a top-class chef so genuinely excited by the ingredients he was given the opportunity to work with was a reminder of why dining out can be such a thrilling experience.

As boxes of fresh fish hurried down the chute, Richard examined each in turn, selecting the best specimens to trim personally: silver-skinned salmon, with their freshness showing in the pink hue of their gills; huge plaice with their own freshness revealed in the telltale covering of slime; and, best of all, crates and crates of lobster from the Scilly Isles, still alive with their powerful claws banded together to prevent the loss of a kitchen porter's finger. After the fish came the deliveries of meat: saddles of roe deer, which Richard would again butcher himself; grouse, shot on land owned by Rules, plucked and ready to be roasted for lunch; beef from their own herds of Belted Galloway cattle, reared until three years old and slaughtered to their specification.

'If you can't get excited about ingredients like this,' Richard shouted above the combined din of the kitchen and the deliveries, 'then, quite frankly, you must be dead. You shouldn't be working in a kitchen and certainly not this kitchen.' It was one of the most impressive sights I had seen on my journey so far. I had visited many restaurant kitchens in the past, but usually towards the end of service and after a meal. I could not recall being in such a large professional kitchen when it was in full flow and certainly not one that had been in place for over 200 years.

Gary, one of Richard's sous chefs, had been at Rules for over eleven years and headed the section in charge of plating up the cold starters. When I arrived, he was busy smoking thick fillets of salmon over Lapsang Souchong tea ready for the lunch service. As soon as I had donned my chef's whites and an apron, he led me across to his station to demonstrate how to prepare the Rules version of potted shrimp. The mix of Morecambe Bay and Dutch shrimp had been seasoned and dried a little to remove excess moisture and then set to one side. Gary then placed a large amount of diced, chopped shallots in a saucepan, spooning over them a good helping of the lobster oil that had taken so long to prepare. 'It has carrot, celery, ginger, garlic and olive oil in it,' he explained, 'as well as the shells from all our lobsters. They've been roasted off in the oven to intensify the flavour.' After adding a handful of finely chopped tarragon, ginger and garlic to the mix he placed it on the side of the stove to cook gently until the shallots had softened and then began to mix them with the shrimp until each of the sweet pieces of seafood was fully coated with the mixture.

'Now,' he said, reaching for a plastic jar as if it were a piece of the True Cross, 'this is the important ingredient, mace. It's as rare as hen's teeth right now, so I have to keep it under lock and key.' He took two good spoonfuls of the ground spice, taken from the outer casing of the nutmeg, and mixed it into the buttered shrimp, then finally added exactly twenty-four twists of white pepper and covered the bowl to rest. 'We like to make them the night before, so the flavours have time to marry,' he added, reaching into a low refrigerator for some that he had already prepared. They had been set into rings and topped off with a little more lobster oil to complete the shellfish overload. He began to plate it up on instantly recognizable Rules tableware with its enamelled red outer ring. 'The portions shouldn't be too big. It's an incredibly rich dish, so you only need a small amount.'

After he had dressed the plate with some mixed leaves, a twist of pepper and half a lemon, wrapped in muslin, he brought the potted shrimps over for me to sample, leaving them on the pass, the place in every professional kitchen where dishes get the chef's final approval before being served to the customer. I tucked in eagerly, even though I must have eaten the same dish dozens of times before, breaking through the buttery shell to reveal the shrimps inside. I sprinkled a little lemon juice on them to cut through the richness of the casing and began to eat them, using a little toast as my cutlery.

They tasted different from any other occasion I had tried them at Rules. I could taste the distinct flavour of each ingredient: the sweetness of the shrimp, the buttery richness of the lobster oil, the sharp hit of mace and white pepper and the subtle back notes of the tarragon. I was certain that my accentuated appreciation came from the time I spent watching Gary prepare them and a better appreciation of all the effort that had gone into making the dish. I was also certain that I would be ordering them again the very next time I set foot in Rules, my favourite restaurant in London.

# 27
## Cromer Crabs

When asked how he was finding his day trip to Cromer in Norfolk, Sir Winston Churchill apparently replied with the words, 'I am not enjoying myself very much.' After my two days there, I know how he felt.

I suffer horribly from motion sickness and a long journey on a coach, the steep bank of a plane as it comes in to land or sitting with my back to the engine on a train can all turn me alarming shades of green. As a child, even the short car trip from Rotherham to Sheffield, a mere twenty minutes, would induce at least one outpouring of my stomach contents. My parents would prepare for the worst by carrying a small, yellow seaside bucket in the boot of the car whenever I set out on a journey with them. It was usually my younger brother Jeremy who would draw the short straw of sitting next to me in the back seat of the car, himself turning ever greener with each of my loud stomach heaves. The car always smelled of new leather as my father insisted on buying a new one every year and this, combined with the scent of my own contribution and the attendant noises, made these short hops something that every member of the family came to dread.

I no longer have to carry the 'sick bucket' around with me as I did as a child, but the thought of it can still make me queasy. All of which made the vision of me clutching the side of a small fishing boat for dear life as it headed out to sea from the coast of Norfolk, on a brisk morning, all the more unlikely a sight.

When it comes to fish and seafood, the seas around the UK provide an abundant source and although much of what is caught by our dwindling fishing fleets is still shipped abroad to fill the stomachs of the grateful French and Spanish, an increasing amount is finding its way into our own shops and on to our own tables. On my trip so far, I had already tasted the sublime smokies of Arbroath, the kippers of Craster and the potted brown shrimp of Morecambe and was now turning my attention to another of our great seafood treasures, the legendary Cromer crabs.

Crabs have been caught off the coast of Norfolk for centuries. Originally it was a summer occupation, with the rest of the year's fishing being taken up with harvest-ing herring and cod. However, in the last thirty years, primarily because of restrictions and quotas on those two fish, the Cromer fishing fleet has made the emptying of their pots a year-round affair. Even this business has come under more recent threat and while there used to be scores of boats heading out to sea each morning, now this number has dwindled to under a dozen, each managing to collect between 200 and 400 pots apiece.

The crabs they catch off the coast of Cromer are smaller than their peers in other waters around the coun-try, I am told, because they grow in shallow waters with beds primarily made of chalk. They are noted not only for their incredible sweetness but also for the higher pro-portion of white meat to dark found in the native brown crab.

John Davies, in his forties, Cromer born and bred, is a tenth-generation fisherman. He invited me to join him and his crew for a day as they headed out to empty, re-bait and re-set 250 pots. 'It'll be an early start, boy,' his voice crackled down the phone. 'We want to be out by 5.30 a.m.' I made plans to arrive early the afternoon before, which not only gave me the chance to look around the town, but also to have an early night in preparation for such an early start.

Cromer is a seaside town, which, while it exudes an air of faded grandeur, still retains architectural remnants of its heyday when its clean airs brought well-to-do Victorians from industrial London at the end of the nineteenth century. Although there is an element of what my mother would have called the 'fish and chippy' about the resort, it was still an agreeable place to spend an afternoon, grab a couple of pints and walk them off with a long stroll along the seashore before heading to bed. On the way back to the B&B, I stopped at a small local chemist for some strong drugs of the anti-motion sickness variety. Their purchase was prompted by a raised eyebrow from the landlady of my accommodation when I told her why I would be long gone by breakfast time. With my past history, I wasn't taking any chances.

I called John to check that the weather would be clement enough for us to set out to sea the next day. 'It shouldn't be too rough, boy,' he assured me in an unmistakable Norfolk twang, before adding with an unnecessary chuckle, 'well, for us.' As I put down the phone, I reached for the packet of tablets in anticipation of a trip I was already beginning to think had not been such a great idea. I was even more convinced the next morning when I woke, after a fitful sleep, to hear the sound of sea spray lashing against the windows of my room. The bed and breakfast was not far from the shore and while the day before had been clear, as I left my room and deposited my bags in the boot of my car, the wind whipping around my ears almost convinced me to return to my room, go back to sleep and not face what I was now certain was going to be a bit of an ordeal.

I gathered my courage and arrived at the slipway to the harbour at the same time as the crews for the fishing boat fleet pulled up in their weather-beaten pick-up trucks. It was still pitch black apart from the light from their car headlamps and in the beams I could see the salty spray, which was wetting my face and depositing salt on my lips. By the time I found John's boat, he and his two crew, Steve and Charlie, had already pulled on their fluorescent yellow waders and were loading crates of stinking fish carcasses on to the boat to re-bait the crab pots once they had been emptied. John gave me a wave and then slowly looked me up and down before asking, 'Have you ever been on a booot before, boy?'

I am not sure what gave away that I was a landlubber; it might have been the fact that my seagoing outfit consisted of a pair of jeans, trainers, T-shirt and a flimsy jacket from Gap or it might have been that even taking into account the lack of light he could see the look of dread on my face. I had to admit that the last time I had been on a boat had been on a twenty-minute ferry journey from the Asian to the European side of Istanbul that had managed to put me quite off my planned lunch of mutton kebabs.

Despite his obvious reservations, I was ushered aboard

and John suggested I sit in the small cabin at the front of the boat as a large tractor began to push us out through a sea of worryingly large waves that were bashing against the shore. The dawn light was appearing over the horizon and, as we cleared the first sections of waves, John booted up the powerful engine of the boat and pointed us out towards the sea. 'We don't go out too far,' he shouted above the noise of the motor. 'It's pretty shallow around here, so we set our pots out about a couple of miles, sometimes where the water is only about five metres deep.'

I was actually feeling rather good at this point. The wind on my face was cold and refreshing, the sea was not as rough as I expected and my stomach was behaving itself remarkably well. I even managed to share a joke with John and the crew as they prepared their equipment to haul the pots from the seabed, empty them and re-bait them. I even scoffed along with them when they described a very well-known TV chef who had made the same journey as me and had spent the whole trip being violently ill over the side of the boat. What a sap, sucker and ne'er-do-well. No such shenanigans from yours truly who, thanks to the wonders of modern medicine, was feeling on top of the world.

Then it began. My first indication was a slight lurch of the stomach. 'Okay, nothing to concern myself about there,' I reassured myself as I kept a smile fixed to my face. The next lurch was a little more decided and the smile dropped from my face long enough for John to recognize that something was amiss with me sea legs-wise. 'You all right, boy?' he asked, although he probably already knew the answer. It was too late; by the time the words left his mouth vomit had already left mine. I lurched to the side of the boat and began heaving wretchedly into the ocean. It was a mighty deposit, the remains of a fish and chip supper added to the three shortbread biscuits I had wolfed down that morning in lieu of breakfast. I staggered back to the cabin where John, prepared for every eventuality, had taken a bucket from a cupboard for my own special use. Oh, God, it was the same yellow colour as the 'sick bucket' from my childhood and the mere sight of it began to make me want to hurl once more.

I wish I could tell you more about the trip after that point, about how Steve hauled up the pots and handed them to John who emptied them. How he checked the crabs were the right size and tossed the ones that were too small back into the sea before passing the pots to Charlie who baited them with fish carcasses and threw them back over the side. I really wish I could tell you what an extraordinary sight it was to see one of my favourite things to eat being caught at sea, but I can't.

We were only twenty minutes into our trip when I began to realize that everything was not okay, and for the next five and a half interminable hours I stayed rooted to a seat in the cabin, my head buried in the bucket and longing for death. John refused my generous offer to pay him the amount his catch would be worth just to go back to shore right away with a slightly more evil chuckle than I thought the suggestion merited and, at one point, when the overdose of useless sea sickness medication had finally kicked in to give me five minutes of blessed release, I opened my eyes to find him standing over me, smiling and saying, 'It's not a nightmare, boy, you're still out here.' He was right, I was still out at sea, the time dragging as if weighted down with lead as they dealt with each of their 250 pots before finally turning the boat back towards the harbour.

As we approached the shore, John cut the engines and let the boat drift in far enough so that it could be attached to the tractor and be hauled back to the slipway. By now, after nearly six hours of championship vomiting, I was dehydrated and unsteady on my legs. The crew covered their smirks and practically carried me from the boat, propping me up against a wall as they turned their attention back to sorting through their catch. Once they were finished they drove away in John's truck, each giving me a cheery wave and a slightly sarcastic thumbs up through the windows. I was shivering with cold and exhaustion and rested against the wall where they had left me for forty long minutes until I felt able to stand upright without its support. I staggered to the nearest café and forced down some breakfast to restore my blood sugar levels. The woman who served me had obviously seen it all before and just sighed, 'Been out on the boats this morning, have you?' as she placed a cup of steaming hot chocolate and a slice of ginger cake in front of me.

I nursed my drink for an hour before I had the strength to trudge to John's fish shop, just off Cromer's busy high street. I wanted to buy some of the catch, which had already been boiled and dressed since we landed that morning. John, having deposited his catch, was long gone, but I collected two prime specimens. I returned to my car for the journey back to London. By now the early start coupled with the drowsiness caused by the motion sickness tablets had finally kicked in, and as I left Cromer

I felt a wave of tiredness and nausea sweep over me. I pulled into the first lay-by and shut my eyes for a few moments. I awoke five hours later wondering where I was until the vomit stains on my jacket reminded me of my day's misery.

That evening, I sat with TGS in our flat and shared with him the spoils of my morning's labours. He, of course, showed precious little sympathy for what I had endured as he picked the sweet white meat of the crab from the shell with his fingers and then lifted it to his mouth to lick it completely clean of the dense brown meat. 'It's bloody good,' he declared. I was sure he was right, but I couldn't bring myself to sample it. I could barely bring myself to look at the crab let alone try eating one without my stomach giving up its contents one more time. Even now, months after the physical horrors of the day have faded, I still cannot face the thought of eating one even if the respect I have for those who catch them is much greater than it was before my journey.

The people of Cromer, with characteristic Norfolk wit, had carved Sir Winston's disparaging words into a plaque on the seafront. Looking at a photograph I had taken of it, I could only imagine that someone had taken him crabbing.

## 28
# Smoked Salmon

Okay, let's start this chapter with a bit of word association.

If I say the words 'smoked salmon' what is the first thing that comes to mind? Did you think of Scotland? Well, of course you did. Where else would your mind wander when reminded of those wafer-thin pink slices of delicately smoked wild fish flesh, but to the rugged landscape and rushing streams of Scotland? After all, that's where the very best smoked salmon in the world comes from, isn't it? And little wonder, because that surely is where it originated, right? Well, a big black cross in the 'wrong' box for anyone who sat back and sucked on a thoughtful tooth as they pictured the glens. Smoked salmon, as we know it in the UK today, has its origins not in Scotland but in London and the very best I tried on my journey was to be found not while I was a-roamin' in the gloamin' but in the East End of London.

I had my doubts too as I bundled up to the door of H. Forman & Sons at 7 a.m. one midweek morning. I had decided that in lieu of the gym session I would normally be enduring at that time, I would walk from my home in Shoreditch to the fish-processing plant of H. Forman on Fish Island near Bow. The hour-long stroll served only to remind me that although London is becoming gentrified at an alarming rate, thanks in no small part to people like me, there are still pockets of resistance where locals live perfectly happily without worrying about the location of their nearest tapas bar or source of single estate oolong tea. With development of the area still to reach full pace, many of the remaining buildings serve to remind you of London's proud industrial heritage.

However, if the chimneys and blackened bricks of the Victorian factories remind you of the capital's past, towering over the area was a reminder of London's future in the shape of the 80,000-seat stadium for the 2012 Olympics. London's victorious bid in 2005 may well have given us a few memorable moments of television pleasure as we watched our dearest friends, the Parisians, cry tears of bewildered disbelief. But in the East End the joy soon turned to anguish as the compulsory purchase orders started flying in all directions and locals were told that they would have to move homes and uproot their businesses. One such order flew in the direction of Lance Forman, the latest in a long family line heading up fish smokers H. Forman & Son. Soon after Lord Coe had led the London bid to victory, Lance Forman and the other businesses of the Marshgate Lane Industrial Estate were informed that they would have to move. It was a double blow for Forman as they had not long moved to that location after fire had destroyed their original factory.

Despite these setbacks and an enforced move to the third location in their history, H. Forman & Sons has prospered since 2005. Their new premises, a javelin throw from the Olympic Stadium, provided not only room for the expansion of their smoking business, but also for Forman & Field, a wholesaler of the best products

from around the UK, as well as an impressive new restaurant. It was there I had my first introduction to Lance
Forman, when I visited with TGS. We had begun, of
course, with a plate of their famous smoked salmon.

By this stage of my journey, I have to admit I was a
little smoked out. I would soon be at the stage of removing shoes and socks to count the number of smokehouses
I had visited and, much as I had adored Craster kippers
and Arbroath smokies, the thought of another plate of
smoked fish could have sent me over the edge. TGS
insisted, 'It's the best there is and we have come all this
way.' He was right, of course, and when the plate arrived,
all salmon-related weariness disappeared. How could I
not be excited about an item of food this alluring?
Around the edges of the plate there were the traditional
accompaniments: capers, buckwheat blinis, a little sour
cream and some artfully placed mounds of sea salt and
freshly ground black pepper. At the centre, the main
attraction, a few thin slices of blush rose-pink salmon.

We divided the plate equally, as we have done since
childhood. The notion of one of us getting less than our
fair share of anything during a meal can cause tantrums
too horrible to behold. We both tore a small strip of
smoked salmon from our portions and sampled it in
unison so we could compare notes. The flesh of the wild
fish had retained its natural fats and oils during the smoking process and began to dissolve on our tongues as we
let it sit, trying our best to discern and articulate the flavours. The taste was more delicate and subtle than other
examples I had tried during my journey, and the salt used
during the process had not overpowered the fish. We
polished off most of what was on our plate, retaining

only one small square each to use with the otherwise unnecessary accompaniments. TGS was right. Annoyingly, he usually is.

As we moved on to our main courses, two more superlative fish dishes, Lance Forman wandered in to the dining room, keen to see who had made the long haul out to visit the new enterprise. We chatted about the salmon and the Olympics, the new stadium rising into the skies a few hundred yards away from where we were sitting, visible through a large picture window. We swapped cards and later, as we were leaving, Lance invited me to revisit a few weeks later so I could see the salmon being prepared.

As I arrived, daylight was only just beginning to win its battle against the darkness and the chimneys of the Victorian factories formed long shadows across the road in the streetlights. Like many of his workers, Lance Forman had already been at work for some time, making sure that the deliveries of salmon were ready to be sent out as soon as possible to the hotels and restaurants of London and to be packed for shipping across the UK and around the world.

Donning the prerequisite sterile clothing, we moved from the offices on to the smoking floor as Lance gave me more of an introduction to H. Forman & Sons. It was obviously a story he had told many times before and he went into a well-rehearsed routine. 'A lot of people think that smoked salmon in Britain originated in Scotland,' he began. I nodded as, quite frankly, I had always believed the same. 'But in fact it started in London in the late nineteenth century, with the influx of Jewish immigrants from Eastern Europe.' I nodded again; the impact of

Jewish arrivals in London on British food was not lost on me as I had recently been researching the history of fish and chips. They brought with them their skills in smoking and set up businesses in London using Baltic salmon, which they imported in barrels of brine. Later, when they discovered they could get fresh fish, they began to use wild salmon from Scotland. When word got back to the smokehouses north of the border, they started to make smoked salmon for themselves.

The company was founded in 1905 by Harris Forman, a recent immigrant, but it was his successors, Louis and Marcel, who built up the business and also began to promote smoking salmon as a delicacy as opposed to just a method of preservation. Now in charge of the business, Lance has continued the tradition of expansion, adding not only Forman & Field, the fine foods mail order business, and the restaurant, but also a kitchen, which produces dishes for hotel banquets and conferences. However, although H. Forman & Son has many aspects to its business, it is the long history of salmon smoking and the end result of which Lance is quite rightly most proud.

'We receive deliveries of tonnes of salmon a day,' he told me as he slid back the door to an enormous freezer room.' In the summer we use it immediately and we freeze stocks for the winter months.' We walked to a large open–plan space where most of the preparation work was taking place. The salmon was filleted and trimmed, and then given the traditional London Cure created by the founder of the company who was keen for the taste of the salmon not to be hidden by too much salt and smoke. The fish is given a light covering of salt before being laid flat for twenty-four hours. 'We lose about 15 per cent of the weight of the fish during this process,' Lance told me as we moved across the room to the smoking kilns, adding, 'Wild salmon is about three times more expensive than farmed salmon,' in case I had any lingering doubts about the quality of their product.

The production methods may be traditional, but Lance is not afraid of modern techniques as long as they can fit into his determination to produce in small batches. He proudly showed off their latest German-made kilns, which instead of creating smoke through slow-burning embers, produced it through the friction created when whirring steel wheels ground against blocks of oak. 'It means we can control the amount of smoke we produce for each batch depending on the type of end result we need.' After smoking, the fish are removed and then hung until they are ready to be sliced. Slicing is done in the traditional manner with long slices taken from the top of the fillet or in a D Cut where a short, swift motion cuts through the fillet to produce the rounded slices that give the cut its name.

'The finest part of the whole fish,' Lance explained as he led me to a small marble-covered table, 'is the smoked belly.' On the table were thick strips of smoked fish, over half an inch thick and glistening with the sheen from the oils that were being released. 'It's like any animal, the belly does little work and is fattier so it has more taste. It's my favourite bit of salmon.' With that, he took a long sharp blade and cut two thin slivers, leaving one on the counter for me and lifting the other to his lips. I did the same and could see immediately why it was so prized and why Lance had dubbed it their 'Royal Fillet'; the thick layers of fat that marbled the meat gave away its wild origins, the light smoke from the London Cure added a depth of flavour I had never experienced in any other smoked salmon and it dissolved on my tongue like a perfect piece of sashimi.

Where once the aim of smoking food was to dry and preserve, now smoked salmon should be eaten as fresh from the kiln as possible. 'Freshness is the key,' Lance confirmed laughingly, adding when I asked him about some rival's claims to mature their fish, 'Fish doesn't mature, it goes off.'

He wrapped up the remaining belly from which he had cut the two slivers for tasting and slid it into a cardboard sleeve, which proudly carried the company logo. I left him to head back to work and set off on my long walk home, the Royal Fillet safely stored in my backpack, making plans for what to do with it on my arrival.

It was a little after nine in the morning. The roads were busy with cars filled with people on their way to work or on the school run. I thought about breakfast. I had not yet eaten that morning and the idea of smoked salmon with creamy scrambled eggs sitting on top of a slice of hot buttered granary toast entered my head and refused to budge. As soon as I arrived at my apartment, I took the salmon from my bag and tore open the packaging. I broke two large eggs into a bowl and whisked them gently with the edge of a fork, adding a little salt and pepper. While I waited for a large knob of butter to heat up in my dedicated scrambled egg pan – sad but true, I have a dedicated scrambled egg pan – I cut a sliver of salmon from the fillet as a pre-breakfast treat. Immediately I ate it, I stopped, turned off the stove and put the bowl containing the beaten eggs in the fridge for later in the day. Smoked salmon this good did not need anything to accompany it.

I sat down on my battered old sofa and cut slivers as thin as possible from the fillet with a sharp chef's knife. I wanted this treat to last as long as I could. I managed to eke it out for forty-five minutes, slicing each piece and chewing it as I slowly savoured every nuance of flavour. It was one of the most enjoyable forty-five minutes of the whole *Eating for Britain* journey.

I have not tried them all, so I cannot say for certain that this is the finest smoked salmon in Britain, but it is certainly the best I have ever tried and, just to remind you, it comes not from Scotland but from the East End of London.

Despite attempts to convey being the bravest of little soldiers, it may surprise you to know that I am in fact a total wimp. Show me a spider in the bathtub and I will show you the scorch marks on the carpet as I make tracks for the door. Show me a picture of cute puppies and fluffy kittens and I will make noises that will make you suggest I should have a gender test. And, God forbid, should I ever injure my hand during some ill-advised experiment with home repairs, I will emit a wail so piercing it will only be audible to animal-kind. How can I put it more plainly? I am a big old softie.

None the less, I have a remarkably pragmatic approach to my food. I am not one of those people who compartmentalize the food they love eating from the fact that something usually had to die to provide supper. I don't believe that my meat comes in prime cuts on polystyrene trays bearing a sell-by date and I have no problem facing down a whole fish whose eyes look back as if to say 'why me?' as it flaps out its last breaths. The food chain is a natural part of life and until some new species comes along that finds bits of humans to be a tasty little treat, I am afraid Brer animal is going to have to watch its back, er, and its loin, and its belly and, well, you get the general idea.

But hunting, that's just wrong, right?

I mean, it's all about drunk toffs dressed in their Pinks chasing some poor helpless fox around the countryside, aided only by twenty or more of their friends on horseback, a pack of ravenous dogs and a few bugles, whose length probably compensates for the huntsmen's small penises. Hunting is all about bigwigs from the City shooting thousands of birds on a corporate junket, the majority of which will be buried and precious few will end up in a pot. Hunting is about hare coursing, where, for no apparent purpose other than the amusement of a few, poor wild creatures are chased around by dogs until, too exhausted to move any more, they are ripped apart. These are blood sports and, of course, if you were to look at them in isolation, you could easily understand why hunting ranks just below child molestation and mass genocide in the opinion of the general public.

However, looking at it from a different direction, you can get another perspective if you listen instead to the views of the men and women of the countryside, of the farmer whose crops are blighted by pigeons or whose cattle and other livestock are made lame by rabbit holes. To them hunting, or more properly field sports, is not only the most efficient form of pest control, but also provides an added source of food for the table and added income from sales to game dealers. Given my own love of the feathered and furred, I also have to admit that without them our menus would be much the poorer. Quite simply, if God had not wanted us to hunt and eat them, he would not have made most animals so tasty. I did, however, take a brief moment to reconsider my opinion as Stuart Blackman tossed the last of four plump rabbits close to where I was standing. Although he assured me it was dead, its feet were still flailing, Thumper-like, banging out a rhythm against the leg of my jeans as it tapped out its last death throes.

Stuart had invited me to spend a day with him near his home in Hertfordshire to introduce me to the fine art of ferreting. He had been involved in countryside pursuits since he was a small child and, after what he described as three 'wasted' years at university and even more a job that merely got in the way of his true passion, he jumped at the chance to take redundancy to set up his one-man operation, the Country Bumpkin, which offered city folk like me the chance to join him for a day's instruction in foraging, shooting and cooking in the lush green countryside close to where he lived.

Stuart was all set when I knocked on his front door at some ridiculous hour in the morning. His gundogs were by his side, ready for the day, and a frantic scratching noise was coming from a small box on the floor in the hallway. 'That's the ferrets.' Stuart nodded towards the box. 'They know they are going out hunting, so they are getting excited.' He lifted one of them from the box. 'This is the older one, she knows what she's doing.' He held her firmly beneath her front legs and dangled her long wriggling body towards the floor, supporting it with his other hand. The furry creature twitched her nose eagerly, keen to get on with the day's activities, as Stuart returned her to the box and pulled a pair of well-worn wellington boots over his feet.

For a nation whose current view of rabbits seems informed almost entirely by the works of Beatrix Potter and that awful song by Art Garfunkel, the thought of eating bunny can be an uncomfortable one, let alone the thought of actually killing one. However, Stuart left me in no doubt that as far as he was concerned rabbits were vermin, pests whose vast numbers can, if they remain unchecked, cause considerable damage to the country-side. 'I am not going to claim that I don't enjoy hunting,' he acknowledged, 'but, without pursuits like ferreting, the rabbits would simply overrun the place. It may be fun, but it is also good animal husbandry.' Ferreting is actually illegal in many countries, but it remains a popular method of pest control in Britain and Ireland where rabbits number in the millions. While there may be other methods of killing rabbits, including shooting, gassing and snaring, compared to ferreting they are ineffectual. Ferreting is one of the most efficient ways of dispatching a rabbit and also has the added benefit of avoiding the use of chemicals, which can contaminate farmland.

Ferreting also has a long history, with the earliest mentions of the animals being domesticated and used for hunting going back as far as the works of Greek historian Strabo who around 30 BC recounted a plague of rabbits in the Balearic Islands causing a famine and finally being dealt with by a small animal brought from Libya and bred specifically for the purpose of hunting. Although we now think of ferreting in Britain as a working-class pastime, historical records from the thirteenth century show that there was an official ferreter to the royal court and that even to own a ferret you had to prove an annual income of over forty shillings, a considerable amount. The added ability of ferrets to catch rodents in growing towns and even for the navy onboard ships at sea was probably the main reason they moved from being the rich man's hunting toy to being the working man's tool.

With the switch from a rural-based economy to an industrial one in the nineteenth century, traditional hunting skills like trapping and ferreting began to be lost and it was not until the Second World War and the advent of rationing and the limited availability of ammunition that people found the need to rediscover these lost crafts. In his superb *British Food: An Extraordinary Thousand Years of History* Colin Spencer argues that rabbits provided a 'salvation for many in a low income group' at that time.

For some who lived through the Second World War and the years of rationing that followed, rabbits and other cheap sources of meat like offal may have been a salvation, but they also appeared on the menu so often that even now, two generations later, the very thought of them can turn the stomach. Their prevalence no doubt contributed to the disappearance of many traditional dishes from British cooking as people turned with some relief to the prime cuts that began to appear on the shelves. It is only in recent years that dishes like rabbit pie have been reintroduced on the menu although it's ironic that the ingredients, which were once thought so plentiful as to avoid rationing, are now being sold at premium prices.

For Stuart, however, ferreting was just a way of life. 'I'd be out here all day every day if my girlfriend let me,' he said with a smile as he pulled his Land-Rover into the field a few short miles' drive from his house. It was not hard to understand why. In the early morning, the air was clear and apart from the rustle of a few tall trees there was no noise but our own breaths forming vapour clouds as they escaped from our mouths. Making sure that the gate was firmly closed behind us, we unpacked our hunting gear from the back of the car. Apart from the animals themselves, ferreting for rabbits requires scarcely any equipment other than a handful of nets, another possible reason why it became so popular with the working classes.

Stuart strode off across the muddy field leaving me, and his gundogs, to trot obediently behind him. He stopped once he had reached a small copse. 'There,' he said, pointing at a handful of telltale holes in the ground covered over with the tangled roots of trees. 'Don't walk around too much, it will let the rabbits know we are here,' he added as he began to lay his nets down on the ground next to the warren. Ferreting nets, or purse-nets, are pegged securely over the hole to ensure that if and when a rabbit does bolt at the sound and smell of the ferret, the net closes behind it on a drawstring and it cannot escape. 'The key is to catch and dispatch the rabbit as quickly as possible,' Stuart told me as he began to peg out the nets. 'Just because we are hunting them, there is no reason the animal has to suffer unduly.' Stuart lifted the lid to the ferret box and brought out the older of the two, carrying her gently as he walked back to the largest opening in the rabbit warren. Lifting one of the nets, he allowed her to wriggle free from his hand and she disappeared quickly beneath the surface.

'Now we wait,' Stuart announced. At first nothing seemed to be happening. We waited for a few more minutes and the small, sharp snout of the ferret appeared from another hole then disappeared again back down into the warren. 'She's on the scent.' Stuart stood ready for the emergence of the first rabbit. Almost as soon as the words had left his mouth there was a sudden rush of activity. A young rabbit bolted from the warren straight into one of the nets, which closed immediately behind it, preventing its escape. Stuart was on to it at once and, as I stood to one side, he released the rabbit from its cord prison and sent it on its way with a swift pull, dislocating its neck.

'It's dead,' he said, waving it at me, 'look at the eyes.' He was correct, they were glazed over and there was little doubt that the animal was already in bunny heaven. Its hind legs, however, had not yet received the bad news and were still trying to run away, twitching on the ground where Stuart had tossed it. The violent and rapid transition from life to death, even of an animal I was looking forward to eating, was a surprisingly visceral moment. It took me a moment or two to regain my composure and to notice that Stuart was already casually replacing the net as if it were the most natural thing in the world, which for him indeed it was.

We caught two more rabbits in rapid succession, both dealt with in the same unsentimental manner by Stuart who explained, 'You can't hesitate, or the animal will suffer. This way it is dead seconds after it comes from the ground.' He was right, but when he asked me if I wanted to have a go I declined. Not, I hasten to add, because of any sentimentality on my own part; I was already anticipating what we were planning to prepare with our catch. It was more that as a novice I did not feel confident that I could dispatch the animals with the efficiency that Stuart showed and I would cause them undue stress.

Stuart nodded in understanding and methodically carried on laying his nets until we had four perfect specimens on the ground and he declared that our hunting for the day was over.

Back at Country Bumpkin HQ, Stuart got to work gutting and skinning the rabbits. 'Look at that,' he said, pointing at a thick strip of fat around the belly of the animal he was cleaning. 'You can see that it led a good life for nearly two years and then it was killed quickly. Not a bad way to go.' He removed all the flesh from the bones with a practised precision until all that was left was a clean carcass. 'Now,' he said, 'we can make a rabbit pie.' His was a simple version. He tossed the meat in seasoned flour before cooking down with chunks of onion and carrot, adding the carcasses to give even more flavour. When it was time to roll the lard-based pastry crust on top of the pie and place it in the oven, delicious savoury smells were filling the kitchen and I was already salivating.

'Seasonal' and 'local' have become buzzwords in British cooking over the last decade as we strive to re-establish the connection with our food that was fractured so badly during the war years. Unfortunately, the words have been hijacked by the media and by marketing gurus to the extent that using them has become almost meaningless, more a tool to sell product than to promote quality. Leaning against the Formica top of Stuart's kitchen with a cup of tea in my hand as he prepared the pie, I began to understand what these words really mean.

Stuart apologized as he removed the pie from the oven and put the final result in front of me, stating, 'There're no airs and graces with my food.' He had no need to be sorry. It was delicious. This rabbit pie was real food, the sort of dish that would have *Masterchef*'s Greg Wallace saying 'deep' and 'savoury' until his head exploded. It was all the more enjoyable because of the long day we had spent hunting and because the results of our efforts were there before us to sample. I sat in Stuart's living room, eyeballing his hunting dogs, while forking the chunks of meat, gravy and pastry into my mouth until the pie was gone. Forgetting where I was for a moment, I lifted up the dish to my lips and tipped it, pouring the last dregs of meaty gravy into my mouth. 'You enjoyed that then?' Stuart interrupted and he was right, I had. Rabbit pie is definitely back on the menu.

You may not be fortunate enough to spend a day as I did, ferreting with Stuart Blackman, the Country Bumpkin, but if you do fancy a bit of bunny action, here is my own recipe for rabbit pie.

## — *Rabbit Pie* —

(MAKES I LARGE 17CM PIE)

*For the pastry*

---

*1 standard block frozen shortcrust pastry will do perfectly well, but if you want to make your own (and why not?) you will need:*

225g plain flour                55g butter
1 pinch of salt                 3–5 tablespoons cold water
55g lard

*For the rabbit filling*

| | |
|---|---|
| meat from 1 rabbit, cut into pieces (you can include the kidneys for richness if you still have them); retain the carcass | 3 large carrots, cut into large dice |
| | 2 celery sticks, sliced |
| | 1 teaspoon tomato purée |
| 3 tablespoons seasoned flour | 1 teaspoon English mustard |
| 25g lard, butter or vegetable oil for cooking | 1 pinch of salt |
| | 1 pinch of white pepper |
| 6 rashers of smoked bacon in strips (or small cubes of belly pork) | 2 teaspoons fresh thyme |
| | 1 glass of punchy red wine |
| | 300ml water or chicken stock |
| 1 medium-sized white onion, sliced in half moons | 1 glass of Somerset cider brandy (or any brandy you may have to hand) |
| 1 garlic clove, finely minced | |

*For the glaze*

| | |
|---|---|
| 1 egg yolk | 2 tablespoons milk |

First make the pastry. Sieve the flour into a large bowl and add the salt. Add the lard and butter and work them into the flour until the mixture resembles breadcrumbs. Add the water a tablespoon at a time and stir with a cold knife or spoon until it forms a smooth dough. Add more water by the tablespoon if necessary.

Wrap the dough in clingfilm and refrigerate for at least 30 minutes or until ready to use.

Toss the rabbit meat in the seasoned flour. Melt half the lard in a deep-sided frying pan and cook the rabbit in batches until it is all sealed. Remove and place in a colander to drain off any excess fat.

In the same pan add the remaining lard and the bacon. Cook gently for 5 minutes. Add the onions and garlic, cooking until they have softened but not taken on colour. Put in the carrots and celery and cook gently for another 5 minutes.

Mix in the tomato purée, mustard, salt, pepper and thyme. Return the rabbit meat to the pan together with the carcass. Pour in the red wine and the water or stock.

Cook gently until the meat is tender and the sauce has reduced by half. Add more water or stock if it becomes too dry. This should take around 20 minutes.

When the filling is ready, remove the carcass and discard, flame the cider brandy in a ladle and pour over the pan. Allow the alcohol to burn off and then transfer the filling to a suitable pie dish.

Remove the pastry from the fridge and roll out to the relevant size. Place on top of the pie dish and trim, allowing at least 1cm of pastry to drape over the side.

Mix together the egg yolk and milk for the glaze and brush over the pastry. Bake in a moderate oven, preheated to 170°C/325°F/gas mark 3, for 30–40 minutes until golden brown.

Serve with boiled, buttered new potatoes and steamed greens.

# 30
## Steak and Kidney Pudding

Steak and kidney pudding is one of the great dividers in British food. You are, they say up north, 'either for or agin it'. I will give you one guess which side of the great divide my size tens are firmly planted.

Steak and kidney pudding, with the usual caveat of when it is well made and with great ingredients, remains one of my favourite things to eat and, indeed, to cook. Yet it is also one of the dishes most cited by foreigners as the final evidence of Britain's inedible cuisine, even though most of the people who say, 'It's a pudding and it has kidneys in it?' have never actually eaten one. It is true that beef and offal boiled for hours in a pastry made from fat taken from around a cow's kidney may not sound like the most appetizing of dishes. The end result, however, with its outer suet crust breaking to release tender chunks of beef and soft melting kidneys in a glistening juice created by the slow cooking, is something that has to be tasted to be understood and fully appreciated.

Although records of steamed puddings date back to the 1600s, the heyday of the steak and kidney pudding was in the mid-nineteenth century to the early years of the twentieth century. References to steak puddings, oyster puddings and kidney puddings abound in literature and the image of household cooks, captured perfectly by Angela Baddeley's sublime portrayal of Mrs Bridges in

277

*Upstairs Downstairs*, has become familiar, giving some idea of the workings of an Edwardian kitchen and the importance of the ability to make a good pudding.

The pudding was not just important in the well-to-do houses and a good kidney pudding, plumped out with cheap and plentiful oysters, was also a staple part of the working man's diet, being a perfect combination of fats, carbohydrate and protein for those whose days were long and laborious. The other benefit was that once the pudding was wrapped in its pudding cloth or covered basin and set to steam, it could be left for a number of hours allowing the cook to tend to other chores.

The decline in popularity of the steak and kidney pudding, as with so many dishes, links back to the impact of the Second World War. The place of women in society began to change for good as they moved from being homemakers and into the workplace, their efforts required to supplement those of the few men who had not been sent to the battlefront. Originally their work would have been in munitions factories, but after the war, as the economy began to rebuild itself, there were ever more opportunities for employment. Though the freedom from the home may have been a welcome one, the inevitable consequences were a decrease in the time women had available to spend preparing meals and a disruption to the process by which traditional recipes were handed down from mother to daughter.

Often, these two changes combined to mean that these dishes were only to be found in ready-prepared versions, which began to appear on the shelves of a new generation of shops, the supermarkets. Despite the manufacturers' claims that they tasted as good as home-made, they were inferior in every way. In addition, a preference for lighter dishes, spurred on by nutritional concerns, and a more sedentary office-based society, together made these dishes increasingly unfashionable.

It is only in more recent years, as chefs have unapologetically mined Britain's culinary past, that puddings have begun to see a resurgence in popularity and have appeared once more on restaurant menus, alongside other traditional dishes like savoury pies.

When I returned to the basement kitchen of Rules to find out how London's oldest restaurant would make one of Britain's oldest dishes, sous chef Paul Fiton was already at work preparing the ingredients for the thirty steak and kidney puddings they would expect to serve that evening. 'It's arguably the most popular dish on the menu and we have people who order it every time they come to eat here,' he told me as he lugged sizeable containers of chopped beef to the back of the kitchen.

For my home version, I fill a suet pastry crust with raw meat and vegetables and steam for up to four hours. Given the number of puddings it serves, Rules does not have the luxury of time on its hands, added to which, Paul did not believe that beginning with raw ingredients gave the best end result. 'You need to cook the meat first to get some real colour and flavour into the dish,' he told me as he started to cook.

In front of us were two trays containing large chunks of diced meat: in one, flank steak, which would break down slowly releasing fat to keep the dish moist; in the other, pieces of fillet steak to add luxurious succulence to the final result. Both had been marinating overnight in a bath of rich dark ale along with caramelized onions, salt and pepper and a small amount of Rules's 'secret' ingredient, Marmite, and had taken on the rich, dark colour of mahogany. Paul poured some beef dripping into a large Bratt pan, a sink-like cooker capable of holding the quantities we were working with. It began to smoke immediately and he tossed in the flank steak.

It sizzled on contact and steam billowed out from the pan. I worried that it might burn, but Paul looked unconcerned. 'If you stir it too quickly,' he said, nodding towards the meat, 'it releases all its juices and then stews rather than seals.' The beef was already depositing a deep brown residue on the bottom of the pan as the natural sugars on the surface began to caramelize. When all sides had been seared, Paul added the fillet steak to do the same. Once all the meat was seared he added sliced onions and began to sweat them down until they too were a golden colour. Finally he added 'beef boil', a special Rules stock made from roasted beef bones, to deglaze the bottom of the pan and make sure all the juices from the meat were captured to add flavour to the final gravy. 'Now we wait,' he shouted above the increased clattering of pans as the kitchen continued to ready itself for service. 'It'll take a good few hours to cook until all the meat is tender.' When service began, the filling would be added to pastry cases and only then would the kidneys be added. 'If we add them too soon, they can toughen up like little bullets,' Paul explained.

While Paul busied himself preparing for service, I spent two hours moving from one section to another taking the opportunity to see a professional kitchen in full flow. None of the staff seemed in the least perturbed as I flashed away with my camera or captured their work on video to review later.

By the time Paul came to find me the meat filling for the pudding was ready. It was thick and dark, the colour of bitter chocolate and the taste spoke to its long hours of slow cooking and the attention Paul had given to sealing the meat. Small ramekins had already been lined with its crust in the pastry section of the kitchen. The crust was speckled with yellow flecks of suet, the fat surrounding the cows' kidneys. It was another perfect example of the ability of British cooks to put every last scrap of the animal to good use. It is not just a worthy addition, however, as suet in a steamed pastry is vital. It adds a sublime texture to the finished crust while it is cooking as the fat melts to combine with the pastry. Paul filled each case in turn to the brim then covered them with a final round of pastry and placed them in the kitchen's convection oven.

By now I had been on my feet in the kitchen for hours. They were throbbing with a dull ache and I was longing to head home to flop with a mug of tea and a custard cream. Yet every one of the chefs had been in for at least an hour before I arrived and every one of them would be toiling in the heat of the kitchen long after I went home to complain about my hard day. Before I left, however, the steak and kidney pudding had been plated ready to be sampled.

I leaned over the plate and took a long, deep sniff, luxuriating in the aroma as I broke open the casing of the pudding with my fork. Immediately beefy vapours rose to meet my nostrils and the glistening filling of the pudding began to tumble on to the plate with the chunks of tender beef and kidney wrapped in a silky gravy. I tucked in. First eating the meat on its own, which retained a bite but soon melted in the mouth into beefy shreds. Then the kidney, added later and with a lingering taste of offal. Finally the pastry, which I used to scoop up the sauce in a perfectly British combination. The pudding was small, but the contents so rich and full of flavour that the portion size was ample, particularly when served alongside a bowl of creamy mashed potato and a side dish of crunchy green beans.

Service was now in full swing and I stood to one side clutching my plate of pudding, watching with added respect as the team dealt professionally with the onslaught of service. The restaurant was, as always, fully booked and order tickets filtered out of the computerized machine like ticker tape. Paul, in charge by the pass, called them out to the waiting chefs, earning the immediate response of 'yes, Chef' as they prepared for their tasks. When the dishes were ready, they were placed on the pass, under heated lamps, while Paul cast one last critical eye over them before calling 'service' and sending them out to be whisked upstairs by the liveried staff.

It was time for me to go and leave Richard and the kitchen staff at Rules to get on with what they do daily and do so well. It had been a remarkable few hours. If anyone ever tells you that being a chef is a glamorous occupation, just get them to spend a day in a professional kitchen. It is not glamorous, it is bloody hard work. The hours are long and the conditions cramped, hot and uncomfortable. The pay can be miserable and, unless you are lucky enough to work under a chef like Richard

Sawyer, the treatment you receive can be worse than that of cattle going off to slaughter.

I spend half my life criticizing what comes out of restaurant kitchens, but after that morning I was sure I would look upon my plate with a different eye. No more forgiving, because I am still the punter and they have a contract to put something decent on my plate for the money they extract, but perhaps more aware of the pressures they are under. One thing is for certain: a simple steak and kidney pudding will never taste quite the same again.

# 31
## Chicken Tikka Masala

There were few foods I found on the *Eating for Britain* tour that didn't owe at least some thanks for their existence to Britain's long tradition of trade and immigration. It is part of our lot as a small nation that not only are we dependent upon imports from other countries to supplement our own insufficient production of food, but also that our inbred desire to travel and our tolerance of the lifestyles and religions of others should bring with them the food of other lands together with the people who cook it.

Those who expound 'rivers of blood' scare stories about the current influx of immigration and who hark back to some mythical pure Anglo-Saxon era of the glory days of Albion should spend less time pushing excrement through the letterboxes of terrified Bangladeshis and more time learning to read. Then they might discover that immigration has been a part of Britain's character as far back as history has been recorded, and that we British would never have reached great heights without it. Our food would also be a lot less interesting than many people already claim it is.

If the politics of immigration to Britain could not have been further from my mind as I walked through the West End of Glasgow, pulling my coat collar around my neck to shelter me from the sheeting rain, then the evidence of it was all around me. Glasgow claims to be the curry capital of the UK and even though the West End has obviously undergone considerable gentrification, I still passed enough restaurants to support that theory in the face of strong challenges from Bradford, Southall, Manchester and Birmingham.

I had taken the first flight from London that morning, which meant a 4 a.m. start and being herded like cattle on to a budget airliner for the short one-hour flight from Stansted. As I exited the plane, rain slapped me in the face helped along by a sharp blast of air cold enough to make me realize why I don't visit Scotland more often. None the less, despite the weather's best efforts to dampen my enthusiasm, I still felt a genuine sense of excitement at being back in Glasgow. I was following up on an invitation to meet the creator of one of Britain's greatest food exports and what has been called by many our national dish: chicken tikka masala.

The spluttering of pedants can probably be heard everywhere as they squeal, 'But chicken tikka masala is Indian,' and it is a misconception that is held by many who hold sacred their weekly visit to a local curry house. But they are wrong, for although chicken tikka, those glorious chunks of poultry marinated in spices and yogurt and then cooked in the searing heat of a tandoor, is ubi-quitous throughout the subcontinent, its coating in a velvety sauce made from spices and tomatoes is as British as fish and chips (except they are not British either, but you get my point). So associated had it become with Britain and even more with the Shish Mahal in Glasgow, that in 2009 Glasgow City Council threw its support behind Labour MP Mohammad Sarwar's attempt to define the dish legally as a 'Glasgow chicken tikka masala' or 'Shish Mahal tikka masala'. It would be easy to dismiss such activities as publicity stunts designed to drive up tourism or at least bring a bit of media attention to the city, but it also shows that this dish, wherever it was created, has become a truly British institution.

As the late Robin Cook, then Foreign Secretary, put it in an excellent 2001 speech about the benefits of immigration to the UK: 'Chicken Tikka Massala is now a true British national dish, not only because it is the most popular, but because it is a perfect illustration of the way Britain absorbs and adapts external influences. Chicken Tikka is an Indian dish. The Massala sauce was added to satisfy the desire of British people to have their meat served in gravy.'

The curry house is a true British institution and should be viewed in an entirely different way from a restaurant trying to recreate authentic dishes from the twenty-eight states of India or the countries of the Indian subcontinent, Pakistan, Sri Lanka and Bangladesh. The curry houses will eschew authenticity in favour of a series of stereotyped favourites that are as familiar to anyone brought up in the UK as the stock characters of a pantomime. Just as we know that the principal boy is always a smoking hot girl, we know that a prawn phal is something to be eaten only if you have asbestos buttocks or a death wish. Just as we know that the pantomime dame is some dodgy old bloke who once appeared in an episode of *The Bill*, so we know that onion bhajis are the size of cricket balls and that a chicken biryani comes with a sliced hard-boiled egg on top. Any connection to dishes that might be recognizable to an Indian expatriate longing for the motherland is purely accidental and to be avoided.

The curry house is now so firmly entrenched a part of British life that it is almost impossible to imagine a high street without a Taj Mahal, Koh-I-Noor or Raj Tandoori and, like the multinational American fast food chains, the reason they have endured is as much down to familiarity as it is down to quality. Step into any curry house in any part of the UK and your experience will be within a naan bread's width of being identical. The bow-tied waiters will be smilingly polite as they deliver a towering plate of poppadums alongside an assortment of lurid pickles. The smooth stylings of Lata Mangeshkar will be forcing their way out of a pair of tinny speakers at either end of the room and, in a nod to modernity, the flock wallpaper that was their hallmark for so many years will have been replaced by a bright lick of paint. Starters will include puri stuffed with prawns, served with a few strips of lettuce and a lemon quarter. The main dishes will all look alarmingly alike, having been prepared with the same base sauce and differentiated only by the amount of sweat they will force from your brow. Breads will be the size of one of the smaller counties and glisten with a slick of ghee. The rice will contain unexplained bits, which you pick at to make certain they are nuts and raisins rather than flies and roaches.

In recent years, things have begun to change. A new influx of immigrants to the UK is arriving from different regions of India, bringing their food with them and Indian restaurants are altering to offer more authentic dishes from these newly arrived cuisines.

Of course, saying 'Indian food' is as nonsensical as

saying 'European food', with the seafood and vegetable dishes of Kerala being as different from the light cuisine of West Bengal as Norwegian food is from Sicilian, and the street food of Pakistani Kashmir being as different from the Portuguese-influenced Goan cuisine as Parisian dining is from the tapas bars of Andalucía. This new breed of restaurant is lifting both the quality and the reputation of 'Indian' restaurants in the UK to a whole new level.

Despite that, there will, however, always be a place for the good old-fashioned curry house. As an industry, it contributes nearly £4 billion to our annual economy and employs over 100,000 people. And, in case you are wondering, let me be very clear about it: I think they can be wonderful things. When the urge hits for a few pints and a meal with friends, nothing else will hit the spot like a good and pleasingly familiar evening in a curry house.

Britain's obsession with Indian food does not, as some may assume, date back just to the wave of post-Independence immigration in the 1950s and '60s although the explosion in the numbers of restaurants certainly does. Even before the granting of a royal charter to the East India Company in 1600, spices were flowing into Britain as a natural part of its trade. By the 1700s curries, a generic term for dishes laced with spices from Asia, were becoming commonplace on dining tables and the first recorded recipe for one appears in Hannah Glasse's *The Art of Cookery Made Plain and Easy* published in 1747. Her recipe would be barely recognizable to any modern curry lover, containing only coriander and black pepper by way of seasoning, although other spices were added in later editions.

By the 1800s both Mrs Beeton and Eliza Acton had got in on the act, with the latter contributing many recipes for curry in the 'Foreign Food' section of her book, *Cookery For Private Families*. In India itself, the growing bureaucracy of the Raj and the influx of administrators from Britain led to the creation of dishes that drew on both the regional cooking of India and the comforting reminders of home. This was the period that gave us kedgeree, an anglicized version of the local dish, *kitchari*, as well as the much maligned mulligatawny soup which derived its name from the Tamil words 'pepper water'.

The rise of the Raj also brought Indians to Britain for the first time in any significant numbers and the majority of restaurants serving Asian food were aimed at feeding these expats rather than the returning British administrators. The first fashionable eating house dedicated entirely to Indian food, the Hindostanee Coffee House, was opened in 1809 by Dean Mahomet and offered 'Indian Dishes of The Highest Perfection'. It did not last long, closing three years later and it was not until the early part of the twentieth century, when Edward Palmer opened Veeraswamy in London's Regent Street as 'The ex-Indian higher serviceman's curry club', that the cuisine began to move into the mainstream and even to gain royal recognition. Fact fans might like to tuck away this little snippet of information: the first time that the classic double act of curry and lager appeared on the same bill was during a meal at Veeraswamy. It was served during a visit by the Prince of Denmark who, if my imagination is to be believed, very probably shouted across the room, 'Oi, Gunga Din, another pint of Cobra and bring some more lime pickle, Jaldi.'

Although the vast majority of these restaurants were to be found in London and the south-east, interest in them began to spread all over the UK, aided by the influx of immigrants from the newly created countries of Pakistan and East Pakistan, later to become Bangladesh. The new arrivals came to Britain to work in factories, steel mills and shipyards, but soon turned their attention to the restaurant trade and Indian food became available in every major city in the country. Brick Lane's array of restaurants was replicated in Bradford, in the Rusholme district of Manchester and, as I was finding out, in the West End of Glasgow.

Ali Ahmed Aslam arrived in Britain from Pakistan in the 1950s and took over the ownership of an existing restaurant called the Taj Mahal, renaming it the Shish Mahal. Despite claims from chefs in other parts of the country, it is Ali Ahmed Aslam who is widely credited with creating the chicken tikka masala. In 1964 the Shish Mahal moved to its current location on Park Road. Just so you know, 1964 is also the year of my birth, which seems appropriate since, at my last doctor's appointment, he announced that I was 'approximately 15 per cent tikka masala', adding, 'We should probably try to get those numbers down.'

The Shish Mahal was already beginning to fill up as I arrived to be greeted by Rashaid Ali, the middle of three sons born to Mr Ali in Glasgow. He had graduated from the nearby university from which much of the customer base of the restaurant still comes and after a stint as a highly paid management consultant in London had returned at the request of his father and older brother to run the Shish Mahal. He pointed me to a seat at the rear of the room and went off to make sure some new arrivals were dealt with promptly, leaving me to eavesdrop on the conversations of my neighbours.

The Shish Mahal was far more than just a standard curry house. I sniffed the air as trays laden with food were brought out to the waiting customers. They looked fantastic. In particular, plates of sizzling lamb chops, which I found out later were marinated in fresh mint and chilli before being cooked to succulent perfection in the tandoor.

When things had quietened down a little, Rashaid returned to sit with me and resume our conversation. 'It was in the early 1970s when my father bought a tandoor that things really started to take off,' he began as a waiter poured me a glass of water from a jug laced with lime slices. 'It was such an unusual thing in the UK then that he had to bring over a chef from Pakistan as no one here knew how to cook with it.' Nowadays, plates of bread and sizzling platters of the meats cooked in these blisteringly hot clay ovens are commonplace, but forty years ago they were a new and exciting part of the dining scene. Indian restaurants would often change their names to reflect the presence of the ovens in their kitchen and menus boasted of the succulence of their kebabs, lamb chops and, of course, that other classic dish, tandoori chicken.

We were joined by Rashaid's older brother, Asif, and, in an act of deference to an elder sibling that I recognized only too well from my own relationship with TGS, Rashaid allowed Asif to take over the story. 'We can actually trace the creation of chicken tikka masala back to a particular day and a particular customer,' he added in a thick Glaswegian brogue, as his younger brother nodded in agreement.

'We have always made fantastic chicken tikka at the Shish Mahal. It's so good it could make you weep, so meaty and moist.' He licked his lips and I felt guilty as I realized that both he and his brother would be in the middle of their daily Ramadan fast as they talked to me about their father's invention. 'One day,' Asif carried on, 'Dad had a regular customer come in who worked on the buses. He loved our food but was in a filthy mood complaining that everything was wrong and even that his favourite chicken tikka was too dry.' He shook his head as if such a thought were barely imaginable. 'Dad was in the kitchen and at the time was suffering from a stomach ulcer. He could only eat tomato soup and had half a can left over from lunchtime which he planned to use for his evening meal.' Asif had obviously told the story many times before and was getting well into his stride. 'He decided to make a sauce out of it using the spices in the kitchen and sent it back out to the customer who loved it. In fact, he loved it so much he kept coming back and insisting we made it again. Sometimes he brought friends with him and, before we knew it, chicken tikka masala was on the menu.'

The dish began to spread to other restaurants in the city, particularly as many were owned by cousins of the same family who realized that there was a market for the dish. From there, it was only a short time before reports of the dish being found across the UK and even in Australia and the USA started to filter back to the Shish Mahal.

'We think it is because people came from all over the

world to study at Glasgow University and ate at the curry restaurants because they offered tasty, cheap, filling food. When they went back to their own countries or other parts of Britain they wanted to eat these dishes again and so they began to appear on menus of other Indian restaurants.' Asif smiled. 'We call it our gift to the world.'

At this point their father, the legendary Ali Ahmed Aslam, appeared to make sure that the tale was being told properly. Slim and well dressed, his grey beard and hair gave away his sixty-five years, but his eyes were still filled with energy as he grasped my hand firmly and asked me if I wanted to join the chefs in the kitchen as they made a batch of chicken tikka masala. There cannot be too many occasions where the person who created a dish that has become popular all over the world offers to show you how it is made and I couldn't help having a small shiver of anticipation as I was shown into the kitchen.

As is the case in many busy kitchens, much of the preparation had been done long before the service began. Large chunks of chicken tikka, charred from their quick cooking in the tandoor, sat waiting for the sauce to be made. A frying pan was heated up on the range until it began to smoke and a paste of ginger, garlic, tomatoes, onions and spices was spooned in to cook down and reduce before the chicken was added.

'Now, the special ingredient,' Rashaid said above the noise of the kitchen. 'But it's a secret, so would you mind turning away?'

I have no idea what the chef added, but a huge spout of steam shot up from the pan, pushing a waft of slightly sour air towards my nostrils. 'Tamarind?' I ventured to

Rashaid, but he just smiled and ignored the suggestion as the dish neared completion.

Ali Ahmed Aslam appeared once again with two large white plates. One was empty, a willing receptacle for the finished chicken tikka masala, while the other was covered with a piping-hot naan bread as big as a queen-sized bed. 'You can't eat chicken tikka masala with a knife and fork; you have to use your fingers.'

Aware that the rest of the staff were probably all still fasting, I was a little reticent about eating in front of them as the chef ladled the chicken on to the plate and then made sure it was given a good coating of the glistening sauce. Rashaid nudged me. 'Go on, tuck in, we made it all for you.' I knew that to turn down their hospitality would have been even more of an insult than to gorge myself in front of them, so, despite the inquisitive stares of the staff, I tore off a large portion of the hot naan bread and used it to wrap a piece of chicken, making sure that I wiped up a slick of sauce on the way from plate to mouth. As I took my first bite, the naan bread gave way to the moist chicken whose juices began to escape from the corners of my mouth and dribble down my chin. There was a hint of sweetness from the tomatoes, followed by a kick of spice and chilli. It was not raw and unpleasant, but still forceful enough to make my eyes water as I worked my way through the sizeable portion they had put in front of me. I cleared the plate. The chef spoke little English but showed his approval with a vigorous nod of the head as he took the plate away.

Although chicken tikka masala is a dish I have eaten on dozens of occasions at restaurants in London and all over the world – I have even eaten it in Delhi at a restaurant that claimed to make it 'just like in Britain' – to eat the sauce at the source, as it were, made this all too familiar dish taste fresh, exciting and new. Perhaps it was the location or the fact that I was eating it in the kitchen of the person who had invented it. Or perhaps it was the generosity with which it was served. But it was a moment I shall treasure. I do know that thanks to my visit to the Shish Mahal boys I will never think of chicken tikka masala in quite the same way again.

My take on this classic dish has been influenced by any number of recipes over the years, but was inspired initially, if memory serves me, by one from Reza Mohammad, chef/owner of the Star of India in London. It may not contain the secret ingredient of the Shish Mahal's version, but it is a real winner and worth trying.

## — *Chicken Tikka Masala* —
### (SERVES 4)

*8 chicken thighs (2 per person), boned, skinned and cut into 5cm dice*

*For the marinade*

| | |
|---|---|
| 2 bunches of coriander leaf (including stalks) | ½ teaspoon salt |
| | 2.5cm piece of fresh ginger |
| 250ml yogurt | 4 garlic cloves |
| 4 fresh green chillies | |

## For the masala sauce

| | |
|---|---|
| 1 cinnamon stick | ½ teaspoon ground cumin |
| 2 cloves | ½ teaspoon ground coriander |
| 3 fresh red chillies, finely minced | ½ teaspoon ground turmeric |
| | ½ teaspoon ground fenugreek |
| oil for frying | ½ teaspoon sugar |
| ½ large white onion, sliced | ½ teaspoon salt |
| 3 garlic cloves | 400g tin chopped tomatoes |
| 2.5cm piece of fresh ginger | 400ml water |
| 1 teaspoon hot chilli powder | 250ml single cream |
| ½ teaspoon ground ginger | |

## To serve

lemon juice
coriander leaf

Blend all the marinade ingredients together to a fine paste, pour over the chicken, mix well, cover and leave to sit for at least 2 hours (more if possible).

Fry the cinnamon stick, cloves and minced chilli in a little oil for 2 minutes. Add the sliced onion and fry until soft and golden.

Blend the garlic and fresh ginger to a paste and fry with the onions for 2 minutes. Add the chilli powder, ground spices, sugar and salt and cook gently for 5 minutes, adding water if they begin to stick.

Add the tin of tomatoes and the water, stir well and allow to cook down until reduced by half. Remove from the pan and blend to a smooth paste. Return the paste to the pan and, off the heat, add the single cream, stirring well, then put the pan back on the heat to reduce a little more.

While the sauce is cooking, place the chicken on a wire rack and grill under a hot grill, turning once until each piece is cooked thoroughly and has a slight char.

Transfer them to the pan with the sauce and toss gently until every piece is coated.

Before serving, sprinkle with a little lemon juice and some chopped coriander leaf.

# 32
## Haggis

There are not many times when I regret being part English. Actually, come to think of it, that's complete rubbish, there are loads of times when I regret being just a little bit English, mainly when sport is involved and I see our national (insert name of any sport here) team humiliated by a group of part-timers from a nation that was only created in the late 1990s and whose population consists of three shepherds, a couple of goats and a woman with loose morals called Katia.

I definitely had some qualms about my Englishness as I entered the ballroom of the Brig O'Doon Hotel in Ayr. It was 25 January, Burns Night, and I had been invited up to Scotland to join the celebrations in honour of the 250th anniversary of Scotland's most famous poet.

As I made my way to a centre table where my name had been written in a careful hand on a place card, I realized that, with one or two exceptions, I was the only man in the room not wearing a kilt, sporran or hiding a dagger in my socks. The women too all seemed to be in full Celtic regalia, with sprigs of heather attached to many an ample bosom and tartan shawls flung over shoulders as if the ladies were about to take flight in some scary demonstration of Scottish country dancing. It was a rather smart affair and even the Scottish First Minister Alex Salmond was in attendance, wearing trews whose material looked under considerable pressure from his impressive girth.

I, perhaps not judging my audience wisely, had chosen to wear an ill-fitting velvet suit over a flowery waistcoat from Liberty of London that may well have been dismissed as 'eccentric' in the capital but received looks like a condom floating in a swimming pool here as we sat to pay homage to Robert Burns. I was definitely out of my comfort zone, but sucked it up as I had come to the party for one reason and that was not to bow the knee to a man who wrote soppy verse. I was hunting down some haggis and where was going to be a better time and place than on Burns Night in the home of his birth overlooking the Brig O'Doon?

It was hard work and although the booze flowed freely, rather too freely, it was not enough to anaesthetize me against the horrors of a series of playlets re-enacting the life of the poet pronounced in a period dialect that I found impossible to decipher. In between these delightful little vignettes attractive young women sang songs, based on verses by the poet in soft, lilting voices and those around me at every table wiped tears from their eyes at the memory of Burns's tragically short life. By the third act of the über-dull rendition, I was almost wishing I could join him.

During one particularly tortuous section of the poet's life entitled, I think, 'Poor Wee Rabbie, How Thin Tha's Got', I had caught sight of the menu slipped between two candlesticks. I scanned it looking for the part when the bagpipes skirled (they do skirl, don't they?), the men in skirts paraded in with a large haggis and people began talking about 'wee timorous beasties' and 'chieftains o' the pudding race'. Slightly concerned, I realized there was no mention of sticking a sword into a bag of offal anywhere on the menu. Surely some mistake; it must have been the beer combined with the champagne combined with the considerable amount of wine I was knocking back to dull the pain of the entertainment that was blinding me to the obvious. I looked again. There was a starter involving seafood in the form of fabulous scallops from the west coast of Scotland. There was a main course involving venison, which I knew would be lovely and there was even a nice-looking pudding. But nowhere was there a mention of a bloody haggis. The hideous truth hit me: I had been brought to Scotland under false pretences. This was a strictly haggis-free zone.

After my discovery, I had to admit that as the evening dragged on I did not behave well. I glugged readily from any passing bottle of booze that came within reach and by the end of the night I was, shall we say, ready to take the night air. As the clock struck midnight, I said my farewells and began the short walk back to my bed and breakfast accommodation. As if to compound God's little joke against any Englishman setting foot north of the border on Burns Night, it began to rain, at first a spittle then with increasing ferocity until I had to wrap my large grey overcoat around me and lean forward to make headway in the increasingly strong wind. Unfortunately, and no laughing at the back, I leaned over just a little too much and, slipping on a wet stone, did a perfect comedy pratfall and landed in a superb spread eagle in a soft and squelchy patch of mud. I managed to right myself with the sort of 'schwooooopsh' noise normally reserved for cartoons and looked down at a mud angel exactly the shape of me that was slowly being washed away by the heavy rain. It had not been my finest moment, nor was it a good start to my journey to look for haggis.

Scotland's most famous dish is, like its English counterpart, black pudding, one of those dishes that causes great consternation in potential diners because it uses parts of the animal that many dismiss and most have forgotten how to eat. I am often accused of eating haggis more from a sense of bravado than from any enjoyment it may bring. The real issue for many who have been brave enough to eat haggis is that it actually has a taste. So much of our food in Britain these days is 'taste neutral', reduced to the anodyne so that it offends as few people and can shift as much volume as possible. Well, no one can ever accuse the haggis of being bland, but when well made it can be a deliciously savoury treat and worthy of sampling even by the most fearful of diners.

Fortunately I had made back-up plans and they came in the unlikely form of a gentleman by the name of Rhidian Creighton-Stewart. Rhidian was the cousin of a good friend and so obsessed with food that he spent much of his free time working in the kitchens of a Michelin-starred restaurant in Edinburgh. He had agreed to meet me a couple of days later in Scotland's capital. He was a big man who exuded all the enthusiasm that you would expect from a Wallace & Gromit character, an impression not hindered by the fact that he waggled his fingers together and giggled whenever he became excited about food, which happened roughly every thirty seconds during our time together.

He had planned a full day's schedule of eating for me,

which included a trip to a local café for breakfast, a huge lunch at a Chinese restaurant, a visit to Edinburgh's ice cream institution, S. Luca, and supper at not one, but two of his favourite fish and chip shops. But, although these all sounded interesting, if a tad challenging to the colon, it was his mid-morning port of call that had me most excited as he pulled his car up outside a small shop in the neighbourhood of Stockbridge.

George Bower, Butcher & Game Dealer was a real butcher's shop. The street-level shop was filled with links of sausages dangling from metal hooks, chiller cabinets packed with meat already cut into Sunday roast-size joints of pork, beef and lamb and one end of the small room was laid out with pies, black pudding and, of course, haggis. This was real haggis too. I was a great fan of the readily available Macsween version to be found in supermarkets all over the country, but this was a whole different beastie, slightly misshapen and looking like it was ready to burst at any moment and spill its offally guts all over the counter. This was what I had been looking for.

Rhidian, who I now had begun to realize was beguilingly nuts, was well acquainted with the staff at the shop. In fact, they told me, in what spare time he had left after working in the kitchens of the restaurant, he would come in to learn how to cut meat. He was already in the staff room giggling with girlish glee; he picked out a long white coat for me to wear, then scurried down a flight of steep stairs like a ferret into a burrow. The basement was where the real action took place and Mark, the son of the original owner, was ready and waiting to guide me through the haggis-making process.

302

The origins of haggis, or at least of stuffing the insides of animals into a casing made of their stomach to preserve them, do not begin in Scotland, whatever the inhabitants may want you to believe. Some believe haggis arrived in Scotland with Nordic invaders, others that it came from the Romans and their love of sausages and some that it had its first mention in Homer's *Odyssey* where it is referred to as 'stomach full of fat and blood', a reference also taken by black pudding makers as the big bang of their own product.

Whatever the origins, there is no doubting that its spiritual home was here in the lower regions of a small Edinburgh butcher's shop. Florid-faced butchers were carrying complete sides of animals to be sliced and diced, others were plucking the feathers from game birds and yet more were making sausages at a machine that appeared to have been in use for decades.

Mark was standing next to a large steaming pot in which the carcasses of game birds were being boiled to make stock. The air was already filled with rich gamey fumes. He reached into a large plastic container and his hand emerged with a link of wobbling entrails. 'We call this the pluck,' he said, waving aloft his gory handful to the considerable amusement of both Rhidian and two more butchers who had walked over to see what the disturbance was. There was a heart, a liver, a couple of kidneys and some intestine. Mark dunked the lot into the simmering pot, returning the lid to let it cook for a few moments while he prepared the rest of the ingredients. In another bowl he had measured out pinhead oatmeal and what he coyly referred to as 'haggis spices', which as far as a quick sniff could ascertain definitely contained lots of white pepper, a familiar spice in many of the savoury dishes I had encountered so far on my trip.

Once the pluck was cooked Mark passed it through a fine mixer, adding fresh onions for their juices and then spooning in the spices and oatmeal to bind it together. It was now my turn to try my hand at haggis-making and, while the resulting mixture was put into the sausage machine, Mark showed me how to rinse out the ox stomach casing he stored in salt. The piping speed was controlled from a pedal pushed with the knee and my first attempts received ill-hidden guffaws from my audience of ageing meat cleavers. By the third attempt, however, I was in the haggis groove and even Mark had to admit that my final try was 'no too bad'; he posed for a picture with me and my bouncing baby haggis then put it back in the bubbling game stock to cook the casing. When he removed the finished article from the pot and placed it on a metal tray, he cut into it with a long, sharp knife allowing a vapour trail of steam to appear which we all leaned over to sniff before digging in with large mixing spoons.

One taste tells you why haggis is one of the food world's great dividers. There is no hiding from the fact that it is made with offal. The lingering gaminess comes through in every single bite. It tastes like heart. It tastes like liver, it tastes like entrails and it is gloriously unapologetic about what it is, much like the Scots themselves. The haggis at George Bower's was the best I have tried anywhere even if I can understand that not every dish has to be liked by everyone. It is very much the way I feel about Robert Burns's poetry.

# PUDDING

The consumption of sweet things by the British is legendary and in 2006 a report showed that per capita the inhabitants of our small island ate more chocolate than anyone else on earth, around twenty-two pounds per person every year. It says a lot about our country that the preference was still overwhelmingly for milk chocolate, an inferior product where milk and extra sugar are added to compensate for using less of the expensively imported cocoa beans. Volume over quality seems to be the British aim, but it does mean that we are among the biggest consumers of sugar in the world.

Cane sugar first came to Britain in the early 1300s when a single pound would cost the equivalent of over £40, making it a luxury available only to the wealthiest members of society. Everyone else, as they had always done, used honey to sweeten food and drink. It was not until the eighteenth century, which brought with it the growth of British territories in the Caribbean and the discovery that sugar could be extracted from beets, that sugar became more widely available, to the point that by the 1800s Britons were consuming over 30,000 tonnes of sugar from various sources.

Nowhere was this love of sugar more obvious than in

the way we chose to end our meal. Pudding, sweet, afters, no matter what your class or location determined you call it, no meal in Britain, however simple, could be allowed to end without something sweet to polish it off. So were created Britain's legendary desserts and baked goods, one area of the world where our cuisine was held in high regard.

Even if it is a piece of bitter chocolate after a sandwich or an overwrought plate of sugar work as the finale to a fine dining experience, the nation's love of sweet things is not to be underrated and I wanted to find a handful of the most famous desserts Britain has to offer to finish off the perfect evening meal.

## 33
# Steamed Puddings

No book about British food would be complete without a shout-out-loud celebration of our glorious steamed puddings. So hats off to the plum duff, three cheers for sticky toffee and a respectful genuflect before the mighty spotted dick. Be warned, phallocentric humour may well pop up (there you go) in the next few pages.

We take our puddings very seriously in Britain. If you don't believe me just ask the catering staff of Flintshire County Council who, in September 2009, decided to change the name of the country's most humorously named dessert to 'Spotted Richard' because they were becoming weary of the constant flow of 'immature' jokes they received while, er, on the job (there you go again).

You would have expected that their desire not to be exposed (one more time) to a constant flow of knob-related jokes would have met with some sympathy, but the reaction was quite the opposite. Instead of garnering support their decision became something of a cause célèbre and the leader of the county council at the offices in Mold found he was on the receiving end of 'abusive letters' and fielding media questions from all over the world. Such was the furore over what was seen as a politically correct challenge to the British pudding that within two weeks spotted dick took its rightful place back on the canteen menu and the staff were just reminded to keep their smart remarks to themselves when they wanted a bit of dick action (I just can't help myself).

Recent visits to the US have confirmed the opinion that steamed puddings are some of our most misunder-stood dishes. Whenever I have mentioned to just about anybody that I was writing a book about British food, there have been two responses: 'Is there anything good to say about it?' and 'Will you be writing about that dick pudding?' The first can be dismissed as most Americans' well-honed ability to be ignorant of anything outside a twenty-five-mile radius of where they live. The second, while also confirming the first point, also goes to prove that we have done ourselves no favours at all when it comes to giving our food names that might make anyone actually want to eat them.

The same people whose noses would turn skywards at the mention of 'faggots wrapped in caul' would swoon if they were described as *farce en crépinette* and those who ridicule those puddings of ours blessed with unfortunate names would take it all back if they were lucky enough to sample the delicious versions I wolfed down one morning as an unlikely breakfast in Susan Green's kitchen at a small farmhouse in Northumbria.

Records of sweet puddings as part of our dining cul-ture go back to medieval times and savoury ones even further back to the time of the Roman invasion of Britain in 55 BC. The legionary soldiers brought with them many culinary skills, which included making sausages cooked in animal casings. It was a skill that, on the one hand, formed the foundation of savoury black puddings and haggis and on the other led to Britain's proud trad-ition of sweet puddings including Christmas pudding and, of course, spotted dick. The name pudding itself is derived from the Latin *botulus* which also gave rise to the French word *boudin*. Through the Middle Ages, puddings were produced in both savoury and sweet versions. They would often contain both meat and suet, and be boiled in the stomach casing of the animal, but the latter would be sweetened by the addition of dried fruits and honey. When casings were not so readily available, the pudding would be boiled wrapped in linen.

Puddings like these continued to be popular through the Elizabethan period and became particularly successful on the dinner tables of Regency Britain. By the Victorian age, they were a staple in cookery books and the very first mention of spotted dick comes in 1850, in the pages of Alexis Soyer's *The Modern Housewife or Ménagère* with the following recipe, which also goes under the name plum bolster: 'Roll out two pounds of paste [a suet pastry featuring elsewhere in the book], having some Smyrna raisins well washed, and place them on it here and there, roll over, tie in a cloth, and boil one hour, and serve with butter and brown sugar.'

A heavy-sounding dish, which explains why to some people steamed puddings represent the very worst of stodgy British food, designed more to fuel than to inspire. None the less, they remained a staple of the British diet right up until the late 1960s when mass-produced versions had taken the quality down as low as it could possibly go and new trends in health made people quake in terror before anything whose ingredients contained the words 'suet'.

More recently, however, the steamed pudding has been making something of a comeback. The sticky toffee pudding led the fightback after it appeared on the menu of Francis Coulson's Sharrow Bay Country House Hotel in the late 1960s and became almost ubiquitous on British menus well into the 1990s. By then, a whole slew of new celebrity chefs, including Gary Rhodes, Jamie Oliver, Antony Worrall Thompson and Brian Turner, were rediscovering British food, and puddings both sweet and savoury began to reappear on fine dining menus everywhere.

My initial plan had been to approach one of these television luminaries to discuss matters pudding-related. However, one morning I received an e-mail giving me the name and number of Susan Green, a Northumbrian farmer's wife and former solicitor who ran a company called The Proof of the Pudding from her farmhouse kitchen outside the town of Alnwick, in Northumbria. She agreed to let me visit and suggested I arrive as early as possible so I could see the puddings being produced.

As I walked through the door after a drive that had seen me leave home before dawn, Susan already had a kettle on the Aga in anticipation of my arrival. We sipped on a restorative brew and she told me how she set up the company at first to supplement declining income on the farm; however, it had become a sizeable local enterprise in its own right and successful around the country thanks to their increasing mail order business.

Despite the growth, the puddings, which came out of her small kitchen bakery, were still made by hand fresh every day and between them she and two staff produced eight different types. Susan had lined up a display of some of them for me to examine. There was, of course, a sticky toffee pudding, a lemon pudding, golden syrup pudding and last, but very much not least, the truly British classic, spotted dick. After much experimentation, Susan had moved her recipe away from using suet in favour of butter, which made the puddings lighter. Also, where possible, she uses ingredients from local producers and even makes a Christmas pudding laced with the local speciality of Alnwick rum, a combination of rums from Guyana and Jamaica that has been blended in the town for nearly a hundred years.

All that would be very laudable, but if the puddings were no good, quite frankly, who cares? However, in the kitchen, you could see the attention to detail and, even at that time in the morning the smells from the steamer ovens were already beginning to make me drool. Knowing that I had endured a very early start and a long drive, Susan offered me the opportunity to enjoy a pudding-based breakfast. Choosing a sample of spotted dick for me, she pulled it from the steamer where it had been cooking gently, unwrapped it from its linen protection and placed the entire pudding on to a large dinner plate and poured a layer of single cream over it in a perfect single drizzle.

The aroma of butter and spice hit me first as I took my initial scoop. It was much lighter than other steamed puddings I had tried and the insides were speckled as they should be with plump currants like dead flies caught on a sticky paper. It was moist and crumbly, possibly the best of its kind I had ever tried and, trust me, one glimpse of me will tell you that I have tried a few. As proof of its quality, I have a picture somewhere of an entirely empty plate. Not bad work for eight in the morning.

After I left, pudding-filled and content, I realized that

eating food like Susan Green's exemplary puddings is what makes me really happy. It would seem that I am not alone and judging from Susan's order books many people are rediscovering pride in the great desserts of Great Britain.

Let us all praise the pudding. But, if we have time, perhaps we can all come up with some better names.

## 34

# Trifle

In an article in the *New York Times* on 27 March 1988 a journalist called Rita D. Jacobs described sherry trifle as the 'quintessential English dessert', going on to say that every time she asked any British person for their trifle recipe they invariably began, 'Me mother . . .', which obviously means she gleaned her vast knowledge of our country almost entirely by watching Dick Van Dyke in *Mary Poppins*. She also states with some certainty in the article that 'men's clubs in Britain always have trifle on the menu'. I suspect by this she was referring to the great gentlemen's clubs of London like the Garrick and the Athenaeum, and not the Greasbrough Working Men's Club near Rotherham where I could get 50p pints of Wards Bitter as a teenager, although I did have to resist the urge to call and ask if they would fax through their pudding menu to test the theory.

'Keith, some lad on t'phone wants to know if we do trifle, what shall I tell 'im?'

'Tell him we're a club and to fook off to Aldi.'

Despite Ms Jacobs's limited knowledge of Britain, there is little doubt that she is correct in one respect. This classic combination of booze-soaked sponge, jam, custard and cream, topped with almonds is among Britain's best loved desserts and is made the world over, one of the few dishes where 'traditional English' is not a cause for concern when used before an item of food. Back in the UK, there can be very few Sunday lunches or Christmas Day celebrations where a meal somewhere does not end with a large glass bowl on the table displaying perfect layers of the correct ingredients.

Trifle takes its name from the French word *trufle,* literally meaning a whimsy or deceit, a small fancy to amuse the diner, the perfect name for something that is one of the great celebratory desserts. There is little or no nutritional benefit in a trifle, it doesn't serve to fuel bodies for a hard day's labour, nor was it born out of necessity to make the most of available ingredients. Trifle is a luxurious wonder. At its very best it should use fine ingredients and should serve no other purpose than to taste great and entertain diners at the end of a meal.

The making of trifle is a tradition that can be traced back to the sixteenth century and has its origins in popular desserts of the day, the syllabub, the flummery and the fool. These were whipped confections made of cream, fruit and juices or alcohol that, because they were served cold rather than hot like sweets such as possets, could be brought to the table in the latest invention of clear glass bowls, which displayed the marbling of their contents for the appreciation of guests at fine dinners.

The first recipe I could find for anything remotely resembling a trifle is in *The Good Huswifes Jewell,* a cookery book written by Thomas Dawson in 1585. Although it bears scant resemblance to the modern trifle, the contents of thickened cream, sugar, ginger and rosewater would still be familiar to most cooks today, as would the method of preparation. 'Take a pinte of thicke Creame, and season it with Sugar and Ginger, and

Rosewater, so stirre it as you would then have it, and make it luke warme in a dish on a Chafingdish and coals, and after put it into a silver piece or bowle, and so serve it to the boorde.'

In the mid-1700s Joseph Cooper, cook to King Charles I, recorded a new addition in the form of a base of biscuits soaked in 'sack' wine, the English name for wines from Málaga and Jerez later to be known as sherry. By the time the ever dependable Hannah Glasse got around to writing her recipe for trifle in the eighteenth century, it was lacking only fruit to make it a dish that could be placed on a modern-day dining table, although the topping continued to be made of syllabub rather than cream well into the nineteenth century.

Like so many dishes in the UK, if people express a negative opinion of trifle it is often a result of their childhood experiences of the dark culinary days of the 1960s and '70s when they were presented with a dish produced from dry, commercially made sponges drizzled with Bird's Custard (I actually like Bird's Custard, but we'll speak of that later), jelly made from a packet, a topping made from Instant Whip and a sprinkling of hundreds and thousands.

Many people will still quake in terror when their dinner host announces that a meal is to be ended with a 'traditional trifle', usually because the tradition they are following dates back to a time not much before the advent of colour television when trifle was the alternative to that other much maligned dessert, Black Forest gateau. However, as I have said time and again in *Eating for Britain*, when well made with the right ingredients and a little patience, the trifle is as delicious and as worthy of respect as any dessert you will try anywhere in the world.

Given that it is such a British creation, it may seem curious to find out that the poor person I selected to help me make the perfect trifle was not British and carried with her the rather un-Albion-like moniker of Signe Skaimsgard Johansen. Signe is, as the name suggests, primarily of Norwegian stock with a bit of American thrown in somewhere along the line. She is strikingly attractive in a willowy Scandinavian with long blonde hair and steely grey-blue eyes kind of way and goes about her daily business entirely unaware of the effect she is having on the half of the world's population that wears Y-fronts. Shallow although I most certainly am, Signe's looks were not my main reason for choosing her as my cooking accomplice. She also happens to be a very accomplished baker and assured me that somewhere in the mix she was at least one-quarter British and that her considerable skills in the kitchen came as much from that small portion of her DNA as they did from the Norwegian root stock that gave her her name and her car-crash-causing appearance.

She had read a post on my blog where I had been pontificating about my firmly entrenched belief that 'real men don't bake'. I should qualify that. It is not that I believe that real men shouldn't bake at all, but only comestibles of a savoury nature. Any sweet, frivolous and fancy creations should, of course, be left to those of the opposite genital grouping. Blame it on my Yorkshire heritage if you will but, as I have mentioned before, I have always found the notion of men baking cakes rather suspect and her enthusiasm to prove to me that I could enjoy making something that did not contain dead animals made me hesitate a little as I began to tie a manly apron (and not a pinny, I deny that completely) across my rounded stomach. I wondered if I would be drummed out of the London branch of the Professional Northerners Club if word got out that I was going to be making a trifle. Signe, however, was having none of it and gave me a trademark steely blue stare until I was suitably clothed and had washed my hands.

Scrubbed up to the high standards her Nordic background demanded, we finally began our preparations. Although I soon realized that my presence was not really required to help make the trifle. I was forcibly pushed to one side and she took total control of the proceedings. My role, it became apparent, was a simple one: to pour enough drinks to keep up with Signe's prodigious appetite for distilled grain and fermented grape. So, as I chilled, measured, stirred, poured and garnished, Signe started by showing me how to make the essential ingredients for all true English trifles, custard. In this case with sugar, the deeply yellow yolks of five free-range eggs and an equal mixture of cream and milk flavoured with flecks from a fresh vanilla pod.

Recipes for custard go back as far as the invading Romans who brought with them to Britain the skill of thickening sauces with eggs, and also more recently to the Middle Ages, where custards could be both sweet and savoury dishes. Some of the latter remain on our menus, like the French parfait, which are in effect little more than savoury egg custards.

Perhaps the most famous character in British custard's history timeline is Alfred Bird. Bird was a Midlands' chemist who first started using cornflour instead of eggs in custard in 1837 because of his wife's allergy to things that had emanated from a chicken's backside. It was only when some was served to guests by mistake at a dinner party that he realized he was on to something and the Bird's Custard that we all know and love was the end result.

As I think I mentioned, I like Bird's Custard. It has all sorts of unexpected uses as well as the rather obvious one of, er, making custard. I was once told by the chef of a respected Chinese restaurant in London that the perfect coating for sweet and sour pork was achieved by tossing the meat in Bird's Custard Powder before frying. Suspecting I was the butt of a joke, I tried it at home. It works a treat. Yet, despite its longevity and the affection in which many people hold the brand, it also carries with it bitter memories of darker times and associations with Britain's food at its very worst. More importantly, as Signe showed me, the real thing made with eggs and cream is so much better and too simple to make for you, me, or anyone else to resort to a packet of powder.

Signe gave a slight shiver as she took her first sip of drink number one, a standard but powerful martini, made with four parts chilled Beefeater gin, stirred with one part dry vermouth served in a frozen glass with a lemon twist. She then returned her attention to scalding equal mixtures of cream and milk until they came to a gentle boil. In a bowl she beat together the five egg yolks and caster sugar, adding them to the milk, which had been allowed to cool so we produced custard rather than sweet scrambled eggs. She stirred the mixture slowly over a very low heat until the eggs had begun to set it enough to coat the back of a spoon. Apart from adding the contents of a vanilla pod, that was it and the custard was made.

I chose that moment to deliver drink number two. As you may well be aware, the second cocktail of any drinking session has been scientifically proven to be the best. This time it was a particularly lethal brew combining gin and fresh lime juice to potent effect. We clicked glasses and both downed half in one gulp, beginning to sway rather alarmingly as we continued our trifling exploits. This probably explains the crooked layering of sponge fingers we placed on the bottom of our presentation bowl and the over-liberal hand as we doused it with sherry.

There are heated arguments in the cut-throat world of trifle-making as to whether you should include fresh fruit, tinned fruit, or even fruit set in jelly. I love jelly and like so many other people of my generation used to wail at my mother until she agreed to prepare it as a teatime treat. This was not so much because of the end result, which I could take or leave, but so I could snaffle a square of concentrated proto-jelly as it was being prepared. However, in a trifle, adding jelly is obviously just wrong on too many levels to discuss here. Anyone who commits such a culinary crime should be shunned from normal society like the Amish would someone with an iPhone. Fresh fruit is just about acceptable but does not take into account the winter origins of the dish. Signe, having done her research, quite rightly had insisted on the very traditional option, adding a layer of her own home-made strawberry jam. When the custard had set sufficiently, she spread the jam on top and then added a layer of thick cream, which she had whipped to a stiff consistency with a hand already unsteady from alcohol consumption.

Drink number three was more of a challenge and I had to improvise, rooting around in Signe's frighteningly sparse collection of spirits until I found some inspiration. I think it was Nick Hornby who once said that men never like staying at their girlfriends' apartments because they have no beer in the fridge, no cable television and lousy music collections. He is spot-on, of course, but should also have added that most women almost always have totally rubbish collections of hard liquor, often limited to curiosities they have found and brought back from holidays to Ibiza. Signe's collection was no different and finally, after working my way through bottles of un-identifiable alcoholic cordials, I settled on a dusty bottle of Johnnie Walker Green Label, which looked like it had been in place since her apartment had been constructed. Using some of the manzanilla sherry that was left from dousing the sponge cake, I made a quirky version of a Manhattan, served in another chilled martini glass, this time with a twist of orange peel.

Signe took a deep gulp of the improvised brew, but by now we were both probably too drunk to care about my cocktail wizardry or the state either we or indeed the trifle were in. She sucked in a deep breath and composed herself enough to dress the top of the trifle with toasted flaked almonds and some sweet blackberries before returning it to the fridge for a final few hours to set. People who know about this sort of thing tell me that a trifle should be left for a day before it is ready to eat. Their reasoning is that this allows the top layers to seep slowly downwards through the lower layers and along the sides of the bowl to produce the marbling effect that is the sign of a truly well-made trifle.

Neither Signe nor I had the time or the inclination to postpone our trifling pleasures for a whole day, and one hour and one more stupidly large cocktail later, we lurched from her living room into the kitchen and retrieved the tempting-looking dessert from the fridge. She scooped large amounts on to two plates with a serving spoon and we swayed our way gingerly back towards the sofa, flopping down while trying not to cover ourselves with a coating of Britain's most celebrated pudding.

As far as my pickled taste buds would allow me to discern, it tasted rather good, better than it had any right to be considering how drunk we were by this stage in the day. When we summoned up enough coordination to get spoon from plate to mouth with some trifle attached, I discovered that the layers had retained enough of their individual identity so that you could differentiate the vanilla custard from the cream and that in turn from the sharpness of the strawberry jam. A Victorian triumph of a dessert, in fact, thanks primarily to the skills of my chum, Signe Skaimsgard Johansen, who showed admirable ability to cook 'under pressure' shall we say?

I played my own part in the whole process too and while I mixed cocktails gave great observation. If I can impart one sage piece of advice to anyone considering embarking upon their own similar pudding, it would be that to make the perfect trifle it is absolutely imperative that you are as soaked in booze as the sponge cake on the bottom.

## 35
# Eccles Cake

There is one very odd group of travellers whose motivation I am afraid I have never quite been able to understand. They are the gastro-tourist. The person, usually and necessarily very wealthy, who flies off solely to eat at the world's fine dining establishments. They use as their Bible the latest Michelin guide or list of the top fifty restaurants in the world as promulgated by *Restaurant* magazine and their aim appears to be to tick off as many of the restaurants on their list as possible, irrespective of whether they enjoy their meals or not. They will often turn down the opportunity of eating at excellent restaurants recommended by locals because there is no kudos to be gained from their peers by dining at somewhere unknown. In the end, the quality of what they eat is less important than the fact they have visited the restaurant itself. They are, to all intents and purposes, train spotters with bigger wallets.

I have a reason for this angsty little diatribe, so bear with me if you will. In the last decade or so, among this rather odd elite group of people, the humble Eccles cake has become a 'must have' dish. It is not, of course, because any of the diners have been or have any intention of ever going to Eccles. Indeed most of them would be unaware that it is a place and struggle to find Britain on the map, let alone Lancashire. The reason why it has become so famous is that the Eccles cake is the dessert of choice at one of London's most famous restaurants, St John. Since the restaurant opened well over a decade ago, Fergus Henderson's nose-to-tail approach to cookery, using every available part of the animal, has made St John a unique part of London's dining scene and a definite for dining list-tickers everywhere. The Eccles cake is served alongside a slab of Mrs Kirkham's sharp and delicious Lancashire cheese and always proves to be the perfect full stop to an interesting meal. Thanks to this adoption by the gastro-tourist crowd, the Eccles cake has become famous, almost revered, which I imagine would amuse the people of Lancashire no end if they cared.

Although I have seen reference to Eccles cakes being banned as too frivolous by the Puritans in the mid-1600s there is no supporting evidence that they were around until a recipe appeared for them in a cookery book entitled *The Experienced English Housekeeper* written by Elizabeth Raffald from Cheshire. Her recipe for 'sweet patties' is very similar to the one we know today and made its way to Eccles where they were also known as church cakes, taking their name from the Latin origins of Eccles's own name, Ecclesia.

According to Alan Davidson's incomparable *The Oxford Companion to Food*, James Birch, a local shopkeeper in this small town near Salford, became the first person to produce Eccles cakes commercially, selling squat cakes made of flaky pastry filled with raisins at his local market in the late 1700s. About twenty years later, his apprentice, William Bradburn, set up his own rival establishment. The cakes became hugely popular and were soon made in other neighbouring towns. Almost as

famous as the Eccles cake are the versions from nearby
Chorley, which have a similar fruit filling but differ in
that they are made with shortcrust pastry and are sold
without the dusting of sugar, a prerequisite of the ideal
Eccles cake.

As when I visited Lancashire in search of the perfect
hot pot I had plenty of options to find the perfect Eccles
cake. I tried them at St John, of course. They were
excellent and good enough for me to buy a bagful to
take away with me. But there was a lingering feeling that
it was still an ersatz version of the real thing, the same
feeling I get when I eat fish and chips in London. They
can be good, but they can never be quite right. The true
notion of eating local food is not just about sourcing
the ingredients, it is also about the context in which the
meal is eaten and so to find the perfect Eccles cake, I
would have to head back up to the wrong side of the
Pennines.

On my way I stopped to visit Bury Market, which is
one of the oldest in the country and according to a sign
at the entrance 'famous', although there is little indication as to why among the grim stalls. In the centre of the
market, I noticed a long line of people outside the stand
of local bakery Harry Muffin's. I joined the queue and
began chatting with the elderly ladies in front and behind
me. Harry Muffin's was selling both Eccles cakes and
Chorley cakes and I asked my queuing companions
which they preferred.

This prompted an improbably heated argument, not
only as to which I should buy (for the record, I purchased
both) but also how they were best eaten.

'I like mine wi' cream, love,' one said, while the others

all shook their heads as if she had instructed me to punch the Queen hard in the face.

There was a sharp intake of breath and another said, 'Not wi' cream, that's barmy. You just want it wi' tea, love, just wi' tea.'

The arguing was still going on when I reached the front of the queue and purchased my cakes. I beat a swift retreat as they looked close to coming to blue-rinsed blows. They obviously take their cakes very seriously in Lancashire.

Whatever the rights and wrongs of how they should be eaten, the cakes from Harry Muffin's were really very good, less luxurious than the St John version, but pleasingly dense and filling. Enough to fuel me for the rest of the journey as I headed back again to the Hastings in Lytham St Annes to put myself in the hands of my new chum, Warrick Dodds. He had not let me down with the hot pot and seemed confident that he could show me how to make the perfect Eccles cake.

In many of the old recipes I found online, the dried fruit filling, which led to their affectionate local nickname of 'dead fly pies', had been soaked in brandy or rum. This may well have increased the length of time they could be stored and there are records of them being exported as far away as the US by the early 1800s. Warrick's version of the classic Eccles cake gave a nod to the modern zero tolerance towards drink-driving and he had instead soaked his dried fruit in a mixture of Earl Grey tea along with lemon and orange zest, sugar and spices.

After the Eccles cake had been prepared, Warrick sat with me in the dining room of the Hastings, watching my face intently as he gently poured a trickle of fresh custard over the golden brown cake with its crunchy caramelized crust.

The first bite tells you all you need to know. It was rich but not stodgy, the soaked fruit gave up the individual flavours of each component of its soaking liquor and the flaky pastry crust was buttery but with a perfect crunch on the outside. It was as good a pudding as you are ever likely to try and is definitely worth trying to prepare yourself.

According to the Eccles Council's website, there is a saying in the town, 'The secret dies with me', showing how fiercely they protect their recipe. Warrick, however, has been kind enough to share his own secret for this sublime Eccles cake and I can tell you that even if you have not been to the required percentage of famous restaurants to be allowed into the exclusive Gastro-Diners Club, it's still well worth trying.

## — *Eccles Cake* —

(MAKES FOUR INDIVIDUAL ECCLES CAKES)

*250fl oz water*
*100g sugar*
*1 teaspoon ground cinnamon*
*zest of 1 orange*
*zest of 1 lemon*
*1 Earl Grey tea bag*
*1kg sultanas*
*1 teaspoon icing sugar*
*4 round sheets of puff pastry (approx. 20cm diameter)*

Boil the water and then add the sugar, ground cinnamon, orange and lemon zests.

Reduce the liquid by one-third and add the Earl Grey tea bag. Allow the tea to infuse for at least 3 minutes and remove the pan from the heat, discarding the tea bag.

Add the sultanas and leave to soak in the tea mixture for 1 hour as it cools and then add the icing sugar to sweeten it.

Dust each round sheet of puff pastry with a little sugar and then place each in a small, shallow 10cm diameter dish so that the pastry overlaps the sides. Put 250g of the sultana mix inside each and flatten with the back of a spoon. Fold over the overlapping pastry so the sultanas are completely covered.

Turn the dishes upside down, allowing your Eccles cakes to fall on to the work surface. Sprinkle with sugar and bake on greaseproof paper in a preheated oven at 180°C/350°F/gas mark 4 until the pastry is golden brown and crisp. This will take 25–30 minutes depending on your oven.

Serve with warm English custard.

## 36
## Bakewell Pudding

If I were to believe all the legends I heard on my travels around the country, just about every dish we love in Britain was created by accident. The farmers of Arbroath, apparently, were unable to prevent their cottages bursting into flames at the sight of a haddock, and the same is true further down the coast in Craster when herring were the piscine culprits. It's usually total nonsense, but a culinary culture is often born of such old wives' tales and in one or two cases there may even be a tiny grain of truth to the stories.

Take the most famous dish of Bakewell, for example. No self-respecting denizen of this small Derbyshire town would ever call their most famous dish a 'tart', dismissing such things as a horror reserved for the shelves of their local discount supermarket. What you get in Bakewell is a pudding and, if the stories of the locals are to be believed, its creation owes a vote of thanks to a culinary misadventure.

The Rutland Arms stands on the main thoroughfare as you enter the town. Originally called the White Horse Inn, it is now circumnavigated by a one-way system, slightly too complex for such a small town. Back in the early 1800s it was one of the first coaching inns carriages would see as they made their way into Bakewell, a welcome sight after crossing the Peak District and a good stopping-off point to feed and water the horses before continuing the journey northwards.

The landlady of the White Horse Inn at the time, Mrs Greaves, was, according to the legend, well known for her jam tarts, which were made with a sweet, rich pastry containing almonds, sugar and eggs. On one particularly hectic day, she had passed the task of making the tarts on to a new cook who, misunderstanding the instructions, used the mixture of eggs, almonds, butter and sugar as a filling for some blind-baked pastry rather than adding it to the pastry itself. As it cooked, the jam rose through the paste of almonds on top and created a skin with a golden-brown glaze. Without the time or the ingredients to make another batch, Mrs Greaves was forced to serve the results to her guests that night and was astonished to find it was greeted with universal praise, but not too astonished quickly to realize she was on to something special and add it to the menu. What we call a Bakewell tart bears precious little resemblance to the original and only became known by the name when manufacturers wanted to persuade people that it was a cake to be eaten with tea rather than, as the name suggests, a pudding to be eaten after a meal.

When Mrs Greaves died, the recipe was handed on, some say to a Mrs Bloomer and others to Mrs Wilson, a local candlestick maker. Both women established shops in the town making the pudding and both shops still exist, a few short steps from each other, and each lays claim to be the original purveyor of fine puddings to the discerning. There is obviously a certain local licence at play in the story since egg tarts, sometimes called fla-thons, had been made in Britain for well over a century before, but this tale does seem to be a more legitimate claim than many I heard as I ate my way around the country.

Until my visit to Bakewell, the wrangling between two tiny Derbyshire bakeries had never really caused me to lose much sleep. I had never been a fan of the mass-market versions of the tart I had been presented with as a child which were a million miles from the real thing: shortcrust pastry filled with frangipane and covered in a slick of icing topped with a strategically placed glacé cherry. However, in the interest of culinary discovery and to maintain my mantra that 'I do it, so you don't have to' I tossed a coin to choose which of the two claimants I was going to visit and found myself knocking on the door of the Old Original Bakewell Pudding Company at a little before 8 a.m. one frosty morning.

I was greeted by Jemma Pheasey who is Bakewell born and bred and has worked at the bakery for over twelve years. She led me up a flight of stairs to a small, smart tearoom above the bakery for a quick history lesson before I went to the kitchens to try to make my own pudding. The Old Original Bakewell Pudding Company is still on the site of Mrs Wilson's candle shop, and Jemma explained that the puddings are still being made in exactly the same manner and with the same ingredients as they always have been since 1820 when the shop was opened. There cannot be too many things, apart from syphilis and an inbuilt dislike of Scousers, that have remained part of British culture for nearly 200 years, so I was keen to see if the real thing lived up to expectation. The smell emanating from the kitchens and making its way up through the gaps in the wooden floorboards to my nostrils was enough to confirm that the baking of the day's batch of puddings was well under way.

Norman, the baker, has been working at the Old Original Bakewell Pudding Shop for over thirty years and every single one of the 4,000 puddings a week the kitchen produces is rolled, filled and baked by his hands. As I watched him turn out pudding after pudding with perfect results, it looked easy enough and I was keen to give it a try myself. Inevitably, it is not as easy as it looks and my own attempts to form a pudding from the simple ingredients of puff pastry, jam and almond paste were enough to draw giggles from the rest of the bakery staff as my efforts were put to one side by Jemma never to see the inside of an oven and probably to be discarded in disgust the moment I left the shop.

Instead, we decided the best option was to sample some puddings that had already been cooking in the oven for forty minutes. As we removed them, they emerged in a waft of sweet steam, the tops a golden brown and the pastry casings curly and misshapen as they should be. Jemma selected two for me to try and we walked back upstairs to the tearoom. Just as there is debate about the origins of the pudding, so there is debate among the locals as to whether they should be eaten hot or cold. Jemma put a plate bearing a cold pudding in front of me. The puff pastry had become slightly more solid as it cooled, so that it cracked under the pressure from my fork and the filling had set to a soft creamy texture. It was delicious, unlike any version I had tasted before, and certainly a million miles from the mass-produced version. But it paled beside the warm pie she placed in front of me next. Steam rose gently from the generous slice, disappearing when it was doused with a thin drizzle of single cream. The pastry this time was still soft, incredibly rich and buttery, flaking in the mouth as I bit into it. The filling melted on the tongue as it dissolved away into an almond aftertaste that lingered until the next bite began the process all over again.

Puddings like this are something we in Britain do better than anyone else on earth and yet, like so many other products, we have allowed mass-produced and debased versions to proliferate until people can declare that 'I don't like X' without ever having tasted the real thing. The recent rush to secure Product of Geographical Importance for British products is helping to stem the tide. It would ensure that only those examples made to a specific recipe in the specified region can carry the name and at least then people could judge whether they liked something or not based on tasting a properly made version.

Jemma waved a thick file at me containing a couple of trees worth of paperwork needed to begin the process of applying for protected status. It's not an easy task and requires cooperation between the rival producers, something often easier said than done. I know for certain that I would not have had the time or the patience to deal with the bureaucracy involved in filling in all the forms but Jemma seemed determined. I can only hope it results in people all over the country having the chance to sample what I was eating as I sat in the small tearoom of the Old Original Bakewell Pudding Company: a delicious British food that goes to prove that sometimes the best things do happen by accident.

— *Drinks* —

Without the skill and ingenuity of the British, the world of alcohol would be a lot less interesting. The dry martini would consist of nothing but warm vermouth if we had not created London dry gin, there would be no Scotch whisky to warm the cockles on a cold winter's day and champagne would not have become a 'go to' drink in times of celebration. Sherry, port and madeira would have remained regional specialities, Bordeaux just another French wine region and the current number of beer brewers in the world poorer by over 600. Britons not only love booze in all its many forms, but we excel at making it.

However, Britain's relationship with alcohol has always been an uneasy one. From the appalling reputation of Elizabethan England's bawdy ale-houses, through the 'dead drunk for tuppence' gin-fuelled nightmare of Hogarth's eighteenth-century London, right down to the contemporary scenes of mini-skirted teenage girls splayed on the kerb after five alcopops too many or louts swilling from cans of cheap lager and using any stationary item available as a urinal.

It is a relationship that has been created by pulpit and parliament and made worse by both over successive generations as drink has been demonized on the one hand and made freely available at ridiculous prices on the other. Only a country with a truly bi-polar attitude towards booze could have sanctioned our antediluvian licensing laws, which restricted pub opening times making drink a race against the clock and at the same time reduced tax to allow supermarkets to promote bulk purchase by often selling distilled and brewed products more cheaply than water.

While the fact that numbers of alcohol-related injuries and illnesses are higher here than in just about any other nation in Europe confirms just how unhealthy a relationship we have as a nation with grain and grape, the fact remains that without our efforts the world of booze would be a much poorer place.

What kind of host would I be if I spent all this time talking about the best things to eat in Britain and did not even offer you something to drink?

# 37
## Beer

It happens just once a year, a rare convergence that puts TGS and me in a singular consensus and gives a joint sense of purpose that could move mountains and defeat armies. Gone are the normal squabbles over the fair portioning of a rib of beef, the failings of an imperfectly prepared martini or the disappearance of a bar of chocolate from the fridge. In their place comes a sense of giddy enthusiasm that can mean only one thing in the Dos Hermanos calendar. It is almost time for our annual visit to the Great British Beer Festival.

The Great British Beer Festival began in 1977 and since then has grown to be one of the largest events of its kind anywhere in the world. In 2009 almost 70,000 people made their way through the doors of Earls Court to sample more than one of the 500 beers on offer, confirming its claim to be the 'biggest pub in the world' and one of the must-not-miss events for beer lovers everywhere.

The festival has become something of a tradition for TGS. Months before the day itself, he is already well in advance with his planning as he scours the website of the Campaign for Real Ale (CAMRA), looking to see which breweries might be the likely contenders for honours at the prestigious event. When the big moment arrives, he will have our plan of attack all mapped out and, by the time the doors open bang on midday on the Thursday of the festival, our traditional day for visiting, he will know exactly to which stand we will be heading for our first of far too many pints.

Like so many men of a certain age in the United Kingdom, the pub has always played a central part in my life. When I hit sixteen, in an all too rare gift from God, I suddenly sprouted enough hairs from my upper lip to allow me to fashion a rudimentary Zapata moustache. It didn't seem to help in my other quest of 'pulling the best lasses', in fact it seemed further to reinforce my ability to repel them. It did, however, act as sufficient disguise to persuade the stout barmaids at our local pub, the New Broom, that I was old enough to be served a pint.

In this case, the beer in question was Sam Smith's Bitter and, if I was being honest, I hated it. The palates of young people are simply not calibrated to enjoy bitter tastes (something to do with protecting babies from eating poisonous food, I am told) and the use of hops in traditional bitter-making would make me shudder with each sip. I may not have enjoyed the beer very much, but I adored the pub. I loved the fact that, like many traditional old-school drinking establishments, it had two rooms. The Lounge Bar was smarter and filled with couples; the men drank pints and the women would sip on halves from a 'ladies glass' with a tall stem. There would be food on offer and the only sound to be heard above the talking would be the occasional clattering as someone won a few quid on the slot machine.

I didn't go into the Lounge Bar much and, to be honest, from the faces of the men trapped there, they would rather have been joining me in the Tap Room.

This was where the real men hung out. A thick fug of smoke clung to the yellowing ceiling like a prayer rising to heaven and everywhere you looked there was activity. Behind the bar, women with muscular right arms drew beer with hand pumps from barrels in the cellar. A fiercely competitive darts game would always be taking place, the scoring done by a man who probably left school at fifteen, but could work out the calculations at a speed that would have come from days spent at the bookie's. At some point during the evening, two men would walk around the bar. One would be selling raffle tickets for some unspecified charity, the other proudly carrying the star prize, a tray of rapidly defrosting meat that would then sit warming up nicely by the till until the draw was made just before closing time.

I sat with my treasured pint in front of me, an outward and visible sign to the whole world that I was an adult. It was in pubs like these that my understanding of what it meant to be a man was formed. Just about every lesson as to what life would require of me could be taught in the Tap Room of the New Broom pub in Rotherham. I was not alone, of course, and for generations boys learned how to become men at pubs all over the country.

FAIRNESS: 'I think this lad was waiting to be served before me.'

COMPASSION: 'She's not worth it, let me get you a pint in.'

RETRIBUTION: 'Did you just knock my pint?'

Move forward nearly thirty years and things are changing. While many traditional pubs still remain, they no longer fulfil such an important role in our society and many have been transformed from places where socialization took place alongside the drinking to being simply a delivery system for alcohol. People are deserting them in such numbers that in 2008 it was reported that over 2,000 pubs had called 'last orders' for the final time, closing their doors as landlords decided they had better things to do with their money than dispense beer and urinal cakes.

The reasons are many, but have their roots back in the late 1980s when Margaret Thatcher's government decided to break the monopoly of 'tied houses' where pubs were contracted to sell only beer from a particular brewery. The government's aim was to promote free trade, but misunderstood that while the breweries obviously wanted a profit, their main aim was to provide a consistent outlet for their product, and within that model there was plenty of room for landlords to make a decent living.

The new model allowed for the creation of 'Pub Companies', publicly owned companies whose only concern was profit and who would replace landlords with tame managers who would do as they were told and sell what they were told to sell. Long-serving staff were replaced by poorly trained staff who did not earn enough to care if you had a good time or not. Worst of all, the product was altered from one that needed care and attention to be served in prime condition to one that could be dispensed by a monkey as long as it could push a button. To this was added the ban on smoking in public places in 2007, which meant that those who had not given up cigarettes, or indeed did not want to, were exiled to the social Siberia of the pavement. And, just to make sure there was a real disincentive ever to visit a pub, the taxation of alcohol was altered to create a huge differential between the cost of buying a drink in a pub and the cost of buying the equivalent in a supermarket for consumption at home.

If all this makes it sound like the world is ganging up on the poor old pub, let us not forget that they too have been pretty active in ensuring their own demise as they face challenges not just from other suppliers of alcohol but also from other forms of entertainment. Pubs can no longer survive just as watering holes for the working man, primarily because, as with Britain's change from a manufacturing society to a service society, there aren't enough working men left to support them and too many have failed to appeal to a wider audience that includes women and families.

It's an unhappy picture and one brought into sharp relief every year by the Great British Beer Festival, because, although our pubs are in real danger of becoming a memory in less than a generation, Britain still produces some of the finest beer in the world and there are over 600 breweries active in the UK.

When the day arrives for our visit to the festival TGS and I are both ready in good time, having squeezed in a quick gym session to put some plus points in the fitness bank for the bad behaviour ahead. We arrive at Earls Court with a few minutes to spare before opening and soon confirm that although the efforts of the organizers to attract women and the younger generation have met with some success, the truth remains that the main demographic of those attending the festival is identical to the one you would get at a Barclay James Harvest reunion concert. Protruding bellies are very much in evidence, usually straining against the flimsy material of printed T-shirts whose messages proclaim the real ale allegiance of the wearer. 'What's the matter, lager boy? Frightened?'

There is more hair protruding from ears and noses than there is from skulls and many of the attendees are carrying flasks and Tupperware boxes, suggesting that the rest of their spare time is spent happily seated on fold-out stools on train station platforms all over the country. The atmosphere is one of excitement and good humour and when the doors finally open the surge forward is not the baying horror of a pop concert or football match, but a patient shuffle as people wave their tickets at the volunteers who man the turnstiles.

In the main hall, the scale of the event becomes apparent. Each section of the arena represents a region of the country and behind the counters more volunteers dispense pints, half pints and tastes. The choice is bewildering and in previous years, where youthful exuberance led us to rush straight to the strongest beers, we peaked too early and by early afternoon could be found sleeping it off soundly on one of the tables provided by the organizers for picnics.

Now, more experienced and with wisdom that comes only with age and regret, we dedicate most of our day to sampling that most unfashionable of beers, mild. Mild beers have been produced in Britain for over 400 years and right up to the early 1980s few pubs did not offer this lower alcohol alternative to bitter or lager. More recently, however, it became hugely unfashionable, being associated with old men in flat caps and would have disappeared altogether had it not been for the rise in numbers of micro-breweries. It is a great shame, because a classic dark mild is a lovely, complex drink. The colour comes from the use of roasted malt barley in the brewing process and can produce a rich, almost chocolate taste that belies its alcohol level which can sometimes even dip below the 3 per cent ABV level. For us, it is the perfect session beer choice and one that allows us to sample a wide range as we walk around the hall looking for the next likely brew.

There has to be food, of course, something to soak up all the booze. While, along with their attempts to attract more women, CAMRA have also added new and more varied food offerings, the idea of Thai fish cakes holds little appeal as we stick to the tried and tested blotting paper of more traditional pub food. That, naturally, can only mean one thing, pork scratchings, those glorious rinds of pork, deep-fried and then, just to make sure your cardiologist has no tears left to shed, tossed in salt; and those sold at the Great British Beer Festival are some of the best anywhere. Big chunks of crispy pork fat to be fought over as we prop ourselves up against a bar and rip open the white paper bag containing our lunch, a perfect combination with a pint of mild.

By mid-afternoon, both we and just about everybody else in the festival are in fine form. The good humour continues and we have enough beer and scratchings in our stomachs to convince us that it would have been a day well spent even if we left now. Then TGS utters those words that I have been dreading and hoped would be forgotten. 'Let's go and have some cider.'

Our day at the festival is split into two very distinct

sections. BC (Before Cider) is a happy time, filled with beardy bonhomie, good humour and jolly fooling. AC (After Cider) is a darker, more challenging time filled with regret, bitterness and not a little self-loathing. The cider here is the real deal, flat and powerful enough to knock you over after one sniff. This is not cider served over ice for pretty people with perfect teeth in television commercials. This is cider for hairy-chested men. It is flat, warm and very, very frightening stuff and the first sip takes me over the edge from what I call 'happily drunk' to 'Mother of God, the walls are closing in'.

It is all downhill AC and, although we usually squeeze in a couple more half-pints, it is soon time to leave the festival and head home, clutching our commemorative glasses for dear life as we sway our way to the tube station. As we leave, one of us invariably makes the observation about how ironic it is that inside the hall there are hundreds of beers being kept in perfect condition and served properly. Yet, outside the hall, you would struggle to find one pub within a mile radius that would serve a half-decent pint.

We may make some of the best beer in the world, but if our pubs don't improve and get some help, soon we will have nowhere to serve it. It's a depressing thought.

# 38
## Gin

I don't think that it is going to come as any great surprise to, well, just about anybody, if I announce that feeding my obsession for food comes at a heavy price. The constant battle against spreading girth is only part of the struggle and, at forty-six years old, my body is showing signs of wear and tear normally expected in someone who watches the letterbox for a telegram from Her Majesty.

Don't laugh, but the main ailment I have to contend with is gout. I told you not to laugh. You are not going to believe me when I tell you that my suffering from this most painful of rheumatic conditions is not just a result of my over-indulgences, but it's true. Gout is one of the generous hereditary gifts from my father to all the Majumdar clan and, although I am sure my intake of red meat has not made matters any better, I can at least take solace in the fact that it would have happened anyway. It usually manifests itself with a dull ache in the middle of the night, which, if you were not aware that it was the onset of gout, would convince you that you had dislocated your toe. Act now, with a strong painkiller and anti-inflammatory and you might just be lucky. Fail to react and within hours even the faint touch of the lightest bedclothes will be enough to have you in tears of agony and the next few days will be spent in the terrified contemplation of pulling a pair of shoes over your swollen big toe. Thanks, Baba.

You may be wondering by now what any of this has to do with gin. Well, as I began my research for this chapter, I was delighted to find out that one of the original uses of gin was as a cure-all for a range of seventeenth-century maladies, one of which was gout. If I had known that when I turned thirty and began to experience my first attacks, I would have been even more inclined to keep a bottle of Beefeater chilling in the fridge than I am now. Next time the doctor complains about me drinking a martini (stirred with a lemon twist, for the record) in his waiting room, I can tell him it is prophylactic.

Although gin is considered the most British of drinks for both good and bad reasons, it actually came to our shores from the Netherlands. It has as a close cousin the local spirit ginever, which was a spirit made with juniper berries from Italy discovered by British soldiers during the Dutch wars of independence, which took place at the end of the sixteenth century. A large glug of the strong spirit was taken by the troops before going into battle, leading to the origins of the term 'Dutch courage'.

Spirit was already being produced in Britain at this time, and in 1638 Charles I had founded the Worshipful Company of Distillers. However, it was not until the accession to the throne of Dutchman William of Orange some fifty years later that production and consumption of gin began to expand rapidly throughout the country. Fiercely Protestant, William's main aim was to cut off revenue streams for Catholic countries by increasing the taxes on imported spirits and reducing taxes to make it easier to produce spirits at home. So easy, in fact, that little more was required than to post a notice of your intent to distil and then wait until ten days had passed before firing up the still.

Unfortunately, the plan was too successful. By the early part of the next century, London in particular had descended into the gin-fuelled nightmare that will be familiar to anyone who has clapped eyes on William Hogarth's apocalyptic picture *Gin Lane*. As the sign above the door of a gin shop put it: 'Drunk for one penny, dead drunk for tuppence. Straw for nothing'. It was the sort of pandemic addiction that would make our current drug problems almost pale into insignificance and by 1720 records show that one in every four residences in London was distilling and selling gin. Such was the consternation of the government at the turn of events that a decision was taken in 1736 to raise taxes to prevent so many people distilling gin. Regrettably, it had the opposite effect, driving legitimate distillers out of business and causing rioting in the streets. Bootleg producers filled the gap left by commercial enterprises and the firewater they produced simply served to fan the addiction of the masses.

The misguided law was finally repealed and redrafted in 1742 with the help of larger-scale distillers and gin began a slow but steady climb to respectability. It was not, however, until the middle of the nineteenth century that it truly found its niche when the invention of the column still allowed for the production of a lighter spirit, which became known as London dry gin, the style of gin for which Britain is known all over the world. It has, contrary to what you might believe, nothing to do with where the gin is made but how it is made. Before the arrival of the new smoother spirit, the standard gin was known as Old Tom, a name taken from a small wall-mounted and cat-shaped machine from which the gin was dispensed. The customer would insert a penny through a slot and place their mouth around a protruding spout through which the purchased gin would be issued.

Old Tom-style gin was much heavier in body and was kept in wooden barrels, which discoloured it, and because of its harsh taste it was often sweetened to make it palatable. London dry was lighter with a slightly fruity note which, although it was still considered a lower-class drink, became hugely popular to the point that by the middle of the nineteenth century there were nearly 5,000 opulent 'gin palaces' in Britain where working people could forget the drudgery of their daily lives.

It was around the same time, 1863 to be exact, that pharmacist James Burrough bought his own distillery in Chelsea for £400 to produce what is now my, and the world's, favourite gin, Beefeater. It was one of a number of fruit-flavoured gins and punches he produced but rapidly became the most popular and the flagship brand of his company. Forty-five years later they made a move to a site in Lambeth and from there to their current home in Kennington.

It was here that I had arranged to meet Beefeater's master distiller, Desmond Payne, who, before his fifteen years with Beefeater, had spent twice as long as the master distiller of another favourite tipple of mine, Plymouth Gin. Desmond is a dapper man, with trimmed grey hair, shoes that never fail to shine and always well dressed in a smart suit. Although his manner is gentle, there is little that hides his passion for his life's work and after issuing a string of safety instructions he took me on a tour of the famous distillery. There has obviously been a move towards modernization over the fifty years they have been at this site, but you can't help but get the feeling that precious little has changed about the drink itself.

Desmond explained the process of taking raw spirit and turning it into one of Britain's favourite drinks. The base spirit is produced out of house and brought in vast quantities to the distillery for the next stage of the process, the addition of flavour. As the base spirit is neutral, any taste the final gin might reveal is only taken on by the addition of flavourings known as botanicals. Juniper is one, of course, and in fact is the only one that has to be used for it to be called gin. Others can be added depending on what profile the distiller is looking for in his final product.

There is a current trend among some of the new boutique gin distilleries to add avant-garde and unusual flavourings like Korean ginseng or Chinese dragon eye to their product. They have their place, and some of the new wave of gins are very fine indeed. There is no room, however, for them in the traditional recipe of Beefeater and Desmond showed me to a room where all the botanicals used were on display. In addition to the boxes of juniper berries there were containers of angelica root and seeds, coriander seeds, liquorice, almonds, orris root and, most importantly, dried strips of orange and lemon peel taken from the company's own orchards near Seville, which give the final gin delicate notes of citrus.

Desmond is often asked how gin and vodka differ,

given that both come from the same base spirit. He explained that vodka would just be made out of the base spirit, to which flavourings could be added. With gin, there is a second distillation added to the process.

What makes Beefeater different from other gins is that the botanicals are allowed to steep in the base spirit for twenty-four hours before this second distillation. Some gins add the flavour to their spirit by passing the fumes of the second distillation through what's known as a vapour box, which contains the dried botanicals. Some cheaper gins don't even do that and rely on oils extracted from the flavourings to give any taste at all to their low-rent attempts. A traditional London dry does not add any flavour to the gin once it has been distilled for the second time. The end result is a clean but complex spirit, layered with flavours that build as they are released on the different receptors of the tongue.

Beefeater has been made the same way since the very beginning and Desmond is keen to promote that his main task is one of custodian. 'My role is to protect the recipe that James Burrough created,' he told me modestly, before leading me to one of the company's meeting rooms to partake in what he called a 'nosing' of a variety of gins. Lined up on the table were six glasses, covered with plastic lids, and alongside them a carafe of water to cut each sample with after our first tasting. 'The water reduces the alcohol content a little and allows the flavours to be released,' Desmond explained.

The supermarket brands were discovered and dismissed pretty easily, their thin aroma and sharp, unpleasant taste a testament to the fact that such things have to be done properly. I pushed two further samples away from me after tasting, deciding they were not at all to my liking. 'Fortunately,' Desmond said with a smile, 'they are our competitors' gins. Not bad at all, but they are not Beefeater.' Finally the last glass, containing the spirit I had seen being made. It had all the hallmarks that had already made Beefeater my favourite gin: delicate notes of lemon and orange, a hit of juniper which while definitely there did not overpower and, even if it was imagination inspired by my tour, a hint of all the other flavours I had seen being added.

I left Lambeth after the tour, but not before I had been presented with a bottle of the good stuff to take home with me. I pondered on how I would sample it for the purposes of this book. My first thought was of an ice-cold martini, my favourite alcoholic beverage of all, but hardly a British classic. Then it hit me. There could be only one drink that summed up the importance of gin to Britain both then and now: the gin and tonic. This was originated by army officers stationed in India. Not content to drink the bitter tonic water for the troops, which contained Peruvian quinine extract to combat malaria, they would mix their 'Indian Tonic' with water, sugar and gin to make the medicine go down, drinking it not in the morning as the enlisted men were forced to do, but as a pre-dinner drink taken as the sun sank over the horizon.

The reasons for drinking gin with tonic may well have changed, but the pleasure in doing so has not. As soon as I returned to my flat, I stowed the gin in the freezer of my fridge where it is always kept in readiness for the times when only a martini will do. I already had a bottle open and nearly finished, what can I say? The times when only a martini will do happen a lot. The glass was chilled too, so was a slice of lime and so indeed was my tonic water, a brand that boasted of still using the same Peruvian extract.

A few cubes of ice in the bottom of the glass, two parts gin to five parts tonic and then topped with a lime wedge squeezed to release its juices to provide a citrus film through which to sip the drink. I moved on to the balcony of my flat and sipped as the sun began to dip under my own particular horizon. Few things could be better, or 'pukka' as the Indian officers and a hugely popular TV chef might put it.

And, what's more, I am delighted to find it was doing my gout the world of good.

# 39
# Whisky

Moments like this don't come along too often in life. In front of every one of the people seated around a long polished dining table was a small commemorative glass, the bottom of which had been barely covered with a liquid the colour of burnished amber. On the outside of the glass were etched in beautiful script the words that told us why we had been given such a small pour and why the tiny amount of alcohol in our glass would set us back about £500 if we were lucky enough ever to come across it in a bar: 'Glenfiddich 50 Year Old Single Malt Scotch'.

On instruction from the malt master of Glenfiddich, David Stewart, we all raised the glasses to our nose and gave a good deep sniff. Even my amateur nostrils could tell that this was a very special whisky indeed, blended from two barrels untouched for half a century and specially selected by David to reflect the best the distillery had to offer. There was an immediate scent of citrus, grapefruit to be exact, and then, released by a gentle swirl of the glass by the stem, more aromas began cascading forward, rose petals, a little spice and even a touch of fresh green tobacco. Noses more expert than mine declared each scent as it appeared and soon we were instructed that it was time to taste this very special drop. I took the tiniest amount on my tongue and let it linger until the flavours blossomed in my mouth. There was more citrus, this time of Seville orange, a little light caramel and at the end a slight hint of smokiness.

Even had I not been surrounded by whisky experts, I would still have been well aware that what I was sampling was a once-in-a-lifetime experience. I made sure that the last drops of the Scotch in the glass were savoured until all that was left was a lingering scent of this magical drink. It was certainly the best whisky I had ever tried and, at £10,000 a bottle to the likes of you and me, it is highly unlikely that I am ever going to put that to the challenge.

The panelled dining room of the Glenfiddich Distillery's visitor centre in Dufftown, with its stunning surrounding countryside, was a far cry from the Adam & Eve nightclub in Rotherham where I had my very first experience of Scotch. I was sixteen and dressed to thrill in a sure-fire 'lady-killer' outfit comprising an ill-fitting tweed jacket of my father's complete with PVC elbow patches, Sta-Prest grey woollen trousers and a shirt with beads embroidered on the pockets, which if my memory serves me had been a staple of TGS's uniform during the 1970s. Although this unique suiting combination was about as potent a contraceptive as a vasectomy, I was convinced that this night, the night of my first sixth form disco, was the night I was going to lose my virginity. I did not. In fact my clothing choices combined with drunken lurching towards anyone of the opposite genital grouping who came within ten yards served as such an active repellent that, by 10 p.m., I was alone and miserable, propping up the bar trying not to look like I was dying on the inside.

I had already drunk my fill of beer for the night, about two and a half pints, for the record, and decided that I was now man enough to battle with the grubby-looking optics behind the bar. Spirits were still new to me, but I had sneaked a few sips from mysterious bottles in the front room drinks cabinet and remembered that the stolen nips of Scotch had not been quite as noxious as those of neat gin and brandy (oh, how times have changed). I ordered a double, adding nonchalantly to the disinterested barman that I wanted it 'on the rocks' because I had seen Martin Shaw doing the same on an episode of *The Professionals*.

The first sip from the clinking glass burned the back of my throat like acid as it went down. I assumed that was perfectly normal and polished it off, ordering another and then another. I have no idea what Scotch it was, some awful cheap blend no doubt, but as I sipped I began to grow in confidence and stand up tall for the passing female folk to admire. I had become a man and, what's more, I was a man drinking a real man's drink, Scotch whisky. From now on, I was no longer just a chubby teenager; men would want to be me and women would want to be with me. Cue the sight three hours later of a sixteen-year-old boy wearing his dad's jacket, now splashed with vomit, feeling very sorry for himself as he knelt in front of a concrete rubbish bin making hurling noises that sounded like a Morris Minor trying to start on a cold day.

It was not a good introduction to whisky, but despite that and my mother's rather prescient warning that my liver would be 'canary yellow by the time you are thirty' whisky became one of my favourite tipples and the small glass of single malt at the end of the day has become one of my most treasured luxuries. It is the perfect full stop to the day and because it has to be savoured to release all its flavours, it has the ability to slow down time and with it bring a sense of relaxation that is not entirely due to the fact that it is 40+ per cent ABV.

Whisky is now being made to expert standards all over the world, particularly in places like Japan whose brands are winning major awards. But, for me, they still don't begin to compare to Scotch whisky, which benefits not just from generations of experience but also from incomparable associations with the surroundings in which it is made. Over the last five years, I have been fortunate enough to visit many whisky distilleries and yet, although the principles of manufacture remain the same at each, every distillery has a distinct character that comes not only from its location but also from the distillers who make the whisky and nurture it through to maturation in oak casks.

The production process may involve the same stages, but in every distillery you will find things to make you marvel. At Glenfiddich it was the colossal washbacks made of huge staves of Douglas fir and each the size of a small semi-detached house. They contained thousands of gallons of 'beer' made from malted barley fermenting away until ready to be sent to the stills for distillation.

In the still room, there were two types of still, working around the clock to keep up with the demand for the world's leading whisky brand. The wash stills, tall and elegant in their copper cladding, take the 'beer' and distil it for the first time into a spirit. The spirit stills, shorter and more round, work to distil the spirit further, using only the middle cut of the run to ensure the fruity new spirit is of sufficient quality to be used to fill the barrels in which the whisky will age and develop character.

Across a paved courtyard, in another cavernous warehouse, was the cooperage, where barrels are restored and repaired ready to be filled. Skilled craftsmen hammered staves of oak, pinning them with hoops of iron with a precision that comes only from years of practice and repetition. More men rolled barrels on to stands to be burned inside with a powerful flame, creating the toasted interior that is integral to the production of flavour and smoothness, and finally the barrels were rolled to the warehouse to be filled with the precious spirit, being left in the cool dark of the stores as the whisky draws colour and flavour from the barrel, while giving up the roughness of the new spirit in return. Originally the barrels would be purchased from Spain, where they would have contained sherry. Now, most distilleries use barrels from bourbon distillers in America who are allowed to use each barrel only once and have developed a lucrative symbiotic industry with the producers of Scotch whisky.

It is a magical process, both to observe in practice and to sample in the resulting spirit. Glenfiddich may lack the charm of some smaller distilleries, and I have heard some whisky enthusiasts dismiss it as a 'whisky factory' because of the volume of whisky it produces, but despite its size there is still something about any whisky distillery that I find enthralling.

Later that evening, when I had returned to my hotel bedroom, I retrieved my notebook from my case and began to write up my feelings about the experiences of the day. The taste of the astonishing and astonishingly expensive whisky continued to linger on my palate, a taste of smoke, of citrus and of half a century of ageing in oak barrels. It was the perfect note on which to end the day and the perfect note on which to end the *Eating for Britain* journey.

## Conclusion

# Cleaning the Plate

At the end of the *Eating for Britain* journey, I took inventory. I had clocked up 13,000 miles on my (usually) reliable Ford Focus. I had sent and received well over 4,000 e-mails. I had stayed in over 100 bed and breakfasts and visited well over 100 different locations in nearly every corner of the country as I searched for the very best food we as a nation have to offer. If I had only been interested in finding good things to eat then the journey would have been worthwhile in its own right. But my remit was to see if what we eat now could tell us anything about who we are as a nation and where we might be going. So, on that basis, did I learn anything?

My travels certainly confirmed the impact on our food of people from overseas. It would be interesting to show those who see the rise of chicken tikka masala to 'national dish' status as a dilution of our traditional British character that immigration has played a role in creating some of our most loved dishes. Without the influx of people to our shores over the centuries we would have no fish and chips, no clotted cream, no cawl, no smoked salmon, in fact no smoked fish at all. We would not have gin if it were not for the Protestant leanings of a Dutch king, nor would we have haggis or black pudding if the Romans had not had a way with a sausage. Trade and later immigration and travel have played a part in all aspects of our history including our cuisine for centuries and our food would be a lot poorer without them.

The impact of rationing from 1940 to 1954 is also still very much apparent in the way we eat now. Although it is easy to overstate the effect or the qualities of our food pre-rationing, there is little doubt that the necessity of feeding the country in the years during and after the Second World War fractured our relationship with food and taught the nation how to eat badly, in volume, at cheap prices. It is a lesson we are still trying to forget even today as quantity over quality still guides many people's choice of what makes a good dining experience. The impact on certain industries was even more keenly felt and, but for the efforts of a handful of passionate individuals, we might all still be eating Government Cheddar.

The rise and fall of Britain as an industrial superpower also played its part. The shifts of population from rural to industrial centres not only had an impact on what we ate, but when we ate it as the natural cycles of the day were replaced by the demands of factory owners which meant that the midday meal, whatever you called it, was the most important of the day.

Wherever people worked, they needed food as fuel and many of the dishes we consider part of our food heritage were designed to be just that. Staffordshire oatcakes were created to feed hungry workers on their way to the ceramic factories of the Potteries and hot pot was perfect for replenishing the energy of those who spent long hours in the mills of Lancashire. What little time they might have for enjoyment could be spent in one of the thousands of public houses that opened on seemingly every street corner.

The decline of Britain as an industrial superpower has posed a threat to many traditional dishes and the places that serve them. There are now only forty bakers of Staffordshire oatcakes where once they could be found in every neighbourhood and, while there are many reasons why pubs are closing at the rate of fifty-two a week, the fact that their key audience of working men has declined has to be a contributory factor.

I found that many producers are turning for protection from the threats they face to the shelter of PGOs and PGIs from the European Union and while attaining such status certainly helps guard against inferior versions from outside the region, I can't help but think that in many cases it is just codifying recipes for the history books rather than protection for the long term. The real issue for many is that the next generation simply doesn't want to get involved in what seems too much like hard work and that when their parents retire the shops will close. It will take more than one generation, of course, but if I were to return to London in one hundred years I would be very surprised if there were any pie and mash shops or stalls selling jellied eels remaining.

If all this sounds dreadfully depressing, and I can certainly understand why it might, I should balance the above by saying that for every sad story I encountered, I found something that filled me with enthusiasm and made me think that while British food still has far to go, it is definitely on the up and up. Along the way, I met farmers, shop owners, restaurateurs, cheese makers, butchers, chefs, distillers, brewers and fishermen who were as passionate about British produce as any people I have encountered anywhere in the world. Their passion would not matter if the food they served me had been lousy, but it wasn't. In fact the last twelve months, putting aside the time I had to eat vegetarian pies for a moment, provided me with tastes that will stay with me for ever: the liver of a freshly killed deer, simply seared, Welsh cakes that brought back memories of my Welsh grandmother, the elegant take on potted shrimps at London's oldest restaurant and a tiny sip of whisky that had been ageing for fifty years just waiting for me to come along and appreciate it.

We still have to be careful, of course; there were also signs that our baby steps into the wide world of food respectability are faltering ones. Every place with a cross-roads and a traffic light seems to think it should host a farmers' market when the plain truth is that we don't have enough great producers to support them. Also food in Britain is currently hijacked by the marketers, food PRs and television producers who see money in celebrity and the promulgation of buzzwords that call for a return to 'seasonal' and 'local' eating. They reference a mythical age of Albion where people never walked more than three metres to buy a carrot and lived for the arrival of broad beans. It is, as far as I can tell, an age that simply never existed, but is useful to hike up prices and promote aspirational purchasing.

Despite all the caveats above, I returned from my trip energized and full of enthusiasm, primarily because of the people I met along the way. I was delighted to find that many of them stayed in touch by e-mail, telling me how they were progressing, requesting status updates on my journey and asking me when I would be visiting again. It is they who are the true legacy of my trip and they who will move British food to the next level.

While writing this conclusion, I turned to my notes from my visit to the Glenfiddich whisky distillery. At the end of the page I had simply written one word to sum up how I felt about sampling such a rare and fine Scotch. The word sums up equally well how I feel about having spent the last year eating for Britain and meeting such amazing people.

The word is 'privileged'.

# The Perfect Day's Eating in Britain

If you had asked me to compile this list yesterday or were to ask me to compile it tomorrow, it might look entirely different. However, as I sit here with a cup of tea in front of me (Taylor's Yorkshire Gold, of course) the following make up my selection for the perfect day's eating in Britain. I hope you are inspired to try at least some of them. If you attempt to try them all, I will not be held responsible for your hospital bills.

## Breakfast

WINNER: The Ulster Fry (The Georgian House, Comber, Northern Ireland)

RUNNER-UP: The King's Liver (The Pot Kiln, Berkshire)

## Elevenses

WINNER: Maddocks Welsh Cakes (Southgate, Wales)

RUNNER-UP: Yorkshire Parkin (Bettys of Harrogate, Yorkshire)

## Lunch

WINNER: Fish and Chips (The Great British Eatery, Birmingham)

RUNNER-UP: Andrew Porter's Roast Beef and Yorkshire Pudding (The Pavilion Hotel, York)

## Afternoon Tea

WINNER: Brown's Hotel (London)

## Snacks

WINNER: Mrs King's Melton Mowbray Pork Pie (Cotgrave, Nottinghamshire)

RUNNER-UP: Cornish Pasty (Chough Bakery, Padstow, Cornwall)

## Supper

*Starter*

WINNER: Potted Shrimp (Rules, London)

RUNNER-UP: Smoked Salmon (H. Forman & Sons, London)

*Main Course*

WINNER: Rabbit Pie (The Country Bumpkin, Hertfordshire)

RUNNER-UP: Chicken Tikka Masala (The Shish Mahal, Glasgow)

*Pudding*

WINNER: Eccles Cake (The Hastings, Lytham St Anne, Lancashire)

RUNNER-UP: Spotted Dick (The Proof of the Pudding, Alnwick, Northumberland)

## Drinks

WINNER: Beefeater Gin and Tonic (London)

RUNNER-UP: Glenfiddich 50 Year Old Whisky (Dufftown, Scotland)

# Bibliography

I have done my utmost to make sure that every book and author whose work aided my research is credited in this section. If I have inadvertently omitted anyone the fault is my own and not that of my publishers. I shall be happy to correct any errors in future editions.

## Books

Davidson, Alan, *The Oxford Companion to Food*

Dickson Wright, Clarissa, *The Haggis: A Little History*

Hawkins, Kathryn, *The Food of London: A Culinary Tour of British Cuisine*

McKay, James, *The Complete Guide to Ferrets*

Openshaw, Julie, *History of Pork Scratchings*

Panayi, Panikos, *Spicing Up Britain: The Multicultural History of British Food*

Pie 'n' Mash Club of Great Britain, *Pie 'n' Mash: A Guide To Londoners Traditional Eating Houses*

Spencer, Colin, *British Food: An Extraordinary Thousand Years of History*

Trigg, Liz, *The London Cookbook*

## Websites

www.answers.com

www.foodtimeline.org

www.ginvodka.org

www.hairybarsnacks.com

www.patchapman.co.uk

www.tastings.com

www.weaselwords.com

# Resource Guide

I have listed below (where available) the websites of the many producers, farmers etc. I mention in these pages. Not only did I glean much useful historical information from their pages, but I also recommend you visit them and check out their exceptional products.

## Breakfast

3. Black Pudding: www.blackpuddingsbury.co.uk
4. Craster Kippers: www.kipper.co.uk
5. The King's Liver: www.potkiln.org
6. The Arbroath Smokie: www.arbroathsmokies.net
7. Staffordshire Oatcakes: www.staffordshireoatcakes.com
8. The Bacon Butty: www.denhay.co.uk

## Elevenses

9. Tea and Biscuits: www.nicecupofteaandasitdown.com
10. Yorkshire Parkin: www.bettysandtaylors.co.uk
11. Welsh Cakes and Pikelets: www.cakesfromwales.com

## *Lunch*

12. Lancashire Hot Pot: www.hastingslytham.com
13. Fish and Chips: www.greatbritisheatery.co.uk
14. Cawl: www.stbridesspahotel.com
15. Lancashire Cheese: www.cheese-experience.com
19. Welsh Faggots and Peas: www.nsjames.co.uk
20. Balti: www.balti-birmingham.co.uk;
    www.visitbirmingham.com

## *Afternoon Tea*

21. Brown's Hotel: www.brownshotel.com;
    www.tea.co.uk
22. Clotted Cream: www.roddas.co.uk

## *Snacks*

23. Cornish Pasty: www.thechoughbakery.co.uk
24. Melton Mowbray Pork Pies: www.mmppa.co.uk
25. Pork Scratchings: www.seasalt.co.uk

## *Supper*

*Starter*
26. Potted Shrimps: www.rules.co.uk
28. Smoked Salmon: www.formanandfield.com

*Main Course*
29. Rabbit Pie: www.thecountrybumpkin.co.uk
30. Steak and Kidney Pudding: www.rules.co.uk

31. Chicken Tikka Masala: www.shishmahal.co.uk;
    www.seeglasgow.com
32. Haggis: www.georgebowerbutchers.co.uk;
    www.visitscotland.com

*Pudding*

33. Steamed Puddings: www.theproofofthepudding.
    co.uk
35. Eccles Cake: www.hastingslytham.com
36. Bakewell Pudding: www.bakewellpuddingshop.
    co.uk

## Drinks

37. Beer: www.camra.org.uk
38. Gin: www.beefeatergin.com
39. Whisky: www.glenfiddich.com

# *Acknowledgements*

The dishes represented in these pages are only a proportion of the meals I ate during the *Eating for Britain* journey. I wish I had room to tell you about them all, but limited space means that I had to restrict myself to the chapters you have hopefully just enjoyed.

*Eating for Britain* would not have been possible without the help of so many of the wonderful food producers across Britain: the chefs, the farmers, the brewers and distillers, the restaurant owners and the fishermen. In just about every instance, my slightly odd request to come and share their lives for a short while was met with curious enthusiasm and generosity. I hope those who are included will take their mentions in the pages of this book as evidence of my gratitude and that those who are not will not be offended by their exclusion. I intend to shill on all their behalves at every opportunity I get from now on.

I would like to thank everyone at my publishers, John Murray, including Eleanor Birne, James Spackman, Polly Ho-Yen, Nikki Barrow, Bernard Dive and Caroline Westmore, for their unwavering support and for thinking that *Eating for Britain* might just be a good idea, and my agent, Euan Thorneycroft and all at A.M. Heath, for agreeing with them. Thanks also to Morag Lyall, my copy-editor.

373

Likewise, I would like to acknowledge my debt to the many whose research I turned to for the historical background and context for my journey around our country. To the mention in the Bibliography and Resource Guide of their books and websites is added a strong recommendation to seek them out for some great reading. I trust that I have not forgotten to credit anyone, but would be happy to rectify omissions in any future editions.

Baba, Robin, Jeremy, Auriel and Matt, Evan and Biba remain the most important people in my life and have been joined by the latest addition, Sybil, who by the time this book is published will hopefully have realized just what she has let herself in for.